Jean-Paul Sartre

Jean-Paul Sartre: Mind and Body, Word and Deed

Edited by

Jean-Pierre Boulé and Benedict O'Donohoe

CAMBRIDGE
SCHOLARS
PUBLISHING

Jean-Paul Sartre:
Mind and Body, Word and Deed,
Edited by Jean-Pierre Boulé and Benedict O'Donohoe

This book first published 2011

Cambridge Scholars Publishing

12 Back Chapman Street, Newcastle upon Tyne, NE6 2XX, UK

British Library Cataloguing in Publication Data
A catalogue record for this book is available from the British Library

ISBN (10): 1-4438-2949-8, ISBN (13): 978-1-4438-2949-6

For Lya; and for Zoé—always
J-PB

To Tom and Ania
BPO'D

CONTENTS

INTRODUCTION

JEAN-PIERRE BOULÉ
AND BENEDICT O'DONOHOE

What does Sartrean existentialism look like in the twenty-first century? We are proposing a multi-faceted portrait which reflects Sartre's mind and body, his words and deeds. We do so cognizant of the fact that these categories could be regarded as tautological. After all, Sartre himself insisted that language was also action, and that no human person was ever more or less than the sum of their deeds, "nothing but what one makes of oneself". He also emphasised the inseparability of mind and body, the embodiment of consciousness, without which, famously, consciousness is nothingness.

Nevertheless, these are useful categories in critical method, the more so as Sartre discovered empirically that the conflation of the two elements of each binary pair was by no means a given. The enactment of language—the transition from the spoken or written word to the making of a real change in the world by deeds—became the mission and obsession of the "committed" post-war philosopher, whether writing epic or satirical theatre and fiction, abstruse dialectics and polemical essays, or visiting Castro in Cuba and the intelligentsia in Japan, or supporting student protest on the streets of Paris, implicitly daring De Gaulle to arrest this twentieth-century Voltaire. Even addressing the proletariat directly, outside the Renault factory at Boulogne-Billancourt in 1972, or visiting Andreas Baader in Stammheim prison in 1974, Sartre could never be confident that his millions of eloquent words had indeed achieved any real change in the world.

Moreover, although Sartre's consciousness was of course embodied, it was rather less so than most. He stood about five feet tall (152 centimetres), tiny for a European male in the mid-twentieth century. If "not quite a dwarf", as he ruefully observes in the autobiographical *Les Mots* (*Words*), he took after his father's side of the family rather than his mother's, to the manifest consternation of his lanky maternal grandfather. Sartre was customarily known to his circle of friends as *le petit homme* (the little man), who also said of him *ça pense tout le temps* (he never stops thinking): a pocket-sized person with a brain the size of a planet, we might say in the modern vernacular. It is as if Sartre's body and mind were in inverse proportion to each other, the condensed and pent-up energy of the former exploding in the hyper-activity of the latter, spilling ink promiscuously over a plethora of genres—and to such effect!

Uniquely in twentieth-century European literature, Sartre can claim masterpieces in philosophy, the novel, the short story, the drama and the polemical essay; to say nothing of literary criticism, biography and autobiography. He also wrote diaries, travelogues, art criticism, journalism, letters—*thousands* of letters—and, with somewhat less distinction, screenplays for the cinema. When the Gallimard Pléiade edition of his *Œuvres romanesques* (*Works of Prose Fiction*) appeared in 1981, he accomplished the childhood dream he had dreamt in his grandfather's library of becoming a name embossed in gold on the spine of a leather-bound book. However, he had also, with characteristically self-contestatory irony, disappeared himself the previous year.

In an attempt to honour Sartre's astonishing polymathic range, we have divided this book into four sections: (i) Sartre and the Body, (ii) Sartre and Time, (iii) Sartre: Ideology and Politics, and (iv) Sartre in Japan. These divisions reflect the interests of scholars from the UK, the US, France, Ireland and Japan, who gave papers at Sartre Society conferences in Tokyo and London in 2009, some with the support of AHRC funding.[1]

"Sartre and the Body" reappraises Sartre's work in dialogue with other philosophers, his predecessors, contemporaries and successors. "Sartre and Time" offers "philosophy in practice" accounts of how this unstoppable "book-making machine" (see *Les Mots* again) actually worked. "Sartre and Politics" uses Sartrean notions of intellectual engagement, political commitment and revolutionary *praxis* to address contemporary questions, including insights into world leaders, past and present—Castro, De Gaulle, Sarkozy, Obama: Sartre, the incorrigible intellectual who simply could not "mind his own business", still has something to say about each of them today. Finally, an important but overlooked episode of Sartre's life—his month-long visit to Japan in September–October 1966—is narrated from two contrasting perspectives: first, that of a young Japanese scholar who has made an exhaustive analysis of Sartre's reception in the media; next, that of a very senior Japanese scholar who, as a young man, was actively involved in that reception both as participant and as interpreter at Sartre's

[1] The Editors duly acknowledge the financial assistance of the AHRC which facilitated, specifically, the participation of Boulé, Noudelmann and O'Donohoe in Tokyo, and that of Nao Sawada and Masamichi Suzuki in London.

various lectures and debates. This truly unique and precious first-hand testimony concludes the volume.

"Sartre and the Body" opens with Dermot Moran who revisits the crucial philosophical problem of embodiment to argue that Sartre's *L'Être et le néant* (*Being and Nothingness*) advances a ground-breaking, but neglected, phenomenology of embodiment. Sartre's account strongly influenced Merleau-Ponty's, but differs from his in important respects. Moran returns to Sartre's original account, discusses his debt to Husserl, and in particular re-examines his analysis of the flesh, the touch, and his critique of the "double sensation" (the experience of one hand touching the other). In "Living and Knowing Pain: Sartre's Engagement with Maine de Biran", Michael Gillan Peckitt explores and challenges Sartre's view of the role of sensation in the body as it pertains to pain. Using the work of the phenomenologist Michel Henry, Peckitt argues that Sartre's "anti-Biranism" needs to be modified—in particular, his notions of *lived* and *known* in application to the body—to accommodate certain quasi-*Biranian* notions, if he is to produce an accurate phenomenology of pain. Peckitt argues a third way of experiencing the body which is *between* the *lived* and the *known*.

Naomi Segal's object of study is the psychic skin, leaning on the work of Didier Anzieu and using his most important theory, that of the *moi-peau* (skin-ego). Segal argues that desire is a component, but not the only component, of love: the wish to be held, in Anzieu's sense, is central. Segal compares elements of the theories of Sartre and Anzieu, revealing some possibly surprising similarities in their theories of love. In the last chapter of this section—"'The Childhood of a Leader' Revisited: *Salauds* and Moustaches"—Gary Cox teases out the range of complex philosophical ideas in Sartre's longest short story, "L'Enfance d'un chef". Primarily, this details one person's slide into the kind of chronic, cowardly and morally repugnant "bad faith" which, for Sartre, characterises the bourgeoisie, whom he denounced *en masse* in his earlier novel, *La Nausée* (*Nausea*), as *salauds* (shits, bastards). Posturing—being a *poseur*—is essential for and to the *salaud*. Cox brings a novel dimension to thinking of Sartre and the body by concentrating upon the moustache as emblematic of the serious-minded, complacent bourgeois: Lucien, the protagonist in "Childhood", completes the construction of his false object-self by growing a moustache.

In the next section, "Sartre and Time", François Noudelmann studies Sartre's time(table) and illustrates how he used his body and his mind. Taking as an example Sartre's work on Flaubert, Noudelmann underpins his own study by explaining that Sartre presupposed that everything makes sense in an existence in order to constitute a life, even what seems to lie outside the individual's intentions. This totalising approach articulates two contiguous and complex notions: life and existence, which Noudelmann then applies to Sartre himself, unmasking his secret temporalities, such as playing the piano, in a detotalising manoeuvre which, through its segmentation(s), (re-)composes the tempos of life. Noudelmann also evokes Sartre's and Beauvoir's seemingly "transparent relationship", and this is the focus of Michel Contat's chapter. Specifically, Contat examines the famous couple's politics of "common time" and how they "worked together". He tracks their partnership in their respective works and concentrates on their one thoroughgoing collaboration, namely a dialogue published by Simone de Beauvoir in 1981, as the second part of her memoir, *Adieux: A Farewell to Sartre*. This dialogue is composed thematically, like Beauvoir's memoir *Tout compte fait* (*All Said and Done*), and Contat's intertextual method brings out the parallels between the two. Working through analyses of themes including "the body" and "music", this dialogue culminates in a reaffirmation of Sartre's atheism as constitutive of his philosophy of freedom.

Sartre's inseparable words and deeds are the focus of the third section, "Ideology and Politics", where a dialogue is set up between Sartre and contemporary political figures. John Ireland analyses two series of articles by Sartre on Cuba, the first of which was published in the French daily, *France-Soir*, in the 1960s, the second of which has only recently come to light. Under the metaphorical title: "Ouragan sur le sucre" ("Hurricane in the Sugarcane"), Sartre anatomised the Cuban revolution, to the unmitigated advantage of Fidel Castro and the merciless detriment of Charles De Gaulle. Ireland argues that Sartre's portrait of Castro as a revolutionary political leader is fashioned *in direct opposition to* his image of De Gaulle. He concludes that these articles opened up a confrontation between, on the one hand, Sartre's high hopes for the Cuban revolution in practice and, on the other, the much more pessimistic prognoses of socio-political change formulated by the theorist of the *Critique de la raison dialectique* (*Critique of Dialectical Reason*), which was in press at the time of Sartre's Cuban visit. Extending the political theme in his chapter, "What Can Philosophers Teach Politicians?", Jean-Pierre Boulé subjects the discourse of French President Nicolas Sarkozy on "May 68" to a Sartrean analysis, revealing that—whilst denouncing the spirit of May 68—Sarkozy in fact appropriates left-wing rhetoric: Sarkozy's aspiration to be a "new politician" is compared and contrasted with Sartre's status as a "new intellectual". Boulé gradually discloses the Gaullist heritage in

Sarkozy's discourse, thereby demonstrating that philosophers can indeed teach politicians—about ethics.

In "Sartre's Concept of Man: Existentialism and Feminism", Nao Sawada confronts Sartre's "word", and the word is "man".[2] He analyses the different ways in which Sartre uses the term "man" in a number of contexts—including homosexuality, femininity and cowardice—concentrating on his major philosophical and literary works, *Being and Nothingness* and *The Roads to Freedom.* After an occasionally surprising itinerary through Sartrean euphemism, innuendo and implication, Sawada brings his argument back to the contemporary world—equally threatened by natural and man-made catastrophe, as recent events have shown all too starkly—and innovatively advocates a "feminine Sartrean existentialism".[3] Steering the conversation towards Japan, Benedict O'Donohoe enquires: "What *is* an Intellectual?" He considers the credentials of Barack Obama (well-known as a convincing candidate—for the presidency, at least), Nicolas Sarkozy (recently converted to Sartre), and Haruki Murakami, whose hybrid work, *Underground: The Tokyo Gas Attack and the Japanese Psyche,* arguably satisfies the criteria set down by Sartre for the writer-*qua*-intellectual in his Japan lectures.

The fourth and final section of this book, "Sartre in Japan", is also concerned with word and deed. First, Masamichi Suzuki's forensic account of Sartre's reception by the Japanese press in 1966 offers both the most thorough contextualisation and the most detailed analysis to date of Sartre's Japan lectures, "Plaidoyer pour les intellectuels" ("Apologia for the Intellectual", already touched upon by Boulé and O'Donohoe). Using press archives, Masamichi Suzuki analyses the Japanese media's role in constructing the image of an "intellectual superstar", before turning his attention to the role of intellectuals in Japan today, where he finds no "charismatic figures comparable to Sartre".

Our volume then closes with a rare document indeed: Michihiko Suzuki—who met Sartre and Beauvoir when they came to Japan and remained in contact with them thereafter—is interviewed by Nao Sawada.

---

[2] To avoid confusion, we have, in this Introduction and in the list of Contributors, deployed the European convention of forename / surname, e.g. Haruki Murakami, Nao Sawada, Masamichi Suzuki, Michihiko Suzuki. Elsewhere, in the relevant chapters, we have respected the Japanese convention of surname / forename.

[3] At the time of final editing (March 2011), we wish to pay tribute to our Japanese colleagues—and to at least one other contributor with family in Japan—who have continued to respond to our last-minute missives with characteristic courtesy and calm efficiency, despite the stresses that they and their compatriots have been placed under by the Sendai earthquake and its terrible aftermath.

In this fascinating eye-witness account of Sartre's and Beauvoir's visit—and their various lectures, debates, and round-table discussions—Professor Suzuki talks candidly, and often humorously, about his own, his contemporaries' and his country's relationships with Sartrean existentialism, over a span of half a century. *En route*, he underscores Sartre's progressive thinking on colonialism, and his remarkable precognition of May 68 with the *Critique of Dialectical Reason*. Above all, thanks to Professor Suzuki's compendious knowledge of Sartre's thought and work, and to Nao Sawada's perspicacious questioning and congenial encouragement, the reader is invited both to participate "virtually" in Sartre's memorable Japanese excursion, and to perambulate through his entire intellectual itinerary. In short, Professor Suzuki demonstrates admirably the extraordinary range, originality and vitality of Jean-Paul Sartre in mind and body, word and deed: "A whole man, made up of all men, worth any one of them, and any one of them worth him."[4]

[4] "Tout un homme, fait de tous les hommes, et qui les vaut tous et que vaut n'importe qui." (Sartre, the last sentence of *Les Mots*.)

PART I:

SARTRE AND THE BODY

CHAPTER ONE

SARTRE'S TREATMENT OF THE BODY IN *BEING AND NOTHINGNESS*: THE "DOUBLE SENSATION"

DERMOT MORAN

Sartre's innovative analysis of embodiment: flesh and intercorporeity

Jean-Paul Sartre's chapter entitled "The Body" ("Le corps") in his *Being and Nothingness*[1] has regrettably been somewhat overlooked as a vital philosophical analysis of embodiment yet it is, by any standards, a ground-breaking piece of great subtlety and originality that deserves a fuller exploration.[2] For instance, Sartre should be credited with introducing the key concept of "the flesh" (*la chair*), which is so fundamental to Maurice Merleau-Ponty's later philosophy, and which is often thought to have originated with him. Another original aspect of Sartre's account is his discussion of *intercorporeity* (*intercorporéité*—a term that Merleau-Ponty employs in his later work—meaning the bodily engagement between lived bodies). While the term "intercorporeity" itself does not

---

[1] Sartre, *L'Être et le néant. Essai d'ontologie phénoménologique* (1943, *Being and Nothingness*, hereafter *BN*, followed first by the English pagination and then by that of the French original). A draft of this chapter was given as a paper at the conference of the UK Sartre Society at the Institut Français, South Kensington, in September 2009.

[2] Of course, one should not assume that everything Sartre says about the body is to be found in the chapter bearing that title. In fact, there are discussions of the body throughout *Being and Nothingness*. In particular, his discussion of hunger and desire, for instance, in the chapter on "Concrete Relations with Others", continues the analysis of the experience of one's own body and of the *flesh* of the other. For recent discussions of Sartre on embodiment, see Katherine J. Morris (ed.), *Sartre on the Body*.

appear in *Being and Nothingness*, nevertheless, the dynamic visual and tactual relations *between* the living bodies of conscious subjects has a central place. For Sartre, the flesh is presented as both the locus of contingency and also as the point of contact with the flesh of the other. Flesh is, as Sartre puts it, "the pure contingency of presence" (*BN*, 343; 410).[3] It is our incarnation in the world in precisely this inescapable manner, our being "thrown" into the world. At the same time, my flesh "constitutes"—as Husserl would say; Sartre uses different expressions—the other's flesh, especially in the acts of touching and caressing:

> The caress reveals the Other's flesh as flesh to myself *and to the Other* [...] it is my body as flesh which causes the Other's flesh to be born [*qui fait naître la chair d'autrui*]. The caress is designed to cause the Other's body to be born, through pleasure, for the Other—and for myself—as a touched passivity in such a way that my body is made flesh in order to touch the Other's body with its own passivity; that is, by caressing itself with the Other's body rather than by caressing her. (*BN*, 390; 459-60)

In fact, in *Being and Nothingness*, Sartre objects to the Cartesian manner in which Husserl claims the other is constituted *within* my own subjectivity (according to the dominant tradition of reading the Fifth Cartesian Meditation). Sartre claims rather to interpret Heidegger's conception of the solitude of *Dasein* when he asserts: "We *encounter* the Other, we do not constitute him."[4] But Sartre also believes that I make myself flesh in order to experience the other as flesh (see the complex discussion at *BN*, 389; 458). I turn myself into flesh, as it were; I become the soft body that greets the other.

Sartre's chapter on "The Body" maps out much of the ground that is later retraced by Maurice Merleau-Ponty in his *Phenomenology of Perception*[5], which appeared two years after Sartre's opus and was deeply influenced by it. Indeed, even Merleau-Ponty's last unfinished project,

---

[3] Sartre develops the notion of the "flesh" (*la chair*) from Husserl's conception of *Leibhaftigkeit*, the bodily presence of the object in perception. Indeed, Sartre already talks about the "flesh of the object in perception" in an earlier 1940 study, *L'Imaginaire* (see Sartre, *The Psychology of Imagination*, 15). The French translation of *leibhaftig* in Husserlian texts (as also cited by Merleau-Ponty and Levinas) is *en chair et en os*, meaning literally "in flesh and bone".

[4] "On *rencontre* autrui, on ne le constitue pas." (*BN*, 250; 307.)

[5] *Phénoménologie de la perception* (1945, *Phenomenology of Perception*, henceforth *PP*, followed first by the page number of the English translation, then by that of the French edition).

published posthumously as *The Visible and the Invisible*[6], is heavily indebted to Sartre's explorations. To name some of the themes which Sartre discusses a few years in advance of Merleau-Ponty, one can point to the discussion of the artificiality of the psychological (behaviourist) concept of sensation; the intrinsic temporality of experience; the Müller–Lyer illusion; the Gestalt figure-ground relation; the "double sensation" (one hand touching the other); and so on. Sartre's overall account of the embodied subject, and of his or her encounters with other embodied subjects, is in many ways more far-reaching that Merleau-Ponty's. It is certainly far more dramatic. It is therefore worthwhile revisiting Sartre's discussion of the body in *Being and Nothingness.*

Sartre's three ontological conceptions of the body

Written in Sartre's customary dialectical and sometimes tortured style, this long chapter is dense, difficult, and confused, yet it also throws up many brilliant insights. *Being and Nothingness* claims to be, according to its subtitle, an "essay of phenomenological ontology"[7], and—as part of this project—in this chapter Sartre is proposing a new multi-dimensional approach to the body that he terms "ontological" in opposition to traditional *epistemological* approaches found in modern philosophy. For Sartre, traditional philosophy has misunderstood the body precisely because it has conflated or inverted the orders of *knowing* and *being.*[8]

Sartre's starting point, of course, is the phenomenological discussion of embodiment as he creatively interpreted it from his readings of Edmund Husserl (drawn presumably from passages in Husserl's then published works—namely *Logical Investigations, Ideas I, Formal and Transcendental Logic*, and *Cartesian Meditations*—since he had no direct access to the then unpublished *Ideas II*, apart possibly from conversations he might have had with his friend Maurice Merleau-Ponty).[9] Sartre also

---

6 *Le Visible et l'invisible* (1964, *The Visible and the Invisible*, hereafter *TVTI*, followed by the pagination of the English translation).

7 William McBride has commented on Sartre's subtitle in his chapter "Sartre and Phenomenology", in Lawlor (see especially page 72).

8 Sartre speaks variously of the "order of being" (*l'ordre de l'être*, *BN* 305; 367), "orders of reality" (*ordres de réalité*, *BN*, 304; 366), and "ontological levels" (*plans ontologiques*, *BN*, 305; 367).

9 Edmund Husserl, *Ideen zu einer reinen Phänomenologie und phänomenologischen Philosophie. Zweites Buch: Phänomenologische Untersuchungen zur Konstitution* (*Ideas Pertaining to a Pure Phenomenology and to a Phenomenological Philosophy, Second Book*, hereafter cited as *Ideas II*, followed by the English

read Max Scheler[10], and was hugely influenced by Martin Heidegger's analysis of *Dasein* in *Being and Time* (which Sartre, following the French custom of the time, translates as *la réalité humaine*, human reality).[11] Sartre's academic formation would also have made him familiar with the established French tradition of physiological and psychological discussion of the body in relation to consciousness that stems from Descartes, and is elaborated in the work of Condillac, Maine de Biran, Comte, Bergson, Brunschwicg[12], Pradines[13], Marcel[14], Bachelard, and others. The idealist Léon Brunschwicg, a professor at the Sorbonne, was one of Sartre's philosophy teachers at the École Normale Supérieure and another formative influence. Similarly, Sartre refers to Gaston Bachelard's *L'Eau et les rêves* in his chapter on the body.[15] Sartre's sources are diverse but he absorbs them into his own original and creative vision. In particular, his interpretation of phenomenology casts it as a philosophy of exteriority, no longer trapped in the epistemological paradigm. Intentionality means being thrust into the world.

The main purpose of Sartre's chapter on the body is to claim that one has to distinguish between different *ontological* orders in relation to the body. He means "ontology" in a phenomenological sense (deeply influenced by Heidegger); the ontological domain is the domain of phenomenality, of

---

pagination, the Husserliana (Hua) volume number and the German pagination). Sartre of course read Husserl's published writings, but had little access to the unpublished drafts, except perhaps through Merleau-Ponty, who was receiving material from Herman Leo van Breda, Director of the Husserl Archives in Leuven, even during the German occupation (see H. L. van Breda, *History of the Husserl Archives*).

[10] For an interesting survey of the role of the body in Scheler's writings, see Daniela Vallega-Neu, "Driven Spirit".

[11] Before writing *Being and Nothingness* (while in the POW camp Stalag XIID at Triers), Sartre read Heidegger's *Sein und Zeit* (1927) and his 1929 essay "What is Metaphysics?", as well as some of his later essays of the 1930s and early 1940s. Although, strictly speaking, the body hardly makes an appearance in *Being and Time*, Sartre interprets the *facticity* and *contingency* of *Dasein*'s "Being-in-the-world" as referring primarily to our embodiment.

[12] See, for instance, Brunschwicg, *L'Expérience humaine et la causalité physique* (1922), which is also criticized by Merleau-Ponty in *PP* (see 54-56; 67-69).

[13] Maurice Pradines, a follower of Bergson, taught Levinas at Strasbourg. See his *Philosophie de la Sensation, I: Le Problème de la sensation* (1928), listed by Merleau-Ponty in his bibliography to *PP* (see also *PP*, 13n; 20n).

[14] Gabriel Marcel, *Être et avoir* (1918–33, *Being and Having*).

[15] Gaston Bachelard, *L'Eau et les rêves: essai sur l'imagination de la matière* (1942, *Water and Dreams: An Essay on the Imagination of Matter*).

the manifest. The body has different modes of manifestation. The body manifests itself within my experience in one way, and there is another quite different experience of the body given from the perspective of the other. Sartre distinguishes the body as it is "for me" or "for oneself" (*pour-soi*) and the body as it is "for others" or "for the other" (*pour-autrui*). These dimensions are, Sartre claims, "incommunicable" and "irreconcilable". The first ontological dimension addresses the way that, as Sartre puts it, "I exist my body" (*j'existe mon corps*, *BN*, 351; 428), the body as non-thing, as medium for my experience of the world, but also as somehow *surpassed* or *transcended* towards the world. This is *le corps-existé*, the body as lived from the first-person perspective, as opposed to *le corps-vu*, the body as seen from the perspective of the other (*BN*, 358; 426), or of myself now in the position of an external observer of my body.

The second ontological dimension of the body refers to the manner in which my body is experienced and indeed utilized by the other (*BN*, 351; 418), and utilized by myself occupying the role of third-person observer of my body. This includes my ready-to-hand equipmental engagement with the world and my body as the "tool of tools". Sartre claims that "the original relation between things [...] is the relation of instrumentality" (*BN*, 200; 250). There are further characteristics of embodiment that relate to these points of view of *mine* and *other*; the body can be experienced as a physical thing, and no more; but it is also an instrument through which other things are disclosed: "Either it [the body] is a thing among other things, or else it is that by which things are revealed to me. But it cannot be both at the same time" (*BN*, 304; 366). For Sartre, I come to understand the other's body as a certain kind of tool for me and then, by analogy, I come to understand my own body as a tool: "The Other's body appears to me here as one instrument in the midst of other instruments, not only as a tool to make tools but also as a *tool to manage tools*, in a word as a tool machine" (*BN*, 320; 384).

Sartre posits a third ontological dimension that is far more complicated: it is the manner in which "I exist for myself as a body known by the other" (*BN*, 351; 419), what Martin Dillon has characterized as "the body-for-itself-for-others".[16] This, for Sartre, captures both the dimension of facticity—I do not control myself completely and have, as it were, to accept its undeniable presence in the public world—and at the same time the *intersubjective* dimension; I have the definite *experience* of my body *as it is experienced* by others, and this is filtered in many different ways in

[16] See Martin C. Dillon, "Sartre on the Phenomenal Body and Merleau-Ponty's Critique", in Stewart, especially page 126.

our "concrete relations with others". Indeed, it is true to say that Sartre has explored the dialectics of this intersubjective co-constitution of my body more than any other phenomenologist (with the possible exception of Levinas). This third dimension of the body includes the manner in which I experience it under the gaze or "look" (*le regard*) of the other, as in the case of *shame* or *embarrassment.* I experience how the other sees me, even in the physical absence of the other: "With the appearance of the Other's look I experience the revelation of my being-as-object, that is, of my transcendence as transcended" (*BN*, 351; 419).

In the first way of experiencing my body, I experience myself primarily, as Husserl puts it, as a series of "I can's", whereby my capacities to do something introduce transcendence into my current situation. I am here but I can look over there, move over there, and so on. This is what Sartre means by "transcendence": I have the capacity from the very intentionality and ontological make-up of the "for-itself" to be always beyond my exact current situation. However, in the public sphere, in relations to others, as in this third way of experiencing my body, my transcending freedom is now inhibited or, as Sartre puts it, "transcended". I am, Sartre says, "imprisoned in an absence" (*BN*, 363; 430). And, similarly, I too inhibit the other: "From the moment that I exist, I establish a factual limit to the Other's freedom. I *am* this limit and each of my projects traces the outline of this limit around the Other" (*BN*, 409: 480).

"Conflict is the original meaning of being-for-others"[17], Sartre asserts at the beginning of his chapter on "Concrete Relations with Others". This mutual relationship of self to the other also intimately involves the constitution of my body which remains, for Sartre, a contested domain. There is—and here Sartre draws heavily on Kojève's reading of Hegel's *Phenomenology of Spirit*—a struggle to the death going on between my desire to impose myself freely and transcend myself towards the situation, and my experience of being defined and delimited by the other, over which I have very little power. My existence places a limitation on the other and vice-versa, but there are many modes of accommodation within this vital dance between us.

Indeed, it is this third intersubjectively constituted ontological dimension of embodiment that has perhaps found most resonance (although rarely with acknowledgement to Sartre) in the social and political language of empowerment, of assertion of one's own sense of self over and against the assignment of meaning conferred by the other, as found in the politics

[17] "Le conflit est le sens original de l'être-pour-autrui" (*BN*, 364; 431).

of gender, for instance.[18] Sartre's account is deserving of much closer scrutiny in this regard. It is surprisingly subtle and sensitive to the complexities of the dynamics of these relations.

The body as "psychic object"

Sartre begins from the concrete, phenomenologically experienced unity of body and consciousness, with the body as lived and experienced *from within* (although that spatial metaphor is shown to be inadequate), from the first-person perspective. This experience cannot be characterized either as pure consciousness or as physical thinghood. The lived, experienced body—corresponding to Husserl's *Leib*—can never be construed purely as a transcendent object (even in the most extreme efforts at *self-objectification*), and certainly not something purely *physical*. In fact, Sartre paradoxically asserts: "The body is the psychic object par excellence—*the only psychic object*" (*BN* 347; 414). The lived body is experienced as something that haunts consciousness through and through. The body dominates the psyche; it is present even in dreams, and the body we experience from within is itself psychically constituted. This is what Sartre means when he states: "I exist my body" (*BN*, 351; 418).

The objectified body of others and the felt body

By contrast, the material, objective body, the body as *idealized* in the natural and life sciences (physics, biology, physiology) is, in Sartre's pithy phrase, the "body of others" (*le corps d'autrui*), that is the body as constituted by the *anonymous* and *collective* other (*l'autre*) in which I also participate. Sartre distinguishes sharply between this body understood as an object in the world, seen from "the physical point of view", the "point of view of the outside, of exteriority"[19], and the body as experienced *from within*. From within, the body as lived is invisible, impalpable, "ineffable" (*BN*, 354; 421). I do not know, for instance, experientially that I have a brain or endocrine glands (*BN*, 303; 365): that is something I learn from others, from science textbooks, from conversations with doctors, from scientific investigations, PET scans, and so on. Likewise, I do not know the precise inner anatomy of my body. I have, as it were, only a phenomenologically experienced "folk" anatomy: where I *think* my

[18] See, however, Jane Duran, "Sartre, Gender Theory and the Possibility of Transcendence".

[19] "[…] le point de vue du dehors, de l'extériorité" (*BN*, 305; 367).

stomach is, where I *think* I can feel my liver, where I *believe* the heart is located, and so on. This folk-map can be more or less well informed by science, more or less accurate, but this scientific map, superimposed on the felt body, does not necessarily coincide with the body *as felt*. I can *visualize* my ulcerous stomach but I *live* its discomfort in a different way (*BN*, 355-56; 423).[20] I feel my heart pounding when I run, but normally I do not apprehend it at all. There is an immediately intuited or *felt* body, Merleau-Ponty's "phenomenal body", *le corps phénoménal*. He writes:

> As far as bodily space [*l'espace corporel*] is concerned, it is clear that there is a knowledge of place which is reducible to a sort of co-existence with that place, and which is not simply nothing, even though it cannot be conveyed by a description or even by the mute reference of a gesture. A patient of the kind discussed above, when stung by a mosquito, does not need to look for the place where he has been stung. He finds it straight away, because for him there is no question of locating it in relation to axes of co-ordinates in objective space, but of reaching with his phenomenal hand a certain painful spot on his phenomenal body [*son corps phénoménal*]. (*PP*,105; 122-23)

Merleau highlights the dexterity of this phenomenal body which has an immediate relationship to itself. Sartre prefers to point up the manner in which objective science challenges our own immediate corporeal self-presence. Thus he writes:

> The disease as psychic is of course very different from the disease known and described by the physician, it is a state. There is no question here of bacteria or of lesions in tissue, but of a synthetic form of destruction. (*BN*, 356; 424)

In this example, Sartre claims my disease is in fact objectified by others who can often apprehend it better than I can.

However, most of the time, this felt body is non-objectified and experienced in a diffuse, amorphous and almost invisible manner (which is precisely its mode of appearing). It becomes obtrusive in certain forms of illness (such as when I become dizzy or nauseous), or failure (the stone is too heavy to lift), or disability (the anorexic *experiences* her body as too

---

[20] Or, for example, in challenging Freudian psychoanalytic accounts of the child's fascination with holes, Sartre claims that the child could never experience his own anus as a hole (as part of the objective structure of the universe). The child learns this from another person (see *BN*, 612-613; 704).

gross), or (as he emphasizes) in the *look* of the other.[21] The other's look is a peculiar form of experience of embodiment. As Sartre writes perceptively, I do not see the other's eyes when I experience his or her look; rather, the other appears to me to be out *in front* of their eyes: "The other's look hides his eyes; he seems to go in front of them" (*BN*, 258; 316).

Furthermore—and this is also Sartre's original contribution—even when I see and touch my body, I am in these situations experiencing my body *from without*, from the point of view of another: "I am the other in relation to my eye". I can see my eye as a sense organ but I cannot, *pace* Merleau-Ponty, "see the seeing" (*BN*, 304; 366). I see my hand, Sartre acknowledges, but only as an external thing. It is simply an object lying on the table like any other object. I cannot *see* the *sensitivity* of the hand or *its mineness*: "For my hand reveals to me the resistance of objects, their hardness or softness, but not *itself*. Thus I see this hand only in the way that I see this inkwell. I unfold a distance between it and me" (*BN*, 304; 366). I see my hand as another object in the world. In other words, my sight (and indeed my touch) manifests my body to me in precisely the same way as it is available to *another*. Here Sartre and Merleau-Ponty are in fundamental disagreement. Merleau, following Husserl, emphasizes the feeling body as a continuing presence in cases of seeing and touching (the body is never absent from the perceptual field); whereas Sartre maintains that our acts of perceiving *objectify* what we perceive and displace the *feeling* onto the *felt*. In Sartre's terminology, thetic or positional consciousness is objectifying or reifying. Physicians and others have an experience of my body, but they experience it as a piece of the world, "in the midst of the world" (*au milieu du monde*, *BN*, 303; 365). This is the body in its "being-for-others" (*être-pour-autrui*, *BN*, 305; 367). Of course, both Sartre and Merleau-Ponty agree that when the body is functioning normally, I do not notice it at all; it does not become salient in my consciousness.

Sartre claims that my own body is primarily present to me in this "for-others" (*pour-autrui*) way, or in what might today be called the *third-person* approach. He writes:

> Now the body, whatever may be its function, appears first as the *known* [...] the body—our body—has for its peculiar characteristic the fact that it is essentially that which is known by the Other. What I know is the body of another, and the essential facts which I know concerning my own body come from the way in which others see it. (*BN*, 218; 270-71)

[21] In *Ideas II*, Husserl had already distinguished between normal or optimal cases of experiencing and impaired ones, e.g. touching a surface with a blistered finger.

Despite this dominance of the *pour-autrui* body, Sartre strongly rejects the view that our ontology of the body should begin from this third-person, anonymous, "externalist" (*du dehors*, *BN*, 303; 365) view. This is, as he puts it graphically, "to put the corpse at the origin of the living body" (*BN*, 344; 411). To invoke a concept from Gilbert Ryle, it would be, for Sartre, a "category mistake"—indeed precisely the mistake made by all previous philosophy—to attempt to unite the first-person experienced body with the third-person "body of others" (*corps des autres*, *BN*, 303; 365), such that the fundamental fissure between the two approaches is elided. This is indeed a profound conceptual confusion, as far as Sartre is concerned.

The invisible body in the primacy of the situation

Rejecting this third-person, externalist, body-of-others approach, Sartre maintains one must start from the recognition that, first and foremost, our experience is not of *the body* as such (or indeed of our own consciousness as such), but rather, of the *world*, or the *situation*: "Our being is immediately 'in situation'; that is, it arises in enterprises and knows itself first in so far as it is reflected in those enterprises" (*BN*, 39; 76). And again: "[T]he body is identified with the whole world inasmuch as the world is the total situation of the for-itself and the measure of its existence" (*BN*, 309; 372). We do not first experience ourselves as embodied and then experience the world as impinging on our bodies, but rather we are completely out there *in the world*: "The concrete is man within the world in that specific union of man with the world which Heidegger, for example, calls 'being-in-the-world'" (*BN*, 3; 38).

It is because of our intentional directedness to the world that we have to overcome, surpass, transcend the body. The whole thrust of human subjectivity is to overcome or cancel itself, to negate or "nihilate" (*néantiser*) itself by *intending* towards the world. Intentionality is world-directed. The embodied consciousness has to "surpass" itself, go beyond itself toward the world: this is the thrust of the long Chapter Three on "Transcendence", which tries to set out the manner in which the *for-itself* transcends. This "surpassing" (*dépassement*) constitutes the essence of intentionality understood as self-transcendence. This surpassing of the body, however, does not mean its elimination: "The body is necessary again as the obstacle to be surpassed in order to be in the world; that is, the obstacle which I am to myself" (*BN*, 326; 391). For Sartre, our transcendence towards the world is part of what he takes to be our original "upsurge in the world": "But it is we ourselves who decide these very dimensions by our very upsurge [*notre surgissement*] into the world and it is very necessary that we decide them, for otherwise they would not be at all" (*BN*, 308; 370).

Sartre frequently speaks of the "upsurge" of the *pour-soi* towards the world, of the "upsurge" of the other in my world, and so on. In a sense, this upsurge is the primal situation: consciousness and world emerging together in one blow. Merleau-Ponty also speaks of the "unmotivated upsurge of the world".[22] For Sartre, this upsurge has both a certain necessity and a certain contingency, this combination he calls "facticity". For Sartre, paradoxically, while the body is that which necessarily introduces the notion of perspective and point of view, at the same time the body is a *contingent* viewpoint on the world. Our body exemplifies the very *contingency* of our being: it is a body *in pain*, or whatever. To apprehend this contingency, is to experience "nausea": "A dull and inescapable nausea perpetually reveals my body to my consciousness" (*BN*, 338; 404). Being embodied brings ontological un-ease (dis-ease) or discomfort which is essential to the functioning of the for-itself. The for-itself can *only* function because it already is a body.

For Sartre, as for Husserl, consciousness requires incarnation, which situates and locates consciousness, gives it a point of view, and makes it possible *as* consciousness. Sartre writes: "[T]he very nature of the for-itself demands that it be body, that is, that its nihilating escape from being should be made in the form of an engagement in the world" (*BN* 309; 372). Moreover, the world in which we are embodied is a world that has been humanized by us: "the world is human" (*BN*, 218; 270): "The body is the totality of meaningful relationships to the world [...]. The body in fact could not appear without sustaining meaningful relations with the totality of what is" (*BN*, 344: 411).

Sartre insists on the synthetic union between body and world. Merleau-Ponty also comments on the remarkable fit there is between my body and the world. The visible world has just that array of colours which my eyes are attuned to register. In *The Visible and the Invisible*, he writes: "[T]he seer and the visible reciprocate one another [*se réciproquent*] and we no longer know which sees and which is seen" (*TVTI*, 139; 181). Similarly, according to Merleau in "Eye and Mind"[23]: "The mirror appears because I am seeing-visible [*voyant-visible*], because there is a reflexivity of the sensible. [...] My outside completes itself in and through the sensible" (EM, 168; 24). And in his "Working Notes" (May 1960), Merleau says that the flesh is a "mirror phenomenon" (*TVTI*, 255; 303). Sartre too sees

[22] "[...] le jaillissement immotivé du monde" (*PP*, xiv; viii).
[23] *L'Œil et l'esprit* (cited as EM with English then French pagination).

the embodied subject as intertwined with the world. On the other hand, he rejects the deep significance that Husserl and Merleau-Ponty accord to the phenomenon of the "intertwining" (*Verflechtung* in German, *l'interlacs* in French) in the double sensation, to which we shall now turn.

Sartre on intertwining and the "double sensation"

As we have seen, Sartre clearly distinguishes between my body as experienced (ambiguously and non-objectively) by me in the first person, and the body as it is perceived or known by me occupying the perspective of another person. These points of view are irreconcilable and indicate an ontological gulf that separates the two dimensions. These different "bodies" underpin different and *irreconcilable* ontologies. Sartre's analysis of the well-known phenomenon of the double sensation aims to reinforce this irreconcilability between these opposing "ontological" dimensions.

Although many philosophers think the phenomenon of the "double sensation" is a discovery of Husserl or Merleau-Ponty, in fact it is a recurrent theme in nineteenth-century psychologies, from Weber[24] to Katz.[25] Husserl discusses the phenomenon of the "double sensation" (*Doppelempfindung*) in his *Thing and Space* (1907)[26] and in *Ideas II* § 36 (152-54; Hua IV, 144-47). For Husserl, when one hand touches the other, the sensations of touching can be *reversed* into sensations of being touched. Husserl calls this "intertwining" (*Verflechtung*), a concept taken up and expanded by Merleau-Ponty until it becomes the very epitome of human engagement with the world.

---

[24] Weber published two studies of touch: *De Tactu* (1834, *On Touch*) and *Tastsinn und Gemeingefühl* (1846, *Touching and General Feeling*). He carefully documented the different sensitivities to touch in various parts of the body, the perception of weight, heat, cold, etc., and the ability of the perceiver to distinguish when being touched by two points of a compass at the same time. In *Der Tastsinn*, for instance, Weber discusses the issue of whether two sensations arise when sensitive areas of the body touch each other. He claimed that the two sensations do not merge into one: a cold hand touching a warm forehead, for example, reveals both heat and cold.

[25] *Der Aufbau der Tastwelt* (1925, *The World of Touch*). The German psychologist David Katz studied at Göttingen under the renowned psychologist Georg Elias Müller and Edmund Husserl, who was one of his doctoral examiners in 1907 and whose seminars he continued to attend. Merleau-Ponty relies heavily on Katz's *World of Touch* for his account of touch in *PP* (see 315-18; 364-68). For more on Katz, see Arnheim, Boring, Krueger and Spiegelberg.

[26] *Ding und Raum. Vorlesungen 1907* (*Thing and Space: 1907 Lectures*, cited *DR* with English then German pagination. This reference is *DR* § 47, 137; XVI, 162.)

In *Ideas II* § 36 Husserl is interested in the manner in which the lived-body (*Leib*) is constituted as a "bearer of localized sensations". These localized sensations or "sensings" (*Empfindisse*, a Husserlian neologism) are not directly sensed but only indirectly by a "shift of apprehension".[27] The touching hand must make *movements* in order to feel the smoothness and softness texture of the touched hand. Husserl says that the "indicational sensations" of movement, and the "representational sensations" of smoothness to the touch, belong in fact to the touching right hand, but they are "objectivated" in the touched left hand. Husserl speaks of the sensation being "*doubled*" when one hand touches or pinches the other. Each hand experiences this double sensation. Furthermore, for Husserl, the double sensation belongs essentially to touch but does not characterize vision (*Ideas II* § 37); there are no comparable visual *sensings*. We see colours but there is no *sensing* colour: "I do not see myself, my body, the way I touch myself" (*Ideas II* § 37, 155; IV, 148). All Husserl allows is that the eye is a centre for touch sensations (the eyeball can be touched, we can feel the movement of the eye in the eye-socket through muscle sensations, and so on). Overall, in these discussions, Husserl employs the double sensation to distinguish touch from vision and to accord primacy to touch. For Husserl (following Aristotle), it is primarily touch that anchors us in the body. He writes:

> Everything that we see is touchable and, as such, points to an immediate relation to the body, though it does not do so in virtue of its visibility. *A subject whose only sense was the sense of vision could not at all have an appearing body*. [...] The body as such can be constituted originally only in tactuality [...]. (*Ideas II*, § 37, 158; IV, 150)

Touch localises us in the world in a way that seeing does not.

Merleau-Ponty discusses the phenomenon of the double sensation most fully in *The Visible and the Invisible*.[28] Since his account is well known, I will not summarize it here, but only say that it follows Husserl closely, except that Merleau-Ponty emphasizes the continuities between seeing and touching and their interconnection.[29]

---

[27] Husserl famously distinguishes between "sensations" (*Empfindungen*) that are interpreted as properties of the object, and the "sensings" (*Empfindnisse*) themselves which he speaks of as "indicational or presentational" (*Ideas II*, 154; IV, 146). See Behnke, "Edmund Husserl's Contribution".

[28] See "The Intertwining—The Chiasm", in *TVTI* (130-55).

[29] For a fuller discussion of the double sensation in Husserl, Sartre and Merleau-Ponty, see Moran in Morris (ed.), *Sartre on the Body*.

In contrast to Merleau-Ponty, however, Sartre claims that the phenomenon of double sensation does not reveal something essential about embodiment. For Sartre, the double sensation is simply a contingent feature of our embodied existence and is not a significant or exemplary phenomenon. Sartre claims the double sensation can easily be removed by morphine which makes my leg numb and insensitive to being touched (*BN*, 304; 366). The intertwining of touching and touched is not revelatory of our being-in-the-world. Rather, for Sartre, to touch and be touched reflect different "orders" or "levels" of being. When one hand touches the other hand, I directly experience the hand that is being touched first. In other words, I am intentionally directed at the *object*. It is only because of the possibility of *a certain reflection* that I can turn back and focus on the sensation in the touching hand. This reflection is not inbuilt into the primary act of intending. Sartre maintains that this constitutes ontological proof that the body-for-me and the body-for-the-other are entirely separate intentional objectivities. Merleau-Ponty's metaphysical use of the double sensation, then, is precisely the opposite of Sartre's. Merleau-Ponty claims that both vision and touch exhibit this "doubling" (*dédoublement*) and, furthermore, that this doubling-up and crossing over, this "interlacing" (*l'interlacs*) and "chiasm" is precisely constitutive of human being-in-the-world. Sartre, on the other hand, wants to prioritize not one hand touching the other, but one body touching or caressing *the other's* body; where a caress is already a touch that has overcome mere touch and which is setting itself up as flesh precisely in order to awaken and reveal the flesh of the other. Primacy, however, is given to *the other* in the caress, not to the reflexivity of self-experience. Intercorporeity, for Sartre, is prior to and is the source and the ground of self-experience. Sartre also appears—although he does not make this thematic—to contrast seeing and touching. "Being-seen" (*être vu*: *BN*, 259; 316) is a particularly informative form of self-experience through the other. I experience myself as vulnerable, exposed, caught in a particular place and time, seized and frozen by the look. Touching, on the other hand, sets up a different chain of relationships.

The other is first and foremost not an object that appears in my visual horizon (although he or she can appear thus) but rather the one who sees me, who characterizes me, who fixes me in the "look". The other does not present himself or herself to me primarily as an object, but precisely as another subject for whom I am an object. In the look of the other, the "I" of pre-reflective experience encounters the "me" as posited by the other's gaze, and I experience the identity between these two as an ontological bond. As Sartre proclaims:

> Thus, originally the bond between my unreflective consciousness and my Ego, which is being looked at [*mon ego regardé*], is a bond not of knowing but of being. Beyond any knowledge which I can have, I am this self which another knows. (*BN*, 261; 319)

In the erotic caress, as opposed to the look, Sartre says, it is not a matter of my taking hold of the other's body as a body understood as an object, defining it—gripping it, as it were—but of placing my body as flesh alongside the body of the other, also construed as flesh. This is not pushing or active touching, but rather an allowing of the other's flesh and my flesh to awaken together:

> Thus the revelation of the Other's flesh is made through my flesh; in desire and in the caress that expresses desire, I incarnate myself in order to realize the incarnation of the Other. The caress, by *realizing* the Other's incarnation reveals to me my own incarnation; that is, I make myself flesh in order to impel the Other to realize *for-herself* and *for me* her own flesh, and my caresses cause my flesh to be born for me in so far as it is for the Other *flesh causing her to be born as flesh* [*chair la faisant naître à la chair*]; I make her enjoy my flesh through her flesh in order to compel her to feel herself flesh. And so *possession* truly appears as a *double reciprocal incarnation* [*comme double incarnation réciproque*]. (*BN*, 391; 460)

This is an extraordinary passage that deserves fuller commentary. It shows that Sartre has an extraordinarily rich sense of what he calls here "reciprocal double incarnation", which is Sartre's equivalent of Merleau-Ponty's later notion of intercorporeity. Of course, Sartre also describes in great detail various deviant forms of possession and desire, as in his discussions of sadism and masochism where the other's body is surpassed in ways that deny the other's original look, the other's free transcendence. Discussion of these topics lies beyond the scope of this chapter.

Conclusion

In this chapter we have only scratched the surface of Sartre's subtle, complex, and many-layered ontological account of the body in its relation to other embodied free subjects. Whilst not as deeply informed by psychological studies as Merleau-Ponty's theories[30], Sartre's account of

---

[30] Merleau-Ponty was deeply influenced not only by David Katz but also by studies such as Jean Lhermitte's *L'Image de notre corps* (1939, *The Image of Our Body*): this introduced the idea of the "body image" which Merleau-Ponty refers to as *le schéma corporel*. For further discussion of these concepts, see Gallagher,

intersubjective embodied relations (such as the erotic caress that expresses desire) is possibly more original, and certainly at least as challenging philosophically. Our analysis also suggests that Merleau-Ponty and Sartre essentially disagree concerning the role of bodily consciousness in perception. Whereas Merleau, following Husserl, emphasizes the ineliminability of the felt body in all perceiving, Sartre maintains that our perceivings *objectify* what we perceive, such that our perceived body belongs to the objective world. Furthermore, he contends that we discover ourselves as the ego that is objectified in the look of the other. Hence, for Sartre, the phenomenon of double sensation—or what Merleau-Ponty calls "touching-touched" (*le touchant-touché*)—is incidental to the point of being irrelevant to our embodiment, and indeed is falsely described in psychology. For Merleau-Ponty, by contrast, especially in the last chapter of his *Visible and Invisible*, this double sensation encapsulates the very essence of flesh and of our inextricable and living entwinement in a sensible world which itself responds reciprocally to our sensitive probings. For Sartre, on the other hand, it is in desiring and caressing the other that we *create* ourselves as flesh; we become flesh for the other as the other reveals his or her flesh to us. There is much to be learned from comparing these rich and still largely untapped explorations of embodiment.

Works Cited

Arnheim, R. "David Katz, 1884–1953", *American Journal of Psychology*, vol. 66, 1954 (638-42).

Bachelard, Gaston. *L'Eau et les rêves: essai sur l'imagination de la matière*. Paris: Éditions José Corti, 1942.

—. *Water and Dreams: An Essay on the Imagination of Matter* (trans. Edith Farrell). Dallas: Dallas Institute of Humanities and Culture, 1984.

Behnke, Elizabeth A. "Edmund Husserl's Contribution to Phenomenology of the Body in *Ideas II*", in Thomas Nenon and Lester E. Embree (eds.), *Issues in Husserl's "Ideas II"*. Dordrecht: Kluwer Academic Publishers, 1996 (135-60).

Boring, Edwin (ed.). *History of Psychology in Autobiography*. New York: Russell & Russell, 1952.

Brunschwicg, Léon. *L'Expérience humaine et la causalité physique*. Paris: Alcan, 1922.

How the Body Shapes the Mind: he explains Merleau's *schéma corporel* as the "dynamic functioning of the body in its environment" (Gallagher, 20).

Dillon, Martin C. "Sartre on the Phenomenal Body and Merleau-Ponty's Critique", in Jon Stewart (ed.), *The Debate Between Sartre and Merleau-Ponty*. Evanston: Northwestern University Presss, 1998 (121-43).

Duran, Jane. "Sartre, Gender Theory and the Possibility of Transcendence", in *Philosophy and Social Criticism*, vol. 30, no. 3, May 2004 (265-81).

Gallagher, Shaun. *How the Body Shapes the Mind*. Oxford: Oxford University Press, 2005.

Heidegger, Martin. *Being and Time* (*Sein und Zeit* (1927), trans. John Macquarrie and Edward Robinson). Oxford: Basil Blackwell, 1962.

Husserl, Edmund. *Ding und Raum. Vorlesungen 1907* (ed. Ulrich Claesges). The Hague: Nijhoff, 1973 (Hua XVI).

—. *Thing and Space: Lectures of 1907* (trans. R. Rojcewicz). *Husserl Collected Works, VII*. Dordrecht: Kluwer, 1997.

—. *Ideen zu einer reinen Phänomenologie und phänomenologischen Philosophie. Zweites Buch: Phänomenologische Untersuchungen zur Konstitution*. (Hrsg. Marly Biemel, Husserliana IV.) Dordrecht: Kluwer, 1991.

—. *Ideas Pertaining to a Pure Phenomenology and to a Phenomenological Philosophy, Second Book* (trans. R. Rojcewicz and A. Schuwer). Dordrecht: Kluwer, 1989.

Katz, David. *Der Aufbau der Tastwelt* (1925). Darmstadt: Wissenschaftliche Buchgesellschaft, 1969.

—. *The World of Touch* (trans. Lester E. Krueger). Hillsdale, N.J: Lawrence Erlbaum Publishers, 1989.

Krueger, Lester. "Tactual Perception in Historical Perspective: David Katz's World of Touch", in William Schiff and Emerson Foulke (eds.), *Tactual Perception: A Sourcebook*. New York: Cambridge University Press, 1982.

Lhermitte, Jean. *L'Image de notre corps*. Paris: Éditions de la Nouvelle Revue Critique, 1939.

Marcel, Gabriel. *Être et avoir* (1918-1933). Paris: Aubier, 1935.

—. *Being and Having*. London: Fontana, 1965.

McBride, William. "Sartre and Phenomenology", in Leonard Lawlor (ed.), *Phenomenology: Responses and Developments. The History of Continental Philosophy, IV*. Durham: Acumen, 2010 (67-85).

Merleau-Ponty, Maurice. *L'Œil et l'esprit* (ed. Lambert Dousson). Paris: Gallimard (Folio Plus: Philosophie), 2006.

—. "Eye and Mind" (trans. Carleton Dallery), in *The Primacy of Perception and Other Essays on Phenomenological Psychology, the*

Philosophy of Art, History and Politics. Evanston: Northwestern University Press, 1964.
—. *Phénoménologie de la perception*. Paris: Gallimard, 1945.
—. *Phenomenology of Perception* (trans. Colin Smith). London: Routledge & Kegan Paul, 1962.
—. *Le Visible et l'invisible* (texte établi par Claude Lefort). Paris: Gallimard, 1964.
—. *The Visible and the Invisible* (trans. A. Lingis). Evanston: Northwestern University Press, 1968.
Moran, Dermot. "Husserl, Sartre and Merleau-Ponty on Embodiment, Touch and the 'Double Sensation'", in Katherine J. Morris (ed.), *Sartre on the Body* (41-66).
—. "Sartre on Embodiment, Touch, and the 'Double Sensation'", *Philosophy Today* (Supplement: Proceedings of 48th Annual SPEP Meeting), 2010.
Morris, Katherine J. (ed.). *Sartre on the Body*. Basingstoke: Palgrave-Macmillan, 2010.
Pradines, Maurice. *Philosophie de la sensation, I: Le Problème de la sensation*. Paris: Les Belles Lettres, 1928.
Sartre, Jean-Paul. *L'Être et le néant. Essai d'ontologie phénoménologique*. Paris: Gallimard, 1943.
—. *Being and Nothingness. An Essay on Phenomenological Ontology* (trans. Hazel E. Barnes). London: Routledge, 1995.
—. *L'Imaginaire*. Paris: Gallimard, 1940.
—. *The Psychology of the Imagination*. London: Methuen, 1972.
Spiegelberg, Herbert. *Phenomenology in Psychology and Psychiatry: A Historical Introduction*. Evanston: Northwestern University Press, 1972.
Vallega-Neu, Daniela. "Driven Spirit: The Body in Max Scheler's Phenomenology", *Epoche*, vol. 9, no. 1, 2004. Also in Vallega-Neu, *The Bodily Dimension in Thinking*. Albany: SUNY Press, 2005 (43-58).
Van Breda, Hermann Leo. *History of the Husserl-Archives*. Dordrecht: Springer, 2007.
Weber, E. H. *De Tactu* (1834), *Tastsinn und Gemeingefühl* (1846), in Helen E. Ross and David J. Murray (eds. and trans.), *E. H. Weber on the Tactile Senses* (second edition). Hove: Erlbaum, Taylor & Francis, 1996.

CHAPTER TWO

LIVING AND KNOWING PAIN: SARTRE'S ENGAGEMENT WITH MAINE DE BIRAN

MICHAEL GILLAN PECKITT

Introduction

> The body is *lived* and not *known*. This explains why the famous "sensation of effort" by which Maine de Biran attempted to reply to Hume's challenge is a psychological myth. We never have any sensation of our effort, but neither do we have peripheral sensations from muscles, bones, tendons, or skin, which have been suggested to replace the sensation of effort. We perceive the *resistance* of things. What I perceive when I want to lift this glass to my mouth is not my effort but the *heaviness of the glass*—that is, its resistance to entering into an instrumental complex which I have made appear in the world.[1]

It is with the above passage that Sartre (in Part III, section 1, of *L'Être et le néant*) characterises, albeit briefly, how we, as embodied individuals, engage with the world, how we sense or experience the world.[2] Sartre, in opposition to Maine de Biran—perhaps the most important Gallic theorist of the body prior to Sartre—denies that kinaesthetic sensation plays a role in our experience of our bodies. Rather we just perceive or experience the "resistance of things", the world appears to us as being "difficult to deal

---

[1] Sartre, *Being and Nothingness* (trans. Hazel E. Barnes, henceforth *BN*), 324.

[2] This chapter—an earlier draft of which was given at the sixteenth annual conference of the UK Sartre Society at the Institut Français, South Kensington, in September 2009—is adapted, with permission, from "Resisting Sartrean Pain: Henry, Sartre and Biranism", in Katherine J. Morris (ed.), *Sartre on the Body*, Palgrave MacMillan, 2010. I would like to thank Dr Minae Inahara for his constructive comments.

with", but we do not experience the effort involved in our attempts to deal with that world.

This denial of the idea that we experience the effort involved in the moving of our bodies has implications for any phenomenology of sensation, but especially for any phenomenology of pain. In this chapter, I will explore and challenge Sartre's view of the role of sensation and the body as it pertains to pain. I will argue, with the aid of the work of the phenomenologist Michel Henry, that Sartre's "anti-Biranism" leads to a confused phenomenology of physical pain, and that Sartre's story needs to be modified to accommodate certain quasi-*Biranian* notions if it is to produce an accurate phenomenology of pain. In particular, Sartre's otherwise useful division between the *lived* and *known*, in application to the body, appears to fall apart when dealing with the issue of pain; for, in pain, the body can be treated as an object, which would imply (according to Sartre's way of thinking) that our own body *can* be known, even if it is not ordinarily experienced this way. I wish to argue that, in pain, we *do* at times experience the sensation of effort: thus, Sartre's claim that, "We never have any sensation of our effort", is at best an over-statement. But also—contra Sartre—I shall argue that this sensation ushers in the possibility of a third way of experiencing the body, which lies *between* the *lived* and *known*.

Sartre states that "[t]he body [for-itself] is *lived* and not *known*".[3] In *Being and Nothingness* Sartre is attempting to challenge a long-standing philosophical prejudice that the body is, and is best understood when viewed as, an *object of knowledge*, that is to say when it is treated as an object that can be analysed in a so-called objective and dispassionate manner. According to the prejudice under attack, human bodies, whether our own or those of others, are to be treated as mere *things*: we should, in short, treat the body as if it were a corpse. This is a conception of the body present in philosophy since Descartes, who, according to Drew Leder, "models the living body first and foremost upon the inanimate".[4]

Sartre is critical of this picture on at least two levels: first, it requires us to put aside the fact that the body—whether our own or another's—is animate, alive, expressive, and affective, i.e. capable of being hurt and receptive to pleasure. But secondly, it ignores the fact that one's own body is *lived*, not known: we *are* our bodies and it is because we are embodied that we experience the world. But, our own bodies are not ordinarily experienced as objects of knowledge or *things*, but in a far more

---

[3] *BN*, 324.
[4] Drew Leder, "A tale of two bodies", 118.

fundamental sense, we experience them *non-positionally*: our bodies are normally in the background without a definite perspective by which we thematise and conceptualise them. Living human bodies in general, for Sartre, are not normally perceived as mere things or corpses, and this includes the body of the *Other*: perception of the Other is, in a sense, perception of the Other's subjectivity. Bodies are not usually objects in this sense; however, the experience of pain seems to challenge this, as I will now elucidate.

This notion of the body as *lived*, as opposed to *known*, is itself challenged by Sartre's discussion of pain. Sartre argues that pain is neither *known* nor accessible by the *lived body* precisely because of the nature of pain. Sartre introduces another way of looking at pain. He takes the example of a person reading a book while his eyes hurt and asks us to imagine that the reader stops focusing on the book and instead focuses on the pain: what he calls "*apprehending* my pain".[5] When we reflect, we transcend or go beyond such categorisations and experience the pain as a "psychic object".[6] It is constantly available to consciousness although distinct from it. As such, we experience pain as having a "life of its own", separate from consciousness, possessing its own characteristics, its own time, its own reality; we relate to it as a kind of object, just as we would when we relate to a book or a computer. This is why, when talking about experiences in this way, Sartre employs the term "psychic object"[7], by which he means to indicate a way of *understanding* a phenomenon. As a "psychic object", pain—the experience expressible as "Ouch!"—is understood as *illness*. As *illness*, pain is distinct from consciousness but is available to it. Thus we can say that "the illness is draining". Yet illness understood as a "psychic object" is not a *mere* object, it is not something "out there" to be grasped, because it remains permanently available to consciousness; unless, of course, the illness has passed, in which case the psychic object will no longer be available since the pain has "gone". After this description, it might be tempting to treat the pain *qua* illness *simply* as an object. Certainly whereas, prior to reflection, the pain *was*, in a sense, the body, "for the reflective consciousness the illness is distinct from the body".[8] Yet the "illness is *mine*"[9], it is experienced as mine precisely because I am passive with respect to it, because my relation to it is *affective*. Thus illness is experienced as:

[5] *BN*, 335.
[6] Ibid.
[7] Ibid.
[8] *BN*, 337.
[9] Ibid.

> [...] an object but as an affective object. One directs oneself first towards one's pain so as to hate it, to endure it with patience, to apprehend as unbearable, sometimes to love it, to rejoice in it (if it foretells a release, a cure), to evaluate it in some way. Naturally it is the illness which is evaluated or rather rises up as a necessary correlate of the evaluation. The illness is not known; it is *suffered*, and similarly the body is revealed by the illness and likewise suffered by consciousness.[10]

In the beginning of this discussion, we were examining Sartre's statement that "the body is *lived* and not *known*"[11], paying special attention to the problems that pain might bring to this idea. Whilst one may grant that we do not normally *know* our body, rather we *live* it, pain would appear to cause problems for this idea as pain is, in a sense, the very impossibility of living. However, Sartre has shown that this is only true if we regard pain *purely* as an object available to consciousness, rather than an experience to be endured. It is in connection with his phenomenology of pain that I wish to interrogate the idea that: "We perceive the *resistance* of things. What I perceive when I want to lift this glass to my mouth is not my effort but the *heaviness of the glass.*"[12]

Between resistance and effort: an autobiographical experience

I have cerebral palsy, yet I am lucky enough to be able to walk with a cane for the time being. However, because of my walking I have bad posture leading to chronic back pain. A Socratic definition of "cerebral palsy" might not include "bad posture leading to chronic back pain", but it is commonly experienced by those with certain types of cerebral palsy. Against this brief medical history imagine the following autobiographical scenario:

> I am sitting on my sofa, listening to Tom Waits's *Closing Time* and drinking a glass of Syrah. After some time, I get up and refill my glass and take my seat again. I pick up the glass, but as I raise it to my mouth, I feel shooting pains go through my body, centring on the lower part of my back. I freeze, the glass remains near my lips and yet I am unable to complete my task. For a moment it is *almost* as if I am paralysed, I know how to drink wine, I know how to move my hands, but I am simply unable to move

---

[10] Ibid.
[11] *BN*, 324.
[12] Ibid.

> them, and the wine glass now feels as heavy as a brick. I put the wine back on the coaster, shaking from the weight that the glass has now assumed whilst I am in my painful state. I try to pick up the glass one last time, but now it is as if there is a wall between me and the glass.

In the description given above, there are two aspects that one finds in Sartre's account. First is the *resistance* of the wine glass. My experience of *resistance* comes only *after* the pain has "set in" and when further attempts are made to pick up the glass, whilst *I,* the subject, am experiencing what Iris Marion Young calls "inhibited intentionality"[13]: that is, the withholding of the bodily intentional arc which, at its most severe, can literally "reverse" the Husserlian or Merleau-Pontyan *cogito*, turning the "*I can*" into an "*I cannot*". Of course, I cannot say whether my experiences are shared by others. However, I do believe that I can use my experiences of pain to challenge Sartre's claim that all we feel is the "resistance of things".[14]

Why does Sartre need resistance?

Why does Sartre need to insist on the perception of the *resistance* of things *rather* than the sensation of effort? It is hardly adequate simply to view him as engaging in a Freudian-style patricide of his great predecessor Maine de Biran. He must have reasons for dispensing with the idea of the sensation of effort; after all, one might be able to feel *both* the resistance *and* the effort. Let us remind ourselves of what he said:

> The body is *lived* and not *known*. This explains why the famous "sensation of effort" by which Maine de Biran attempted to reply to Hume's challenge is a psychological myth. We *never* [my emphasis] have any sensation of our effort [...]. We perceive the *resistance* of things. What I perceive when I want to lift this glass to my mouth is *not* [my emphasis] my effort but the *heaviness of the glass*—that is, its resistance to entering into an instrumental complex which I have made appear in the world.[15]

If Sartre's sole reason for dispensing with the sensation of effort is that "the body is *lived* and not *known*"[16], Sartre has, I claim, made two interesting assumptions. First, that *lived* and *known* are distinct, and secondly, things which are *known* are just that: *things* or objects of

[13] I. M. Young, "Throwing like a girl", 265.
[14] *BN*, 324.
[15] Ibid.
[16] Ibid.

knowledge. This indeed is the basis of the distinction between the lived body and the *known* body: something which is "lived" is experienced, not treated as an object of knowledge. Sartre does go on to give an impressive theory as to how *lived* is different from *known*, yet it is difficult to see how this distinction can work with the sensation of pain, which was, ironically, just the kind of experience for which Sartre intended this distinction to account. If, as I have stated above, it is possible to experience *both* the resistance *and* the sensation of effort, then the possibility of Biran's "sensation of effort" is put back in play. To explore this possibility, I shall turn to the work of Michel Henry.

Henry's phenomenology of life

Henry's main project is an attempt to counter the idea that the "what" of experience must be separate from the self that experiences it. Why is such a division necessary for a satisfactory concept of the self? In Dan Zahavi's terms:

> Obviously, self-manifestation or self-awareness has been analysed in the course of time, and particularly within phenomenology one can find detailed analyses of a pre-reflective, non-objectifying self-awareness. But according to Henry, all of the previous analyses have failed to conceive of self-manifestation in a sufficiently radical manner. If one approaches Husserl, Heidegger, Sartre, Merleau-Ponty, Levinas and Derrida one will repeatedly encounter the claim that division, separation and opposition are structural elements in all kinds of manifestation, including self-manifestation, and that even self-manifestation therefore implies a form of *ekstasis*, a form of internal splitting, self-alienation or self-transcendence, or as it is also sometimes put: self-manifestation presupposes a confrontation with radical otherness [...].[17]

It not merely that Henry cannot see why such a self-division is necessary; he also thinks it limits the scope of phenomenology since, as long as the self is divided, separated, split or in some form of *ekstasis*, the phenomenon of phenomenology will always be external, out there and worldly. For Henry, this is mistaken because it makes an assumption about the nature of the phenomenon that he calls *Ontological Monism*: "[…] the assumption that there is only one kind of manifestation, only one kind of phenomenality.

[17] Dan Zahavi, "Subjectivity and immanence in Michel Henry", 134.

It has thus been taken for granted that to be given is always to be given as an object."[18]

Even after Sartre's critique emphasising the *lived* nature of the bodily self, the bodily self which we encounter pre-reflectively is still a kind of object for Henry, for it is external to the self. The idea of a phenomenon that is interior has been lost. Sartre in particular is offering the kind of account of the self that Henry rejects. Sartre is of course totally opposed to the idea that the self can coincide with itself, the idea of pure presence. Rather, Sartre defends the view that "self-awareness and self-transcendence are interdependent". In his view, subjectivity is characterised by a pre-reflective self-awareness of "not being the object of that which, at the same time, it is intentionally conscious".[19] In *Being and Nothingness*, Sartre begins by arguing that the very notion of presence involves some kind of division, and this is no less true of self-presence, where there is a division within the subject itself:

> Concretely, each *for-itself is* a lack of a certain coincidence with itself. This means that it is haunted by the presence of that with which it should coincide in order to be *itself*. But as the coincidence in Self is always coincidence with Self the being which the For-itself lacks, the being which would make the For-itself a Self by assimilation with it—this being is still the For-itself [...]. What must be noted here is that the For-itself is separated from the Presence-to-itself which it lacks and which is its own possibility, in one sense separated by Nothing and in another sense by the totality of the existent in the world, inasmuch as the For-itself, lacking or possible, is For-itself as a *presence* to a certain state of the world.[20]

Thus, according to Sartre, human subjectivity is never a whole, present to itself, and can never be so. For Sartre our notion of human subjectivity is constituted by a division between what we are, our facticity on the one hand and our transcendence on the other, our possibilities. As (living) human subjects we will *always* lack the latter since there will always be more possibilities, hence, for Sartre the human subject can never achieve self-presence. This separation within this duality between facticity and transcendence is pernicious. For Sartre, because of its facticity, the human subject is self-aware, but this self-awareness cannot be viewed in terms of self-identity, because to attempt self-awareness is to attempt transcendence through intentionality. Hence, there is *always* a division between self-awareness and self-identity, a "fissure" within consciousness.

---

[18] Zahavi, *Self-Awareness and Alterity*, 51.

[19] Zahavi, "Subjectivity and immanence in Michel Henry", 134.

[20] *BN*, 100, 102.

Henry, pure immanence and ipseity

The account given by Jean-Paul Sartre would be abhorrent to Henry. Henry accepts no fissure, fracture, separation, division or self-alienation within the subject. Nothing but Absolute Subjectivity where the Self *completely* coincides with itself will do. The motivation behind Henry's radical conception of the subject is, as we have seen, to combat *ontological monism*, the idea that in order to show itself, the "phenomenon" of phenomenology must be an object, exterior, or "ec-static"—in effect, worldly. This insistence on the ontological priority of the world leaves us with a concept of "phenomenon" that is severely limited, doomed always to be worldly. One way of understanding Henry's critique is through Edmund Husserl who, in his famous "principle of principles", states that: "*Whatever presents itself in 'intuition' in primordial form* (as it were in its bodily reality), *is simply to be accepted as it gives itself out to be,* though *only within the limits in which it then presents itself.*"[21]

Henry has no problem with the idea that phenomena are given to the subject and that the good phenomenologist should bracket the question of the "world": questions as to where the phenomena may have come from. The only real problem with Husserl is that he does not go far enough in keeping transcendence, and thus some notion of the world, in play. Henry would prefer to bracket the world entirely, but this is not to deny that phenomena are not *given* to the subject, and in this Henry remains faithful to the principle of principles: *the phenomena that are given need not be worldly, but rather interior, immanent to the subject, where there is no notion of the world.* As John Mullarkey states, for Henry:

> [...] Husserl plays with different and incompatible forms of immanence and transcendence in order to stabilise phenomenalisation into an object and a subject, thus missing its radicalism. The transcendence suspended by the *epoché* is only of one, special variety, namely the "empirical world", with the "psychical ego [*moi*] inscribed within it". An outside, albeit empty, world as such remains—one that Henry emphasises as a specular, as a "view". The idea of immanence concomitant to this empty but still present outsideness becomes that which is not the empirical world but which aims at it emptily. This is a mitigated, half-immanence, *not immanent enough.*[22]

---

[21] Edmund Husserl, *Ideas Pertaining to a Pure Phenomenology*, § 24, 92.
[22] John Mullarkey, *Post-Continental Philosophy*, 51.

Absolute subjectivity is immanent to itself, and the essence of its ipseity, Henry insists, is affectivity, which he begins to describe in *L'Essence de la manifestation* (*The Essence of Manifestation*):

> Affectivity reveals the absolute in its totality because it is nothing other than its perfect adherence to the self, nothing other than its coincidence with self, because it is the auto-affection of Being in the absolute unity of its radical immanence. *In absolute unity of its radical immanence, Being affects itself and experiences itself in such a way that there is nothing in it which does not affect it and which is not experienced by it, no content transcendent to the interior experience of self which constitutes this content.*[23]

For Henry, the absolute subject which appears through self-affection is not worldly, it is immanent to itself, affects itself, experiences itself *as* itself without interference from outside. It is therefore not experiencing sensations or affections, in the sense of feeling *the smoothness of paper*, for that would be to bring in the world and commit the sin of ontological monism. It experiences itself *as* itself, and this experience is entirely interior.

Henry has more to say about this absolute subject, despite its *unworldliness*: its ipseity, he claims, is to be understood as *suffering*. Suffering, for Henry is passively experienced by the self and as such admits of no Other, no divide. When one suffers, whilst there may be an external cause or reason for the suffering, one's *experience* is "one's self" alone, it is experienced by "me" and no other. Nor is it initially subject to reflection: one does not have the opportunity to contemplate suffering, one merely receives it. Hence affectivity understood as suffering is called by Henry "original ontological passivity"[24]:

> [T]his is what the passivity of suffering means, this is what happens in it; the effectiveness of Being given. In it, in its original passivity with regard to the self, feeling takes possession of its content, experiences it, experiences itself, enjoys the self and in this enjoyment of the self as pure enjoyment, as constitutive as such of its Being, arrives at this Being and places itself in it in effectiveness. *In the helplessness of suffering the power of feeling is born.*[25]

---

[23] Michel Henry, *The Essence of Manifestation*, 682 (all emphases are Henry's).
[24] Ibid., 468.
[25] Ibid., 475.

The experience of suffering giving rise to the "power of feeling" does not, for Henry, give the subject access to the world, but rather to the essence of subjectivity as affectivity: "*The subjectivity constitutive of Being and identical to it is the Being-with-self, the arrival in the self of Being such as it occurs in the original passivity of suffering. The essence of subjectivity is affectivity.*"[26] The understanding of ipseity *as* affectivity *qua* suffering in turn leads Henry to the conclusion that: "Every life is essentially affective, affectivity is the essence of life."[27]

Thus the phenomenology of life is born (or rather self-affected). Henry has a very specific notion of life. First, life is absolute and transcendental, that is to say it is not empirical. When Henry speaks of life, he does not mean to refer to individual persons or empirical egos, and in this way he parts company with Heidegger and to some extent with Husserl. Life also has nothing to do with Being: life is "not", it is not anything to do with "the world" or "Being", it has the characteristic of "Nothingness", or "Not-Being".

Pain and life: living and knowing the body with Henry

Some might take the fact that Henry's account is an account of the self prior to its Being-in-the-world as a negative aspect. I would admit that Henry gives the reader very little idea of what it would be like to experience such subjectivity, although it should be made clear that he never denies the existence of the world or Others. In fact, in *Philosophie et phénoménologie du corps* (*Philosophy and Phenomenology of the Body*), Henry states: "Certainly, subjectivity is always a life in the presence of a transcendent being."[28]

Henry acknowledges that there *is* the Other, the non-ego, whether it be the world, or in a very Fichtean sense the Not-I, that even his work leaves something unanalysed, untouched; but this may just be a methodological move in order to talk about the Self with philosophical rigour. In his later work, Henry goes on to theorise how the self relates to the world. Perhaps he does not do this in his earlier work because he felt the need to make sure the ground was firm before moving on to the world, rather as Descartes does not talk about the existence of the world or others until he has affirmed the *cogito*. Henry offers an account of subjectivity where the self has no separation or duality, where there is nothing akin to Sartre's

---

[26] Ibid., 476.
[27] Ibid., 477.
[28] Michel Henry, *Philosophy and Phenomenology of the Body*, 187.

idea of facticity and transcendence; the self coincides with itself, in that it is completely immanent to itself. Indeed the absolute self *lives* and *knows* itself. This is not, of course, the *living* or *knowing* that Sartre has in mind, but—and this is the crucial point for our argument—it does allow the possibility that there is a "sensation of effort" back in play. Henry's self, after all, being immanent to itself, would experience its own feeling. Whilst to talk of sensations would be to admit the "outside", as outlined above, Henry does talk about pain and suffering, as that which reveals affectivity as the essence of ipseity to the Self.

Thus, Henry's account of absolute subjectivity could be helpful in understanding experiences such as pain. In pain we are not experiencing an outside force or another person, but our own self; pain, in other words, is self-experience. Whilst in pain we are experiencing the pain and ourselves through the pain, and in that sense we experience the *effort* of pain—although, admittedly, not as a sensation, for that would be too "worldly" for Henry. Rather, it is that we experience pain as *existential* process, a process given to the subject whereby we come to understand ourselves and our essence, a process which we ourselves experience. It is here that a certain kind of Biranism about pain is located. It is through the experience of pain that we have complete *knowledge* of what we experience or *live*, as it is an experience of self where the self is *completely* unified. It is this process which cannot be captured by Sartre's lived / known distinction when discussing pain. There is a sense in which pain is *both* lived *and* known, although these two terms do not do it justice. It is experienced, felt, and it is in the "feeling" that the "sensation of effort" appears. Thus, Sartre cannot say that we *never* experience the "sensation of effort", and must allow Maine de Biran back into the debate on pain.

Conclusion: towards a new phenomenology of pain

It still remains a mystery as to why Sartre is so quick to dismiss Biran without much explanation or analysis of his work. It may indeed have been because of the need for Sartre to present his own work as saying something new, and he did succeed in this—but he did not need to attack Biran in order to do so, and I do not believe this to be the reason. I believe that Sartre was using Biran to make a distinction between living and knowing the body, to say that these are two different ways of approaching the body. The notion of the lived had, except in the works of Husserl and of Heidegger—notably in *Sein und Zeit* (*Being and Time*)—remained largely untheorised until Sartre wrote about it. However, as I have argued in this chapter, the picture may not be clear and simple: we cannot so easily draw a line and say that some cases are cases of experiencing the body as lived, and others are cases of viewing the body as an object. The experience of pain blurs this picture; it may be possible to talk about pain *both* as an experience which is lived, *and* as something which is known.

This is not an argument for dismissing Sartre's phenomenology; I have no interest in my own act of philosophical patricide. However, I do believe that it is worth returning to thinkers such as Biran, Ravaisson and Bergson (amongst others)—part of Sartre's philosophical inheritance—in an attempt to develop a phenomenology of pain. What I have attempted to develop here is merely the groundwork or foundations for such a phenomenology, by asserting that the lived / known distinction can be questioned and possibly even collapsed. What would take its place, I envision, would be a phenomenology which can account for both the lived and the known, *without* placing them in opposition to each other, *or* dismissing the importance of one in favour of the other.

Works Cited

Grøn, Arne, Iben Damgaard and Søren Overgaard (eds.). *Subjectivity and Transcendence*. Tübingen: Mohr Siebeck, 2007.

Henry, Michel. *The Essence of Manifestation* (trans. Girard Etzkorn). The Hague: Martinus Nijhoff, 1973.

—. *Philosophy and Phenomenology of the Body* (trans. Girard Etzkorn). The Hague: Martinus Nijhoff, 1975.

Husserl, Edmund. *Ideas Pertaining to a Pure Phenomenology and to a Phenomenological Philosophy. First Book: General Introduction to a Pure Phenomenology* (trans. Fred Kersten). The Hague: Martinus Nijhoff, 1982. (Original German publication: *Ideen zu einer reinen Phänomenologie und phänomenologische Philosophie. Erstes Buch: Allgemeine Einführung in die reine Phänomenologie*, 1913).

Leder, Drew. "A tale of two bodies: the Cartesian corpse and the lived body", in Donn Welton (ed.), *Body and Flesh: A Philosophical Reader*. Oxford: Blackwell, 1998 (117-30).

Morris, Katherine J. (ed.). *Sartre on the Body*. London: Palgrave MacMillan, 2010.

Mullarkey, John. *Post-Continental Philosophy: An Outline*. London: Continuum, 2006.

Sartre, Jean-Paul. *Being and Nothingness: An Essay on Phenomenological Ontology* (trans. Hazel E. Barnes). London: Routledge (1948), 1969.

Welton, Donn (ed.). *Body and Flesh: A Philosophical Reader.* Oxford: Blackwell, 1998.

Young, Iris Marion. "Throwing like a girl", in Donn Welton (ed.), *Body and Flesh: A Philosophical Reader.* Oxford: Blackwell, 1998 (259-73).

Zahavi, Dan. *Self-Awareness and Alterity: A Phenomenological Investigation.* Evanston: Northwestern University Press, 1999.

—. "Subjectivity and immanence in Michel Henry", in Arne Grøn, Iben Damgaard and Søren Overgaard (eds.), *Subjectivity and Transcendence.* Tübingen: Mohr Siebeck, 2007 (133-48).

CHAPTER THREE

JEAN-PAUL SARTRE AND DIDIER ANZIEU: CONSENSUALITY

NAOMI SEGAL

This essay is derived from my most recent book, *Consensuality: Didier Anzieu, Gender and the Sense of Touch*, which is a study of the psychic skin, leaning on the work of Didier Anzieu, whose most important theory—that of the *moi-peau* (skin-ego)—was first broached in the mid-1970s, and published in book form twice, in 1985 and 1995.[1] The skin-ego is both a metaphor and a reality. Anzieu writes: "[…] by 'Skin-ego' I am referring to a configuration used by the child's ego during its early stages of development to represent itself as an ego containing psychic contents, based on its experience of the surface of the body."[2]

In its earliest days, the baby not only receives care but also gives out signals to its family circle. In the mother-child dyad it is no passive partner: by a sort of "feedback" process, it solicits as much as responds

---

[1] A draft of this chapter was given as a paper at the conference of the UK Sartre Society at the Institut Français, South Kensington, in September 2009. All translations into English, unless otherwise attributed, are my own. In order to avoid the "generic masculine" I have occasionally changed a French singular to an English plural, where no meaning is lost, and I generally use the pronoun "they" in reference to ungendered singulars. With all translated quotations, reference is given to the original text. Further references to a cited text appear in footnotes before quotations; passages without page reference are from the last-cited page, and page-numbers without specified text are similarly from the one last named. Unless otherwise stated, all italics are the authors'. Parts of this chapter have appeared in others of my recent publications: see Segal, *Consensuality*, and "To love and be loved". I am grateful for permission to reproduce these elements.

[2] Anzieu, *Le Moi-peau*, 61, hereafter cited as *AMP*: "[…] par Moi-peau, je désigne une figuration dont le Moi de l'enfant se sert au cours des phases précoces de son développement pour se représenter lui-même comme Moi contenant les contenus psychiques, à partir de son expérience de la surface du corps."

and can withdraw as much as be neglected: exchanging looks, smiles, noises and sense-impressions, it "acquires a power of endogenous mastery that develops from a sense of confidence into a euphoric feeling of unlimited omnipotence"[3]; such over-confidence is necessary for it to move forward to further affective and sensori-motor enterprises. Touch is the first sense-faculty to develop embryonically and thus "the skin is the basic reference point for all the various sense data"[4]; and because touch is the only reflexive sense—I feel myself feeling, touch myself touching—it gives rise gradually to the reflexivity of thought. Thus, "to have an ego is to fold in upon oneself".[5] The baby develops the phantasy of a "skin common to the mother and the child, an interface with the mother on one side and the child on the other".[6] But this illusion can fail in various ways: the common skin can appear too tight, too loose or violently torn away, leading to pathologies of the skin-ego.

In the course of normal development, as Anzieu describes it, there is the "double taboo on touching"[7], which every child encounters and without which there is no possibility of moving from the skin-ego stage to that of thought; it precedes the Œdipal taboo, which would be impossible without it: "Tactility is fundamental only on condition that, at the right moment, it is forbidden."[8] Thus the child is not allowed to touch itself or other people on certain parts of the body, is required to keep away from fires or windows, and made to hold an adult's hand when out of doors. The taboo on touching is what sends us from an early echo-tactile form of communication towards a skin-ego that becomes a "space of inter-sensorial inscription".[9] As for psychoanalysis, it uses the circumscribed setting *where touch is forbidden but talk is free-flowing* to recreate the effects of tactile contact by the very work of replacing the physical by the psychical.

---

[3] *AMP,* 80: "acquiert un pouvoir de maîtrise endogène qui va d'un sentiment de confiance dans ses entreprises à un sentiment euphorisant de toute-puissance illimitée".

[4] *AMP,* 83: "la peau est le référent de base auquel sont spontanément rapportées les diverses données sensorielles".

[5] *AMP,* 84: "avoir un Moi, c'est pouvoir se replier sur soi-même".

[6] *AMP,* 85: "peau commune à la mère et à l'enfant, interface d'un côté de laquelle se tient la mère, l'enfant étant de l'autre côté".

[7] *AMP,* 161, 179: "double interdit de toucher".

[8] *AMP,* 165: "Le tactile n'est fondateur qu'à condition de se trouver, au moment nécessaire, interdit."

[9] *AMP,* 178: "espace d'inscription intersensorielle".

A dual surface turned both inwards and outwards, the skin-ego has a number of "functions" including containment, holding, protection against excitation, sexuality, toning and—the term I have used for the title of my book—"consensuality", which stands for the coexistence and correspondence of the bodily senses, all sited on the skin. By extension, I am using this term too for the meeting of skins which occurs in desire and which may be both co-sensual and based on consent: con-sensuality.

In this short essay I am going to compare elements of the theories of Sartre and Anzieu, showing some quite surprising similarities in their theories of love. Desire is a component, but not the only element of love: the wish to be held, in Anzieu's sense, is central.

Beginning with Sartre writing about the caress in *L'Être et le néant* (*Being and Nothingness*), we find a theory of the surface which has some interesting parallels with the *moi-peau*. I give three quotations, none of which is typical of the "nasty, brutish and short" idea of the love-relationship that we might expect from Sartre:

> The caress is not a simple floating touch: it is a *fashioning*. When I caress another person, I create their flesh by my caress, with my fingers. The caress is that set of rituals that *incarnates* the other. [...] The caress creates the other as flesh both for me and for themselves. [... It] reveals the flesh by divesting the body of its action, splitting it off from the possibilities that surround it.[10]

> In the caress what caresses the other is not my body as a synthetic form in action, but my fleshly body which creates the flesh of the other. By means of pleasure, the caress is able to create the body of the other both for them and for myself as a *touched* passivity, in the sense that my body becomes flesh in order to touch their body with its own passivity—in caressing itself against it rather than caressing it. This is why the gestures of lovemaking have a languor that one might almost call studied: it is not so much that we *take hold of* a part of the other's body but that we *bring* our own body up against the body of the other. Not so much pushing or touching, in an active sense, but *placing up against*. [...] By *realizing* the other's incarnation, the caress uncovers my own incarnation to me. [...] I make the other person taste my flesh through their own flesh in order to make them

[10] Sartre, *L'Être et le néant*, 430, hereafter cited as *SEN*: "La caresse n'est pas simple effleurement: elle est *façonnement*. En caressant autrui, je fais naître sa chair par ma caresse, sous mes doigts. La caresse est l'ensemble des cérémonies qui *incarnent* autrui. [...] La caresse fait naître autrui pour moi et pour lui-même. [... Elle] révèle la chair en déshabillant le corps de son action, en le scindant des possibilités qui l'entourent."

> feel themselves being flesh. In this way *possession* is revealed as a *double reciprocal incarnation.*[11]

Sexual desire, here, brings the body to the fore in a way that its everyday existence, a means of enacting projects in the world, cannot. It creates two selves of flesh. It does this because of the peculiar "impenetrability" of the other's body, the caress being closer than a "floating touch" but farther off than a penetration: a placing-up-against that slides briefly along the smoothness of the other's otherness. However, unlike the appropriativeness of knowledge, sport or art—for which Sartre also uses the term *glissement* (a slipping or sliding)—desire creates, through the caress that makes them flesh, an encounter of two bodied freedoms.

"In love, the lover"—despite Sartre's masculine noun in the French, which I borrow for simplicity here, what he says is not conditioned by gender, simply a subject / object relation—wants to be "everything in the world" to the beloved. He continues:

> This means that he is putting himself on the side of the world; he resumes and symbolizes the world, he is a *this* that contains all other *thises*, he is and agrees to be an *object*. But on the other hand, he wishes to be the object in which the other's freedom agrees to lose itself, the object in which the other finds their second facticity, their being and *raison d'être*, the limit-object of transcendence, the one towards which the other's transcendence transcends all other objects but which it cannot itself transcend. And everywhere, he desires the circle of the other's freedom; this means that at every moment, in the other's acceptance of this limit to their freedom, he wants that acceptance to be *already* there as its own motive. He wants to be chosen as an end that is an *already* chosen end. This shows us what the lover fundamentally wants from the beloved: he

---

[11] *SEN,* 431: "Dans la caresse, ce n'est pas mon corps comme forme synthétique en action qui caresse autrui: mais c'est mon corps de chair qui fait naître la chair d'autrui. La caresse est faite pour faire naître par le plaisir le corps d'autrui à autrui et à moi-même comme passivité *touchée* dans la mesure où mon corps se fait chair pour le toucher avec sa propre passivité, c'est-à-dire en se caressant à lui plutôt qu'en le caressant. C'est pourquoi les gestes amoureux ont une langueur qu'on pourrait presque dire étudiée: il ne s'agit pas tant de *prendre* une partie du corps de l'autre que de *porter* son propre corps contre le corps de l'autre. Non pas tant de pousser ou de toucher, au sens actif, mais de *poser contre.* […] la caresse, en réalisant l'incarnation de l'autre, me découvre ma propre incarnation […] je lui fais goûter ma chair par sa chair pour l'obliger à se sentir chair. Et de la sorte apparaît véritablement la possession comme *double incarnation réciproque.*"

does not want to *act* upon the other's freedom but to exist *a priori* as the objective limit of that freedom.[12]

What I want when I love, according to Sartre, is to be "the object by whose proxy the world exists for another; in another sense, I am the world. Instead of being a *this* standing out against a background [*fond*] of world, I am the object-background against which the world stands out."[13] Bearing in mind how the Sartrean caress creates a psychical membrane for the lover who is held by becoming the world-as-object for the beloved, I want to move on now to Anzieu's work, to see what goes on there.

In Anzieu's writing, the word "caress" is mentioned rather rarely and I am going to by-pass these references to look directly at his discussion of love. Again, this is not at the centre of the argument of any of his books, but appears in margins, at endings, sometimes in multiple comparisons. Here is one particularly resonant description of love: it "presents the paradoxical quality of allowing us to experience simultaneously, with the same person, the deepest psychical contact and the best epidermal contact".[14]

As Anzieu presents them, two people in love share both surface (sense) and depth (psyche). On the one hand they may be brought together by a need to conjoin "at points where their psychical borders are uncertain, inadequate or failing"[15], they may invest in each other in a "compensatory

---

[12] *SEN,* 407-408: "Dans l'amour, [...] l'amant veut être 'tout au monde' pour l'aimé: cela signifie qu'il se range du côté du monde; il est ce qui résume et symbolise le monde; il est un *ceci* qui enveloppe tous les autres *ceci*, il est et accepte d'être *objet*. Mais, d'autre part, il veut être l'objet dans lequel l'autre accepte de trouver comme sa facticité seconde, son être et sa raison d'être; l'objet limite de la transcendance, celui vers lequel la transcendance d'autrui transcende tous les autres objets mais qu'elle ne peut aucunement transcender. Et, partout, il désire le cercle de la liberté d'autrui; c'est-à-dire qu'à chaque instant dans l'acceptation que la liberté d'autrui fait de cette limite à sa transcendance cette acceptation soit *déjà* présente comme mobile de l'acceptation considérée. C'est à titre de fin déjà choisie qu'il veut être choisi comme fin. Ceci nous permet de saisir à fond ce que l'amant exige de l'aimé: il ne veut pas *agir* sur la liberté de l'autre mais exister *a priori* comme la limite objective de cette liberté."

[13] *SEN,* 409-10: "l'objet par procuration de quoi le monde existera pour l'autre et en un autre sens, je suis le monde. Au lieu d'être un *ceci* se détachant sur fond de monde, je suis l'objet-fond sur quoi le monde se détache."

[14] *AMP,* 32: "présente ce paradoxe d'apporter à la fois avec le même être le contact psychique le plus profond et le meilleur contact épidermique".

[15] *AMP,* 113: "là où leurs frontières psychiques sont incertaines, insuffisantes ou défaillantes".

relationship"[16], believing in the fantasy of being "glued by love".[17] On the other they may, like the mother-child couple, be jointly part of a "homeostatic system [...] closer to a pair of twins than a complementary dyad".[18] This idea of being twinned or suspended together is particularly characteristic of the young couple in love, who see themselves as having "a common ideal ego [and being] fused inside a single psychic skin".[19] In the following passage, Anzieu moves through two versions of the common skin fantasy, ending with a different kind of membrane:

> I prefer to think of the two lovers as linked in imagination by the fantasy of a common skin, a duplication of the common skin between the mother and the child—touching, holding or embracing each other all the time, aren't they expressing the need to share a single piece of cutaneous surface between them? This interface, in the position of a diameter internal to their couple, is a surface for the inscription of signs, an organ of direct communication, without mediation, which supposedly lets each of them know immediately the thoughts, impressions and affects of the other. In addition, the couple in love shut themselves inside a bubble, trying to function in a closed system, *in camera*, cut off as far as they can be from the demands and intrusions of the outside world. That is a different kind of psychic envelope from the surface of inscription, an envelope of protection against stimuli that is total, global and, in my view, double so that it can be more resistant: the lovers make it out of the imaginary skins of their respective mothers (or primary carers) which they took away when they separated from them.[20]

---

[16] *AMP,* 116: "relation de compensation".
[17] "[...] le collage amoureux", Anzieu, *L'Épiderme nomade*, 38, hereafter *AEN*.
[18] *AMP,* 81: "système homéostatique [...] plus proche de la paire de jumeaux que de la dyade complémentaire".
[19] "[...] un moi idéal commun [et être] soudés à l'intérieur d'une même peau psychique", Anzieu, *Créer/Détruire*, 248, hereafter *ACD*.
[20] *ACD,* 254: "Pour ma part, je préfère me représenter les deux amoureux imaginairement reliés par le fantasme d'une peau commune, reduplication [*sic*] de la peau commune à la mère et à l'enfant: n'éprouvent-ils pas le besoin, en se touchant, en se serrant, en s'accolant sans cesse, d'avoir un même morceau de surface cutanée en partage? Cette interface, en position de diamètre intérieur de leur couple, est une surface d'inscription des signes, un organe de communication directe, sans médiation, censé procurer à chacun la connaissance immédiate des pensées, des impressions, des affects de l'autre. Par ailleurs, le couple amoureux s'enferme à l'intérieur d'une bulle, cherchant à fonctionner en système fermé, en huis clos, coupé le plus possible des exigences, des intrusions de la réalité extérieure. Il s'agit là d'un type d'enveloppe psychique différent de la surface d'inscription, d'une enveloppe pare-excitation globale, totale et, à mon sens, double afin qu'elle soit plus résistante: les amoureux la constituent avec les peaux

This fantasy includes the wish, described in *Le Penser* (1994), to be "an introjectable kernel which spreads out into an envelope. This is a first paradox: that the other should be at one and the same time the centre and the periphery, the shell and the kernel."[21] Part of this is the

> double belief that the partner is the object that counts above everything for me and that they also have the desire to be that primordial object for someone, who happens to be me—just as the mother wanted to be this for her baby who, in its turn, put her in the place of being its object.[22]

This exchange of objecthoods within a closed spherical membrane is an idyll of mutual passivity, freely accepted. It is, as we shall see, the common skin as reciprocally inclusive "in which each of the lovers, holding the other in their arms, envelops the other while being enveloped by them".[23]

There are two last words that Anzieu offers on the theme of love; both are gentle and sane. One really is virtually his last word: at the end of his last book, *Beckett* (1999), he leaves a "Finale" that includes the phrase: "To sustain love in the gap between abandonment to the other and abandonment of the other."[24] For love to survive disillusion and even loss, this principle is essential. The other, some years earlier, appears at the end of the interviews with Gilbert Tarrab that make up *Une Peau pour les pensées* (1991):

> *GT: I'd like to quote what you said in the notes you wrote in preparing for this book. You said about yourself: "In his public life, he liked three things: making people think, making them laugh and making them dream. In his private life, one thing mattered to him above all: being loved." Being loved, yes—but what about loving?*

---

imaginaires de leurs mères respectives (ou de leurs tenant-lieu) qu'ils ont emportées avec eux en se séparant de celles-ci."

[21] Anzieu, *Le Penser*, 67, hereafter *AP*: "[…] un noyau introjectable qui se déploie en enveloppe. C'est sans doute là le paradoxe premier: que l'autre soit à la fois le centre et la périphérie, l'écorce et le noyau."

[22] *ACD,* 254: "double croyance que le partenaire est l'objet qui compte par-dessus tout pour moi et qu'il a lui-même le désir d'être cet objet primordial pour quelqu'un, pour moi en l'occurrence—comme la mère a voulu l'être autrefois pour son tout-petit qui, de son côté, la mettait en place d'être cet objet."

[23] *AMP,* 85: "selon lequel chacun des deux, en le tenant dans ses bras, envelopperait l'autre tout en étant enveloppé par lui".

[24] Anzieu, *Beckett*, 289: "Maintenir l'amour dans l'écart entre l'abandon à l'autre et l'abandon de l'autre."

DA: That phrase came to me spontaneously. I thought when I wrote it that you'd ask me this question, and it's quite a poser. But I decided not to alter the phrase my unconscious had dictated to me. It didn't actually surprise me that much: all through my childhood and adolescence I lived with the feeling of not being loved by my mother.
GT: I don't want to go on too much about this, but your phrase has many levels. I'm trying to understand. The reader will also want to understand, I'm sure.
DA: I wouldn't have spoken to you about the richness, power and complexity of the feeling of love, as I did at the end of our sixth interview, if I hadn't had personal experience of it, but I do believe that this question, when it is broached in public or for an audience, must be treated soberly and discreetly. That is my first comment. The second is that love may be used well or badly. Love is not simply generosity: one can crush or stifle someone with the poisoned gifts one gives them. Love is not just accepting the other person's suffering—including the suffering the two people inflict on each other, which sometimes comes to fill the whole stage of their drama. Love shows that it is intelligent when it helps to create, for the child, the friend, the partner in life, a supple and firm envelope that delimits and unifies—a bark for their trunk, oxygen for their leaves, a living skin for their thoughts. That, if you don't mind, will be my last word.[25]

---

[25] Anzieu, *Une Peau pour les pensées*, 147, hereafter *APP*: "*GT : J'aimerais citer ce que vous avez écrit dans la note de présentation de vous-même préparatoire à ce livre. Vous écrivez, à votre propre sujet: 'Dans sa vie publique, il aima trois choses : faire réfléchir, faire rire, faire rêver. Dans sa vie privée, il trouva satisfaction à une seule: être aimé.' Être aimé, oui, mais aimer, alors?* / DA: Cette phrase m'est venue spontanément. J'ai pensé, en l'écrivant, que l'on me poserait cette question, cette 'colle'. Mais je me suis refusé à modifier la phrase que l'inconscient m'avait dictée. Elle ne m'a pas complètement surpris : j'ai trop eu le sentiment, tout au long de mon enfance et de mon adolescence, d'avoir été mal aimé de ma mère. / *GT: Je ne voudrais pas insister outre mesure, mais votre phrase est à plusieurs niveaux. J'essaie de comprendre. Le lecteur aussi, sans doute, essayera de comprendre.* / DA: Je ne vous aurais pas parlé de la richesse, de la force, de la complexité du sentiment amoureux, comme je l'ai fait avec vous à la fin de notre sixième entretien, si je n'en avais pas l'expérience personnelle, mais je maintiens que cette question, quand on l'aborde en public ou pour un public, doit être traitée sobrement et discrètement. C'est ma première remarque. La seconde est qu'il y a un bon et un mauvais usage de l'amour. L'amour n'est pas que générosité: on peut écraser ou étouffer quelqu'un sous les cadeaux empoisonnés qu'on lui fait. L'amour n'est pas qu'acceptation de la souffrance de l'autre, y compris de celle que les deux partenaires s'infligent mutuellement et qui vient parfois occuper tout le devant de la scène d'un couple. L'amour fait preuve d'intelligence quand il contribue à construire, chez l'enfant, chez l'ami, chez la compagne ou le compagnon, une enveloppe souple et ferme qui le délimite et l'unifie—une écorce

This "last word" is a description of *intelligent* love, a capacity for mutual holding without illusion; but the penultimate word—dictated by the unconscious, that is, by fantasy—was still the desire to be not so much its subject as its object.

I want to return now to the fantasy of the common skin with the mother, which has hovered over the whole of this discussion. My view is that, although this appears more between the lines than within them, Anzieu has a number of different versions of the common skin, and each of these has a distinct relevance to the question of love. Lack of space prevents me from showing how these develop: all I can do here is point to the last and, in my view, most startling version. Not simply two beings either side of a tangential membrane, or even involved in a feedback circuit: in this version, the mother and infant may be perceived in fantasy as *mutually containing*, exactly like lovers in their fantasy.

This is derived from life in the womb, in which the child "knows" the mother as "phantasized as the object containing all objects [...] the mother-space-everything".[26] But this uterine containment is strangely reversible. Talking of the psychology of groups (one of his long-standing interests), Anzieu describes the fantasy of "a proto-group which is fantasmatic, undifferentiated and reversible: the group of children inside the womb of the mother, or that of the mother in the womb of the children"[27], and in the Tarrab interview he speaks of his determination to use psychoanalysis "to care for my mother in myself and other people".[28]

This version of the common skin, combining the system of exchange and reversible containment of the sphere, is also found in Anzieu's idea of "mutual inclusion" or "reciprocal inclusion".[29] In this image, "my mother surrounds me and I surround her at the same time".[30] Anzieu sometimes describes this as a system of embedding, like Russian dolls, and it can be viewed as having only two dimensions, but essentially it is a *projective*

---

pour son tronc, de l'oxygène pour ses feuilles, une peau vivante pour ses pensées. Ce sera, si vous le voulez bien, mon dernier mot."

26 *AEN,* 93: "fantasmée comme l'objet contenant tous les objets [...] cette mère-espace-tout".

27 Anzieu, *Le Groupe et l'inconscient*, 108: "[...] un proto-groupe, fantasmatique, indifférencié et réversible, celui des enfants dans le ventre de la mère, celui de la mère dans le ventre des enfants".

28 *APP,* 20: "pour soigner ma mère [...] chez moi et chez les autres".

29 *AMP,* 59 and *passim*: "l'inclusion mutuelle"; *AMP,* 262 and *passim*: "l'inclusion réciproque".

30 *AEN,* 61: "ma mère m'entoure et je l'entoure en même temps".

effect, "a double process of sensorial and fantasmatic projection"[31], and thus, I would argue, a sphere rather than a phenomenon of tangential surfaces.

With all this material from Anzieu, I would like now to return to Sartre's theories of love and see what parallels can be found. First of all, the creation of the other as flesh through the caress—and Sartre's term *faire naître* underlies it—is a version of the creation of a psychic envelope which implicitly continues that of the other's infant environment. It is, like the common skin, a circuit—"the caress creates the other as flesh both for me and for themselves"[32]—and a mutual inclusion: a "*double reciprocal incarnation*".[33] And it is essentially a relation of passivity; here we recall Anzieu's stress on "being loved" rather than loving.[34] For Sartre, the "languor" of lovemaking—its reversal of the motive of grasping or taking hold, one's body "caressing itself against [the other's body] rather than caressing it"—these are the gestures of the wish to *be loved*.

The second passage I cited from Sartre goes further, again in a similar vein to Anzieu, for it describes love as a structuration of the world. The motif of passivity continues: each of the partners wishes to be the object for the other. In the same way, Anzieu writes of "the double belief that the partner is the object that counts above everything for me and that they also have the desire to be that primordial object for someone, who happens to be me".[35] This rather strange phrasing represents, I think, the miracle, if it occurs, of two subjectivities having the good luck to desire one another at the same time. The object they each agree to be is "everything in the world"[36], and that means both the container of "all other *thises* [...]" and the "limit-object of [the other's] transcendence [...] the circle of their freedom"[37], with the other freely accepting this limitation as though it had always been so: "[T]his shows us what the lover fundamentally wants

[31] *AMP,* 59: "un double processus de projection sensorielle et fantasmatique".

[32] *SEN,* 430: "la caresse fait naître autrui comme chair pour moi et pour lui-même".

[33] *SEN,* 431: "*double incarnation réciproque*".

[34] *APP,* 147: "être aimé".

[35] *ACD,* 254: "la double croyance que le partenaire est l'objet qui compte par-dessus-tout pour moi et qu'il a lui-même le désir d'être cet objet primordial pour quelqu'un, pour moi en l'occurrence".

[36] *SEN,* 408: "« tout au monde »" (the « scare-quotes » are Sartre's).

[37] "[...] tous les autres *ceci* [...] l'objet limite de la transcendance [...] le cercle de la liberté d'autrui".

from the beloved: he does not want to *act* upon the other's freedom but to exist *a priori* as the objective limit of that freedom."[38]

I have likened this idyll to the common skin of mutual inclusion in which lovers, in their "bubble"[39], envelop each other. But actually it is something very much larger: a membrane coterminous with the imaginable world. This fantasy is uterine, to be sure, a version of the "mother-space-everything"[40], and the combination of centre and circumference cited earlier; but it is also a projection. A projection must fall somewhere: this membrane is the screen or backcloth on which it falls. Sartre's term is *fond* (background), Anzieu speaks of a *toile de fond* (backcloth). But again, let us recall, we are not talking about a two-dimensional backdrop but a membrane coextensive with the outer limit of the "freedom" that is each individual's psychic world.[41] Anzieu writes:

> In relation to all other sensorial registers, the tactile possesses a distinctive characteristic which not only makes it the origin of the psychic system, but also allows it to provide the latter permanently with something one might call the mental background, the backcloth on which psychic contents are inscribed as figures, or perhaps the containing envelope which allows the psychic apparatus to be capable of having contents.[42]

The sense of touch is reversible, "bipolar"[43], creating internal and external perceptions—and it is the backcloth to everything else. So, when Sartre describes love thus: "I am the world. Instead of being a *this* standing out against a background of world, I am the object-background against which the world stands out"[44], he could be talking about the skin-ego as

---

[38] "[C]eci nous permet de saisir à fond ce que l'amant exige de l'aimé: il ne veut pas *agir* sur la liberté de l'autre mais exister *a priori* comme la limite objective de cette liberté."

[39] *ACD,* 254: "bulle".

[40] *AEN,* 93: "mère-espace-tout".

[41] See my discussion of Peter Weir's 1998 film *The Truman Show* in *Consensuality*, 208-12, or my "Hands and worlds".

[42] *AMP,* 106-107: "Par rapport à tous les autres registres sensoriels, le tactile possède une caractéristique distinctive qui le met non seulement à l'origine du psychisme mais qui lui permet de fournir à celui-ci en permanence quelque chose qu'on peut aussi bien appeler le fond mental, la toile de fond sur laquelle les contenus psychiques s'inscrivent comme figures, ou encore l'enveloppe contenante qui fait que l'appareil psychique devient susceptible d'avoir des contenus."

[43] *AMP,* 107: "cette bipolarité du tactile".

[44] *SEN,* 409-10: "je suis le monde. Au lieu d'être un *ceci* se détachant sur fond de monde, je suis l'objet-fond sur quoi le monde se détache."

the site of consensuality: "consensuality", both in Anzieu's primary sense of a place where the senses coincide, and also in my sense, the sense of shared sensuality on a basis of love.

Works Cited

Anzieu, Didier. *Beckett*. Paris: Dunod, 1999.
—. *Créer/Détruire*. Paris: Dunod, 1996.
—. *L'Épiderme nomade et la peau psychique*. Paris: Dunod, 1990.
—. *Le Groupe et l'inconscient*. Paris: Dunod, 1999.
—. *Le Moi-peau*. Paris: Dunod (1985), 1995.
—. *Une Peau pour les pensées*. Paris: Apsygée, 1991.
—. *Le Penser*. Paris: Dunod, 1994.
Sartre, Jean-Paul. *L'Être et le néant*. Paris: Gallimard, 1943.
Segal, Naomi. *Consensuality: Didier Anzieu, Gender and the Sense of Touch*. Amsterdam and New York: Rodopi, 2009.
—. "Hands and worlds: the membrane of desire in Sartre, Anzieu, Jane Campion and Peter Weir", in Francesca Vidal and Johan Siebers (eds.), *Träume gegen Mauern / Dreams against Walls*. Ernst Bloch Jahrbuch, 2009 (267-80).
—. "To love and be loved: Sartre, Anzieu and theories of the caress", in *Theory-Tinged Criticism: Essays in Memory of Malcolm Bowie. Paragraph*, vol. 32, no. 2, July 2009 (226-39).

CHAPTER FOUR

"THE CHILDHOOD OF A LEADER" REVISITED: *SALAUDS* AND MOUSTACHES

GARY COX

In his career Sartre published only five short stories, a collection that appeared in 1939 entitled *Le Mur* (*The Wall*).[1] The collection was repackaged, translated into English (and censored) some years later with the alternative title *Intimacy*. Before Gallimard published the stories as a collection, some of them appeared individually in Gallimard's journal, *La Nouvelle Revue Française,* around the time of the publication of Sartre's first novel, *La Nausée* (*Nausea*), in 1938. These few short stories, of undoubted literary excellence, are an integral and significant part of the philosophical project and existentialist vision of the early Sartre.

By far the longest story in the collection, and the most sophisticated in terms of the range of complex philosophical ideas it explores, is "L'Enfance d'un chef" ("The Childhood of a Leader"). Extremely detailed yet brilliantly concise, "The Childhood of a Leader" traces the emotional, psychological, social, sexual and moral development of a privileged bourgeois, Lucien Fleurier, from infancy and innocence to adulthood and intolerance. This major piece of work, conceived during the same years as *Nausea* and pointing the way towards it both stylistically and philosophically, has been somewhat neglected by recent Sartre scholars.

The story, briefly, is this: Lucien is a sensitive, intelligent, imaginative child given to fantasising and inventing games. Even as an infant, he worries about his self-identity and the nature of reality. When made to wear an angel costume he worries that he might become a girl, or be permanently mistaken for one. He wonders whether he is real, whether

[1] This chapter—an earlier draft of which was given at the sixteenth annual conference of the UK Sartre Society at the Institut Français, South Kensington, in September 2009—is adapted, with permission, from Gary Cox, *Sartre and Fiction*, Continuum, 2009.

anything is real, whether his parents and other adults are just pretending to be who they appear to be. He often feels he is asleep, that his thoughts are just mist or that he is nothing but mist himself, and he wishes he could wake up to a reality that is clear, certain and solid:

> "What am I, *I* … ?" There was this fog rolling back on itself, indefinite. "I!" He looked into the distance; the word rang in his head […] Lucien shuddered and his hands trembled. "Now I have it!" he thought, "now I have it! I was sure of it: *I don't exist*!"[2]

As he grows, he tries various strategies to overcome his troubling sense of unreality.

As an adolescent Lucien becomes close friends with Berliac, a Jewish youth who is mature and well informed for his age. Lucien and Berliac share confidences, each admitting to a childhood desire for his own mother. Thus, Berliac introduces Lucien to Freudian psychoanalysis, which Lucien then studies avidly. Psychoanalysis appears to hold the answer to Lucien's worries about his identity. It seems he has been unable to find the true Lucien and his lifelong search for him has been misguided because the true Lucien is hidden in his subconscious: "The true Lucien was deeply buried in his subconscious; he had to dream of him without ever seeing him, as an absent friend."[3] He decides, like Berliac, that all his worries are just complexes as diagnosed by Freud.

Much to Berliac's annoyance, Lucien becomes acquainted with Berliac's mentor, Bergère, a surrealist artist in his thirties whose intentions towards Lucien are sexual. Bergère finally succeeds in seducing Lucien who, nervous but consenting at the time, is left feeling disgusted and ashamed of himself. He fears what will become of his respectable, middle-class reputation and his destiny to lead if he "becomes" a homosexual:

> "But suppose I get in the habit?' he thought with anguish. "I could never do without it, it'll be like morphine!" He would become a tarnished man, no one would have anything to do with him, his father's workers would laugh when he gave them orders.[4]

His reaction is to have nothing more to do with Bergère, Berliac or Freud. Raised in an anti-Semitic environment, it is easy for him to convince himself that the dangerous, perverted, Jewish ideas of Berliac and Freud

---

[2] "The Childhood of a Leader" (henceforth TCL), in Sartre, *The Wall*, 99.
[3] TCL, 104.
[4] TCL, 118.

temporarily corrupted his mind and his moral health, and led him to the episode with Bergère.

In an attempt to convince himself that he is heterosexual, he finds a girlfriend, Maud, and loses his virginity, but it is clear that he does not really enjoy heterosexual sex: "[S]he always wanted to sleep with him, it was tiresome; their confused flesh giving off an odour of scorched rabbit stew in the torrid heat of springtime."[5] He embraces the security and respectability of his family, looking forward to the day when he will inherit his father's factory, assert his bourgeois rights and be respected by his workers as a leader of men. He adopts his father's positive view of capitalism, his nationalism and above all his anti-Semitism. He is encouraged to join the French Fascist movement by André Lemordant, a fellow student with a moustache and a mature manner. He helps his Fascist brothers, the *camelots*, to beat up an immigrant in the street in a random, unprovoked, racially motivated attack.

At Pierrette Guigard's eighteenth birthday party, Lucien proudly refuses to shake hands with Weill, a Jew. Lucien leaves the party immediately, his pride melting as he reaches the street. He starts to worry that the Guigard family will never speak to him again, but the next day, to his surprise and relief, Pierrette's brother apologises for having introduced him to a Jew: "My parents say you were right and you couldn't have done otherwise because of your convictions."[6] Lucien is transformed by the thought that he has convictions that other people respect. For the first time in his life, he feels as though he has real substance. He feels powerful and threatening and clearly defined: "Now Lucien felt clean and sharp as a chronometer."[7]

The finishing touch to the transformation and solidification of Lucien's self-image is added when, dissatisfied with his pretty, childish face, he decides to grow a moustache:

> [H]e would have liked to find on his own face the impenetrable look he admired on Lemordant's. But the mirror only reflected a pretty, headstrong little face that was not yet terrible enough. "I'll grow a moustache", he decided.[8]

"The Childhood of a Leader" was conceived during the same period as Sartre's seminal 1938 novel, *Nausea*. The two works complement each

[5] TCL, 143.
[6] TCL, 140.
[7] TCL, 141.
[8] TCL, 144.

other in that they explore many of the same philosophical ideas: contingency, indeterminacy, self-identity and bad faith. Both Lucien Fleurier and the central character of *Nausea*, Antoine Roquentin, are haunted by issues of self-identity and bewildered by existence generally. Their existential anxieties are largely the same. Where they differ is in terms of their response to these anxieties, with each choosing himself as the kind of person the other detests. Antoine detests those who, like Lucien, seek to fool themselves that their existence is necessary, while Lucien comes to detest those who, like Antoine, think and question too much and dwell on their contingency and superfluity. Lucien suppresses his anxieties by striving to *be* something, and eventually becomes a superficial, bourgeois *salaud* (shit, or bastard) steeped in bad faith, very much like one of the *salauds* described in *Nausea* that Antoine so despises.

For his part, Antoine sees through the deluded posturing of the *salauds* and in opposition to them thoroughly indulges his anxieties. Rather than strive, as they do, to *be* something, he strives instead to *be* nothing. Antoine's project of nihilism, however, his attempt to *be* his own nothingness, is, nonetheless, a last desperate attempt to escape his indeterminacy. As such it is as much a project in bad faith as Lucien's *seriousness*. Antoine's bad faith consists in his false belief that he is his own nothingness in the mode of being it, a nothingness-in-itself, when in fact his nothingness is a nothingness-for-itself which he has to be without being able to be it. For a person to believe that "deep down" he is a non-being-in-itself is equivalent to believing that "deep down" he is a being-in-itself. In so far as both attitudes involve considering himself to be a self-identical being, both attitudes are equally in bad faith. In *Pour une Morale de l'ambigüité* (*The Ethics of Ambiguity*), Simone de Beauvoir compares the nihilist with the serious person who seeks to annihilate his subjectivity by treating himself as an object defined by social norms:

> The failure of the serious sometimes brings about a radical disorder. Conscious of being unable to be anything, man then decides to be nothing. We shall call this attitude nihilistic. The nihilist is close to the spirit of seriousness, for instead of realising his negativity as a living movement, he conceives his annihilation in a substantial way. He wants to *be* nothing, and this nothing that he dreams of is still another sort of being.[9]

Antoine, however, remains a far more sympathetic character than Lucien because he strives with a brutal honesty that is genuinely admirable, even

[9] Beauvoir, *The Ethics of Ambiguity*, 52.

heroic, to confront certain hard existential truths that Lucien, as he grows older, strives to evade. Also, Antoine's way of being, his way of being in bad faith, harms only himself, whereas Lucien's bigotry is harmful to others.

Like the young, precocious Sartre himself, Lucien Fleurier is troubled by questions of identity and reality throughout his childhood. In fact, many of the incidental details in "The Childhood of a Leader" are drawn from Sartre's own childhood as later described in his autobiography, *Les Mots* (*Words*). For example, at the start of the story Lucien is wearing an angel's costume: "'I look adorable in my little angel's costume.' Mme. Portier told mamma."[10] In *Words* Sartre writes:

> [I]n a blue muslin dress, with stars in my hair and wings, I went from one person to the next, offering them mandarin oranges from a basket, as they exclaimed: "He *really is* an angel!"[11]

Lucien's childhood and adolescence are characterised by a quest to understand who he is, to find and define himself, to give himself a solidity and reality that will replace the vagueness, indeterminacy and insubstantiality he usually feels. In feeling indeterminate and contingent he is recognising the existential truth that there is nothing that he is in the mode of being it, that, like everyone else, he must play at being what he is because he cannot simply be what he is. As Sartre later wrote in *L'□tre et le néant* (*Being and Nothingness*):

> I can be he only in *representation*. But if I represent myself as him, I am not he; I am separated from him as the object from the subject, separated by *nothing*, but this nothing isolates me from him. I can not be he, I can only play at *being* him; that is, imagine to myself that I am he. And thereby I affect him with nothingness.[12]

Like many people, Lucien does not like to have a sense of his own indeterminacy and contingency, it makes him uncomfortable and anxious. As he gets older he takes increasingly drastic measures to ease this anxiety. He eventually chooses to think and act in profound bad faith, creating the illusion of his own necessity and determinacy and willing himself to believe in it. The crucial episode in the development of Lucien's bad faith is his homosexual relationship with Bergère. His

---

[10] TCL, 84.
[11] Sartre, *Words*, 27.
[12] Sartre, *Being and Nothingness*, 83.

journey into extreme bad faith is in no small part an adverse reaction to this episode.

Bergère awakens homosexual desires in Lucien but, partly as a result of his naivety and partly as a result of bad faith, Lucien refuses to acknowledge his own homosexual tendencies or the true meaning of Bergère's advances: "He had no luck; twenty times, these last few days, he had almost discovered what Bergère wanted of him and each time, as if on purpose, something happened to turn away his thought."[13] In this respect, Lucien is comparable to Sartre's flirt in *Being and Nothingness*, who relinquishes responsibility for herself and her situation, refusing to acknowledge the sexual background of her suitors' attentions.[14] Lucien escapes the burden of his responsibility for himself by allowing himself to exist for Bergère as a flattered, pampered object, a doll. He has fantasised since childhood in a vaguely sexual way about being treated like a doll. Unable to determine himself, Lucien allows himself to be determined as the object of Bergère's homosexual desires: "Lucien slowly removed his slippers and dressing gown and slipped under the covers without a word [...] he told himself, 'I'm his little doll!'"[15]

Although Lucien is a homosexual insofar as he practises homosexuality, he nonetheless shares the deep-rooted homophobic prejudices of his social class. He reacts strongly against his homosexual encounter with Bergère, against his own homosexuality, by making a radical conversion to extreme bad faith. He strives to deny the true meaning of his sexual encounter by treating it as an unfortunate aberration to be blamed on circumstances and other people. In time, he treats it as an aberration to be blamed on the traditional and convenient scapegoat of Jews and their supposedly dangerous, corrupting ideas. Lucien's anti-Semitism is a distraction from his homosexual desires. What he really fears and therefore hates are these desires, but to hate them would be to recognise that he has them, so instead he hates Jews and what he comes to identify as Jewish intellectualism: "And how much he preferred the unconscious, reeking of the soil, which Barrès gave him, to the filthy, lascivious images of Freud."[16]

Maurice Barrès (1862–1923) was a French novelist, journalist and politician, noted for his fervent nationalism, his anti-Semitism and his involvement in the Dreyfus Affair. As an early influence on writers such as Gide, Aragon and Mauriac, Barrès remains an important if controversial

---

[13] TCL, 115.
[14] See *Being and Nothingness*, 78-79.
[15] TCL, 116-17.
[16] TCL, 131.

figure in French literature. In "The Childhood of a Leader", Lucien Fleurier reads Barrès on the recommendation of the racist nationalist, André Lemordant. Sartre clearly despised Barrès, and even lampooned him in *Nausea* as a model *salaud*:

> An excellent portrait, granted. Olivier Blévigne had a little black moustache and his olive-tinted face somewhat resembled that of Maurice Barrès. The two men had undoubtedly met: they sat on the same benches.[17]

Antoine Roquentin even has a dream in which he spanks Barrès until he bleeds: "I gave Maurice Barrès a spanking [...] we spanked him until he bled."[18]

One of the central aims of "The Childhood of Leader" is to show that the slide into anti-Semitism, into any kind of racism, is not first and foremost a political journey, but a personal journey into the self-evasions, the inauthenticity, of bad faith. The story explores a set of personal circumstances—one set among many possible sets—that results in the adoption of bigotry as a means of imposing an illusion of certainty on a morally confused and confusing world. The story was published just prior to the Second World War and was a timely response to the increasing hatred and suspicion that was being directed towards Jews in France and throughout Europe. By the late 1930s, Sartre would certainly have known about the systematic persecution of Jews that was taking place in Nazi Germany but, like most people, he would have been unaware of the true scale and horror of the problem.

In 1946 Sartre returned to the theme of anti-Semitism in *Réflexions sur la question juive*[19], a book largely inspired by his desire to address the taboo subject of French complicity in the Nazi project, at the time of the widely unwelcome return to France of French Jews deported by the Nazis. *Anti-Semite and Jew*, like Sartre's "American" play of the same year, *La Putain respectueuse*[20], confronts the issue that the defeat of German Nazism was not synonymous with the defeat of prejudice and hatred in those western democracies that defeated Nazism.

Lucien's membership of the French Fascist movement, an aggressive, macho, anti-intellectual tribe, makes him feel strong and proud and gives him a sense of belonging. He had formerly searched for his *personal*

---

[17] Sartre, *Nausea*, 135.

[18] TCL, 89.

[19] *Reflections on the Jewish Question*, available in English as *Anti-Semite and Jew*.

[20] *The Respectful Prostitute*, available in English as *The Respectable Prostitute*.

identity, but now he is happy to take on an identity granted and confirmed by the group; happy to be nothing more than his being-for-others:

> "First maxim", Lucien said, "not to try and see inside yourself; there is no mistake more dangerous." The real Lucien—he knew now—had to be sought in the eyes of others.[21]

By fiercely despising Jews, his badge of honour among his fellow Fascists, he not only finds a scapegoat for his past actions, he also sees himself as important and substantial in comparison to those he despises. He prides himself that he is not a member of a despised or humiliated race, but a Frenchman with a good French name and respectable ancestry. His anti-Semitism, unreasonable and unfounded though it is, transforms him into a man of conviction. His racist convictions define him and give him solidity; like religious beliefs, they demand the respect of others: "Lucien's anti-Semitism was of a different sort: unrelenting and pure, it stuck out of him like a steel blade menacing other breasts. 'It's ... sacred,' he thought."[22]

Throughout the story, and in other works by Sartre, such as *Nausea*, the moustache marks out those serious-minded bourgeois who command respect for their convictions, their belief that whatever they choose to believe is true. These men of apparent substance have fooled themselves and others that they exist by right, that they are what they are in the mode of being it: a being-in-itself rather than a being-for-itself. It is not surprising then that Lucien completes the construction of his false object-self by growing a moustache. Lucien Fleurier's fellow Fascist, Lemordant, has a moustache, as does the Fascist *falangista* who takes himself so seriously in "The Wall":

> The *falangista* had a moustache. I said to him again, "You ought to shave off your moustache, idiot." I thought it funny that he would let the hairs of his living being invade his face. He kicked me without great conviction and I kept quiet.[23]

The *salauds* Blévigne and Barrès in *Nausea* also have moustaches.

Sartre is obsessed with moustaches, they recur so often in his fictional writings that we lose count of them. Some of his female characters have them too, although they are excused for not having *cultivated* them. In *Le Sursis* (*The Reprieve*) he writes: "She was a good-looking, buxom

[21] TCL, 142.
[22] TCL, 142.
[23] Sartre, "The Wall", in *The Wall*, 16.

Marseillaise with a shadow of a moustache."[24] He identifies them, on men, as a ridiculous, futile gesture, as superfluous and surreal. They tend to belong to minor characters, to unthinking men with no inner life, to characters that exist as the Other for his main characters. A man cannot see his own moustache, at least to the extent that others see it, so a moustache exists chiefly for others and a man with a moustache is a man who has undertaken to exist for others rather than for himself. In so far as it is typical of the bourgeois to strive to *be* his social role, the moustache, for Sartre, becomes the emblem of the shallow, self-satisfied, respectable, reactionary middle class gentleman. In *Nausea* he writes:

> The fine gentleman exists Legion of Honour, exists moustache, that's all; how happy one must be to be nothing more than a Legion of Honour and a moustache and nobody sees the rest, he sees the two pointed ends of moustache on both sides of the nose; I do not think therefore I am a moustache.[25]

Primarily, "The Childhood of a Leader" details one person's slide into the kind of chronic, cowardly, morally repugnant bad faith that, for Sartre, typifies the French (or any) bourgeois. That is, the faith that his existence is not accidental but essential and that he has sacred *rights* granted by God and his nation, such as the right to have unquestionable opinions and prejudices and the right to have his necessary existence confirmed by the respect of others, particularly the social inferiors he is destined to lead. In *Nausea*, Sartre refers to the bourgeoisie as *salauds*. "The Childhood of a Leader" complements *Nausea* in being about a *salaud* or, more specifically, in being about the evolution of a *salaud*. That is, a pillar of the community who has learnt to deny his inner life by becoming nothing more than a *posturing* before others, a poser: "So many people were waiting for him, at attention: and he was and always would be this immense waiting of others. 'That's a leader', he thought."[26]

We can easily imagine that, like the *salaud*, Olivier Blévigne, in *Nausea*, Lucien will go on to have a portrait of himself painted in which he will appear grander, more significant, more substantial, more perfectly moustachioed and infinitely less contingent than he really is:

---

[24] Sartre, *The Reprieve*, 267.
[25] *Nausea*, 147.
[26] TCL, 143.

> The power of art is truly admirable. Of this shrill-voiced little man, nothing would go down to posterity except a threatening face, a superb gesture, and the bloodshot eyes of a bull.[27]

Works Cited

Beauvoir, Simone de. *The Ethics of Ambiguity* (trans. Bernard Frechtman). New York: Citadel Press, 2000.

Cox, Gary. *Sartre and Fiction*. London and New York: Continuum International, 2009.

Sartre, Jean-Paul. *Anti-Semite and Jew* (trans. George J. Becker). New York: Schocken, 1995.

—. *Being and Nothingness: An Essay on Phenomenological Ontology* (trans. Hazel E. Barnes). London and New York: Routledge, 2003.

—. "The Childhood of a Leader", in Sartre, *The Wall*, (trans. Lloyd Alexander). New York: New Directions, 1988.

—. *Intimacy* (trans. Lloyd Alexander). London: Panther, 1960.

—. *Nausea* (trans. Robert Baldick). London: Penguin, 2000.

—. *The Reprieve* (trans. Eric Sutton). London: Penguin, 2005.

—. *The Respectable Prostitute* (trans. Kitty Black), in *"In Camera" and Other Plays*. London: Penguin, 1990.

—. *Words* (trans. Irene Clephane). London: Penguin, 2000.

[27] *Nausea*, 136.

PART II:

SARTRE AND TIME

CHAPTER FIVE

SARTRE'S TIMETABLE

FRANÇOIS NOUDELMANN

What must the ordinary day of an extraordinary man look like? Sartre stood aside from all élites and left a well-known formula at the end of *Les Mots* (*Words*) to define himself as "[a] whole man, made up of all men, worth any one of them, and any one of them worth him."[1] But Claude Lanzmann rightly pointed out to Sartre that he was "rather more just anyone" than any other man. To which Sartre made this sublime response: "Being just anyone is a task, a mission: you cannot *be* just anyone, you have to become it!"[2]

Ordinary or extraordinary existences?

The ordinary man, therefore, is ordinary as a matter of will, he actively resists the seductions of elitism. However, is this ethic compatible with the idea of *un homme siècle*, a "man of the century"? Sartre wanted indeed to carry the century upon his shoulders, like Frantz, his negative double in *Les Séquestrés d'Altona* (*The Condemned of Altona*). He assumed a total responsibility by theorising and living existence according to the idea of an historical incarnation. Taking up the Hegelian conception of the Objective Mind, he subsumed the singular by the universal. And when Sartre interested himself in individuals, he did not choose just anyone: Baudelaire, Mallarmé, Tintoretto, Flaubert and Genet were men of the Word and of Meaning, they embodied their epoch by their singularity.

---

[1] "Tout un homme, fait de tous les hommes et qui les vaut tous et que vaut n'importe qui." (Sartre 1964, 213.) This chapter—a draft of which was given as a paper at the conference of the Japanese Sartre Society at Rikkyô University, Tokyo, in July 2009—and all quotations are translated from French by the Editors.

[2] "Être n'importe qui c'est une tâche, une mission, il ne faut pas rester n'importe qui, il faut le devenir!" (Lanzmann DVD 2005.)

The understanding of these "extraordinary" existences for Sartre, who had an avowed "passion" to understand human beings, entailed going constantly from the individual to History. In this respect, Sartre was different from Sainte-Beuve because he did not stop short at the biography of the self, and sought the process of constitution more than the connection between the life and the work. The structuralists were not prepared to acknowledge this fact and relegated Sartre to the nineteenth century. However, the author of *L'Idiot de la famille* (*The Family Idiot*) was not claiming to say who Flaubert was: he showed rather how one becomes Flaubert. Historiography, sociology, psychoanalysis, linguistics were all enlisted to serve this ambition: to illuminate the investment in an existence that is endowed with meaning. According to this plan, Sartre wanted to collate all the signs, all the traces of these singular existences in order to inscribe them in a project of meaningfulness. He presupposed that everything makes sense in an existence in order to constitute a life, even what seems to lie outside the individual's intentions. This totalising approach articulated two contiguous and complex notions: life and existence.

Life and existence

What is Sartre concerned with in his monographs? With the *existence* of Baudelaire, Flaubert, Genet… or with their *lives*? Faithful to the existentialist philosophies, Sartre maintains the idea that existence is what is *there*, arising from facticity and contingency, and that it is made up of situations, possibilities and choices. Life designates rather a collection of deliberations, decisions and behaviours. Well into the post-war period, Sartre confined life to the biological given, to the in-itself, to the realm of things. One has to wait until the *Critique de la raison dialectique* (*Critique of Dialectical Reason*) in 1960 to see him attribute a role to need and approach a dimension of life which is no longer reduced strictly to the biological. He incorporates it, nevertheless, with great reservation because he is suspicious of Nietzschean or Bergsonian vitalism.

The distinction between life and existence appears all the more problematic when Sartre describes and analyses his own existence. In *Les Mots*, and also in numerous interviews which he gave on his work and his thought, he displays an ideal of transparency and exhibits a sort of continuous self-analysis. The reconstruction of his existence portrays thereby a life in perpetual formation, and Sartre resorts to dramatisation of his abrupt changes [*ruptures*] and constant reconstructions [*dépassements*], to the point of inventing them, as with his sudden conversion to atheism in childhood. The reader is entrapped because Sartre himself takes charge of his own critique: bad faith, illusions of Salvation, self-deluding individualism, bourgeois trappings... In this way, he reappropriates the movement of his own existence as a self in the process of becoming. Sartre constructs for himself a life in constant revolution, like an anti-biography evading any external attempt to fix it by imposing a narrative. Precisely so: life reveals itself only through "true novels", totalising and detotalising fictions of which the author wishes to remain in control.

The phantom of continuity

The life constructed by these possessive narratives is haunted by the phantom of unity and continuity. Certainly, Sartre insists repeatedly upon *les ruptures et les dépassements.* However, he does so in order to demonstrate more clearly, in retrospect, the coherence of his project, with its fictional "original moment". Such stories echo the philosophical question of the continuity of consciousness, a question which torments Sartre because consciousness is defined as a being in perpetual treachery. It is what it is not and is not what it is. It is no longer what it has been and it is not yet what it will be. How, then, can we be sure that it is always the same consciousness? And what terms can we find to denote its continuity, without fixing it in a representation of the self which would amount to the bad faith of a person who is able to say who s/he is? Authenticity, sincerity, fidelity, self-reintegration [*réenroulement*]—these are the words that Sartre tries out, notably in his *Carnets de la drôle de guerre* (*Notebooks from a Phoney War*).

In this desire to find the meaning of the continuity of existences, and the refusal to accept them as pre-determined lives, Sartre maintains the presupposition that all the elements of an existence have a meaning and that those meanings are connected. His monographs and his autobiography rely upon just such a unifying conception. But are there no facts, no moments, no activities that escape this current of meaningfulness? Sartre's enormous interpretative machinery imposes upon us his totalising vision, which throws light on individualising programmes and promotes his regressive-progressive methodology.

And yet, if we pay attention to moments and activities that are not verbalised, another life reveals itself and shows existence to be, as it were, full of holes or dreamt-up, multiple and discontinuous. Melancholy, depression, sickness, dreams, love, music—all of these involve so many affects and temporalities that resile from the narrative unification of a life.

In these aspects, Sartre revealed himself to be less synchronous with his era, experiencing times which did not follow the great timeline of History.

Sartrean melancholy

The idea of discovering the real Sartre behind the presentation that he gave of his existence would surely be an illusion. Nevertheless, biographical enquiry does enable us to simplify his multiple portraits and to keep his retrospective and unifying vision at a distance. His days were filled by numerous heterogeneous time-slots: friends, writing, women, piano, sleep. Sartre thematised these micro-temporalities. He gave them a meaningfulness, a representation, a conceptualisation. However, several sources enable us to observe a distortion between his "lived experience" [*vécu*]—a notion that he develops in respect of Flaubert—and his narratives. And if it remains illusory to discover an authentic life behind the narrative, it is instructive to observe the discursive construction of these *vécus* and their dissonance with other stories, testimonies, confidences which hint at the unspoken, the holes in temporal linearity. Time is no longer dialectical, it is suspended, made up of "achronisms", moments outside of time.

Against the flow of Sartrean activism—that is to say his valorisation of intention and activity—melancholy signals moments of passivity that are less within our control. The original title of *La Nausée* (*Nausea*) was *Melancholia* and took its inspiration from Dürer. To be sure, Sartre liked to declare that he had never known anguish or melancholy, a way of thumbing his nose at Heideggerian *Sorge*, or "angst". Yet several testimonies, notably those of Simone de Beauvoir, evoke significant episodes of depression in Sartre's life, and not only after his experiments with mescaline. His empathy with Romanticism, detectable in his juvenilia, signals also an attraction towards *la morbidezza*, even if it is denied or mocked. His taste for Chopin's nocturns and his sense of dissolving in the waters of Venice confirm it.

Moments of dreaming are a part of this passive life. In *L'Imaginaire* (*The Imaginary*), Sartre accords little credit to the images of dreams, and stresses his distrust of the interpretation of dreams by psychoanalysis. He had already condemned the surrealist uses of dreams which created the illusion of the autonomy of images. His fascination was nevertheless manifest in his voluntary experiments with hallucinatory phenomena, marked by the slight madness of believing that one can both hallucinate and describe one's delirium objectively—that one can be, at one and the same time, subject and object. However, Sartre confided his dreams to

Arlette Elkaïm. He did not write them down, like Adorno or Benjamin who left accounts of their imaginary activity during sleep. For Sartre, dreams evaded writing and were shared with a woman, doubtless because they did not fit into the project of a controllable meaningfulness.

Flights of fancy

These secret temporalities suggest escapes in Sartre's life. The thread of life, the self-reintegration or *réenroulement* of existence leave no space in which to recount these flights of truancy. Yet the couple Sartre–Beauvoir had privileged a willingness to say everything, to give an account of the least details of ordinary life, with its physical and psychological weaknesses. Their transparent relationship showed forth a highly controlled agreement between a man and a woman telling each other all their amorous adventures. The couple took on board the freedom and the truth of each other's desires. The testimony of third parties shows, however, that this life was not exempt from lies, or from jealousies provoked by multiple and hidden lives. In her love letter to Jean-Paul Sartre, Françoise Sagan explains that the numerous women who pursued him "restored a life to him, the life he had known hitherto, his life as a ladies' man, a philanderer, a liar, sympathetic and amusing".[3] To recount this hidden life is not to attempt to unmask another Sartre, less glorious or more libertine. Rather, the telling of it enables the reader to free her/himself from the self-representation that the author has produced and to observe the work of construction, the narrative crafting of ordinary life.

If there is a domain in which the verbal often fails to take account of the *vécu*, no doubt it is music. Here too, Sartre devoted a large part of his life to a practice which escapes discourse and the great timeline of History: he played the piano daily from childhood, and even at moments of major political engagement, he jealously guarded those moments outside of time. He talks about them in *Les Mots* in order to evoke the complicity with his mother, but when he writes about music, it is in order to situate himself in the avant-garde art scene. He takes care not to recount his intimacy with the Romantics, preferring to comment on Stockhausen, Xenakis or Berio. The affective, imaginative, sensual life he enjoys with his musical instrument has no place in the grand historical discourse of the period.

The timetable of Sartre the man bears witness to a segmentation which differs from the narrative of an active totalisation. It incites the reader to

---

[3] "[Elles] lui restituaient la vie, sa vie de jusqu'alors, sa vie d'homme à femmes, coureur, menteur, compatissant ou comédien." (Sagan.)

free her/himself from the author's discourse on his life. The ethic of control, of transparency, of activity encounters experiences that are irreducible to a unilinear interpretation. Life is composed of tempos, of rhythms, of sequences made up of passivities. These times are stretched, fragmented, dispersed by uncontrollable imaginings and corporeal constraints.

Away from the grand Sartrean formulations on the totalisation of the singular by the spiralling movement of History, individual time is the object of an existential question: how do these scattered temporalities, which Sartre sought to reassemble into a life-story, articulate with each other? It is less a matter of retotalising them than of composing rhythms, for writing possesses that virtue of constructing the tempos of life. It deploys a score in which the self remains accessible to variations, counterpoints, suspensions.

Sartre's activist psyche led him constantly to re-take control of these passive temporalities—of the body, of the emotions, of the dream-world. Thus he sought even to deny sickness, continuing to work vigorously when he was on the very threshold of death. Montaigne, at the end of his life, wanted to retain precious moments, to take full advantage of the present, even to the point of forgetting his Stoical ethic of knowing how to die. For Jean-Paul Sartre, those moments of let-it-be remained in the non-verbal sphere, nestled in the temporalities of the clandestine life.

Works Cited

Lanzmann, Claude, and Madeleine Gobeil. *Sartre, entretiens et témoignages*. (DVD) CBC Radio Canada / BNF, 2005.

Sagan, Françoise. "Lettre d'amour à Jean-Paul Sartre", in *Avec mon meilleur souvenir*. Paris: Gallimard, 1984.

Sartre, Jean-Paul. *Baudelaire*. Paris: Gallimard, 1947.

—. *Carnets de la drôle de guerre*. Paris: Gallimard, 1983.

—. *Critique de la raison dialectique, I*. Paris: Gallimard, 1960.

—. *L'Idiot de la famille, I, II, III*. Paris: Gallimard, 1972, 1973.

—. *Les Mots*. Paris: Gallimard, 1964.

—. *Saint-Genet, comédien et martyr*. Paris: Gallimard, 1952.

—. *Les Séquestrés d'Altona*. Paris: Gallimard, 1960.

CHAPTER SIX

HOW SARTRE AND BEAUVOIR WORKED TOGETHER

MICHEL CONTAT

There are very few studies on how Sartre and Beauvoir helped each other professionally, how they collaborated in the exercise of their craft. After *Les Mots* (*Words*) and the demystifying of his former conception of literature as a means of achieving metaphysical salvation, Sartre kept on insisting that literature is mainly a profession. Certainly a difficult and very demanding one, but nevertheless a profession, that is a combination of knowledge, know-how, techniques and procedures serving the production of a *work*. Sartre and Beauvoir were two professional writers who united their lives to produce works of an intellectual nature.[1]

Sartre and Beauvoir never wrote or signed a book together, their collaboration took other paths, and we have to acknowledge that we know only very few details about their collaboration. Most importantly: they were giving each other an *imprimatur* after careful rereading and without indulgence. Sartre said once that he was enormously lucky as a writer to have someone at his side who knew where he was going and what his goals were, and who approved of them, who judged what he was doing according to his own principles, and who was capable of deciding how well he succeeded. Sartre and Beauvoir discussed their projects both in general terms and in great detail. They submitted to each other different versions of their manuscripts and read them with a great deal of critical attention.

---

[1] An earlier draft of this chapter was given at the sixteenth annual conference of the UK Sartre Society at the Institut Français, South Kensington, in September 2009. A version in French has been published as: "La Collaboration Beauvoir–Sartre", in *The Florence Gould Lectures at New York University*, vol. X (eds. Tom Bishop and Coralie Girard), 2009, 184-202. Adaptation of text and translation of quotations have been, appositely, a collaboration of author and editors.

In the film *Sartre par lui-même* (*Sartre by Himself*), Beauvoir recalls with amusement how violently she criticised Sartre and how he sometimes resisted before he finally had to concede that his "little judge" was right. Sartre's manuscripts very seldom bear a handwritten comment or correction by Beauvoir, which means that her criticisms were mostly made orally. We know that for *La Nausée* (*Nausea*) these criticisms were numerous and important, severe and stimulating. In the manuscript there is only one correction by the hand of Beauvoir, dealing with the repetition of one single word. But it is a final manuscript, made after Beauvoir's initial remarks and advice. Her criticisms thus dealt at the same time with small details of execution and large questions of construction and style. Two of these criticisms had a considerable influence on the work: on the one hand, she criticised the lack of tension in the first versions, which were too philosophical for her taste; on the other hand, she thought his prose displayed an exaggerated use of adjectives and comparisons.

For Sartre's part, we know less about what precisely he critiqued in Beauvoir's early literary endeavours. He made a general criticism of the young female characters who were too influenced by the English novels which Beauvoir was fond of. He encouraged her to draw inspiration more from her own life and to be more self-assured about her own individuality and originality: she, as a woman, was far more interesting than the female characters in English novels. He wanted her to be herself in her books, with the same boldness that she had in life. And he also reproached her for lacking ideas: he wanted her to *think* more, to *work* more, and to come up with original ideas. Beginning with *L'Invitée* (*She Came to Stay*), Beauvoir used a technique that they had forged together by discussing Dos Passos, Faulkner, and Hemingway. The ironical distance that both Sartre and Beauvoir adopted towards some of their characters was directly inspired by Dos Passos's narrative technique in the *USA* trilogy. Thus, it seems that Sartre's criticisms were mostly concerned with the actual realisation of projects whose principles he condoned.

In his war diaries, *Carnets de la drôle de guerre* (*Notebooks from a Phoney War*), Sartre explains how he asked Beauvoir her opinion about his ideas for developing the characters for his novel *L'Age de raison* (*The Age of Reason*), which he wrote as a soldier while on the Eastern Front in 1939. She dissuades him from writing a prologue in which the reader would have learnt how the different characters had experienced childhood. Sartre had wanted to select specific childhood scenes which would have given a key to each one of the characters.

In these war years, only one work seems to have resulted from an actual collaboration, and that is the reportage on the liberation of Paris which Sartre signed in his name alone in the newspaper *Combat*, under the title "Un Promeneur dans Paris insurgé" ("Walking through the Paris insurrection"), during the days of upheaval in August 1944. Sartre and Beauvoir had lived the events together, yet in different places, and this confers a sort of ubiquity upon the author.

Another role that Beauvoir undertook for Sartre was that of an editor. Jean-Jacques Servan-Schreiber, a former director of *L'Express*, describes this in his memoirs. He and Sartre had agreed that Sartre would write a series of articles against De Gaulle in 1958. Sartre was supposed to hand in fifteen pages for each article. The first one he sent from Rome had seventy-five pages—unbelievable! Servan-Schreiber did not know how to cut it to fit just two pages of the magazine, so he called Beauvoir in Paris. She came, and very professionally cut the article to the right size, perfectly. Then she left without a word.

For his part, Sartre greatly encouraged Beauvoir to write *Le Deuxième Sexe* (*The Second Sex*) as an assessment of her own experience as a woman. Later, he helped with her several volumes of memoirs by reading the first drafts and giving her schemes of analysis, offering details on facts about their lives and interpretations of how they had lived certain historical moments together. This collaboration was the result of conversation, discussion and shared reminiscence. In the dialogues she had with Sartre in 1974, Beauvoir goes so far as to say that anything to do with politics in her memoirs was written practically under Sartre's "dictation".

From 1954, they were both embarking on an autobiographical enterprise, and it seems that Sartre had deliberately given to Beauvoir the task of becoming the historiographer of their relationship. What he intended to do was to elucidate the origin of his literary calling, and to understand how he had been driven to write the books he had written and to take the political stands he had taken. He wanted to write the story of an intellectual who was representative of his time. Beauvoir, on the other hand, wanted to write "memoirs", a chronicle of their life as a couple, to which she undoubtedly attached greater importance than he did, probably because she had a more literary representation of what a couple could and should be. The success of the couple as such appears to have been a goal for Beauvoir since the days of her adolescence. Sartre, by contrast, always thought of himself as a bachelor who was pairing up with an intellectual partner for the production of their work. Thus they never conceived a common work, although each collaborated with the other's work by approving it. We are dealing here with two distinct and distinctive bodies of work, each having its own specific affective tonality, whilst being nevertheless connected by a profound intellectual kinship.

Beauvoir took up projects that her companion had abandoned. For example, after their joint trip to China in 1955, Sartre had started a book on China, then dropped it, and Beauvoir wrote *La Longue Marche* (*The Long March*), which today is probably the most embarrassing of her books to read because of its lack of critical distance. Beauvoir also replied to attacks on Sartre when he did not want to engage in polemics. In 1954, she responded to Merleau-Ponty's assault on "Sartre et l'ultrabolchévisme" ("Sartre and Ultra-Bolshevism") by a vigorous and pugnacious article entitled "Merleau-Ponty et le pseudo-sartrisme" ("Merleau-Ponty and pseudo-Sartreanism"). When existentialism is criticised, she defends it with passion and reason. So, the collaboration of these two writers illustrates an ethos of generosity, reciprocity, equality and practical solidarity. It is exactly this "writers' ethic" that Sartre reproached himself for having arrived at in his first phase of moral thought, precisely because it was valid *solely* for writers.

The only work they undertook together as an active collaboration is the dialogue published by Simone de Beauvoir, in 1981, as the second part of *La Cérémonie des adieux*, entitled: *Entretiens avec Jean-Paul Sartre, août–septembre 1974*.[2] They started these dialogues with the idea of collecting material for a sequel to *Les Mots*, which Sartre had announced but, for various reasons, had put off writing. A first follow-up had been the movie *Sartre par lui-même,* which Alexandre Astruc and I had begun to film in 1972 (although final production was delayed until 1976: Beauvoir mentions the project in *Entretiens*, to the effect that it is impossible to know whether it will ever be finished).

In 1974, during their usual summer vacation in Rome, Beauvoir encouraged Sartre, in order to keep him busy—he had lost his sight the previous year and was no longer able to write—to take up his autobiographical project again. She had a model that she had probably discussed with him at the time, and it is the order adopted for *Tout compte fait* (*All Said and Done*), the supposedly last volume of her memoirs. This volume is arranged not by chronological order, but thematically. This is the form she suggested for the sequel to *Les Mots* that she proposed to help Sartre write, and possibly even to write herself, with his guidance. But she never explained how she intended to realise this project in practical terms. That is why, in order simply to collect material, she adopts the posture of an interviewer: a keen interviewer with a privileged knowledge of her subject, it is true, but an interviewer all the same. This means that she very

[2] Paris: Gallimard, 1981. Literally, *The Farewell Ceremony* and *Interviews with Jean-Paul Sartre, August–September 1974*, these are available in English as *Adieux: A Farewell to Sartre*, trans. Patrick O'Brian, Pantheon, 1985 (Eds.)

seldom involves herself personally in the dialogue. Their relationship is not envisaged as a theme in the book, and whenever Sartre tries to speak of it, she cuts him short, saying: "Let's not talk about me."

Perhaps the complete recording of this dialogue will be published one day—I certainly hope so. I do not know whether this recording exists or is technically of good enough quality to be published. But I do know that it is the oral performance of these *Entretiens* that made me realise how good and interesting they are. In 2001, the fascinating French actor Sami Frey gave a performance at the École Normale Supérieure, over a whole week, reading the *Entretiens* in their entirety, and these readings were broadcast by France Culture radio. It was so brilliant, moving and intelligent, that it revealed how Sartre gives himself through these dialogues, in complete good faith. Thus, we become witnesses to a philosophical exercise *en situation* (in real time, as it were), much more than to a mere exercise in reminiscence: Sartre tries, under the questioning of Beauvoir, to reflect upon his life in precise terms, looking for the *mot juste*, in order to extract its ultimate meaning, with a candour that is deeply moving.

Beauvoir herself says very few things about the way she conducted these interviews and edited them. She concludes: "He had come to accept his half-blindness and he was proud to have been able to adapt to it so well."[3] But the dialogues were eventually abandoned for another project: a series for television on the history of the century, as seen subjectively by Sartre. Both he and Beauvoir worked on this project for many months with Benny Lévy (previously known as Pierre Victor), Sartre's new secretary and former head of the revolutionary organisation *La Gauche prolétarienne* (the Proletarian Left), which Sartre had supported. However, this project also finally collapsed, owing to the opposition of political leaders on the right who judged it to be dangerous. When Simone de Beauvoir published the *Entretiens,* she wrote a short preface explaining how they had been conceived. There, she insists that they show the "meanderings" of Sartre's thought in the rough, and the originality of his "living voice". This is indeed what strikes one most in these dialogues: the way that Sartre searches for the right expression of his thought—what I call his enormous good faith—and the sound of his voice that has such an authentic ring to it.

There was also another urgent reason for Beauvoir to publish the *Entretiens*, namely to reaffirm Sartre's atheism in the face of the world, after the publication of his last interviews with Benny Lévy in successive

[3] "Même sa demi-cécité, il avait fini par en prendre son parti et il était fier de s'y être si bien adapté." (Beauvoir 1981, 97-98.)

issues of *Le Nouvel Observateur* in Spring 1980, just weeks before Sartre's death (and subsequently collected and published as *L'Espoir maintenant—Hope Now*—in 1991). In those interviews, Sartre had appeared to renounce his former atheism, and this had made them a subject of immense controversy. Had "the last Sartre" become a religious believer? I shall return to this question in due course.

In the *Entretiens* of 1974, there are very few instances of a reflective attitude towards what Sartre and Beauvoir are actually doing. Near the end, Beauvoir says, almost incidentally:

> I would like you to look at your life in the same way as I tried to look at mine when I wrote the beginning of *Tout compte fait*. That is to say, what has there been in your life in the way of opportunities, risks, moments of freedom, and obstacles to that freedom?[4]

Let us begin by examining how *Tout compte fait* is crafted. In a "Prologue", Beauvoir describes her project as follows:

> In the preceding volumes, I adopted a chronological order. I am aware of its disadvantages. The reader has the feeling that s/he is only ever getting secondary information: preambles. It seems that the essential is always up ahead, further off. [...] Yet I could not proceed in any other way. Living was, for me, a clearly oriented enterprise and to give a true account of it, I had to follow its slow progression. [...] I still have projects that I care about, but [...] I no longer have the feeling that I am heading towards a goal, only that of sliding ineluctably towards my grave. So I no longer need to take the development of time as the narrative thread; to some extent, I will respect chronology, but I will organise my memories around certain themes.[5]

---

[4] "Je voudrais que vous la regardiez [votre vie] comme j'ai essayé de regarder la mienne lorsque j'ai écrit le début de *Tout compte fait*. C'est-à-dire, qu'est-ce qu'il y a eu dans votre vie comme chances, comme hasards, comme moments de liberté, comme obstacles à cette liberté?" (Beauvoir 1981, 539.)

[5] "Dans les volumes précédents, j'ai adopté un ordre chronologique. J'en connais les inconvénients. Le lecteur a l'impression qu'on ne lui livre jamais que l'accessoire: des préambules. Il semble que l'essentiel soit toujours en avant, plus loin. [...] Cependant, je ne pouvais pas procéder autrement. Vivre pour moi était une entreprise clairement orientée et pour en rendre compte il me fallait en suivre le cheminement. [...] des projets me tiennent encore à cœur, mais [...] je n'ai plus l'impression de me diriger vers un but mais seulement de glisser inéluctablement vers ma tombe. Alors il ne m'est plus nécessaire de prendre pour fil conducteur le déroulement du temps; dans une certaine mesure je tiendrai compte de la

Those themes are the following: the opportunities she has had in life, and the turning-points of freedom after a "good start". The rebellion against her milieu came after she discovered the really hateful nature of the bourgeoisie when her friend Zaza died. Her death, according to Beauvoir, was due to the authoritarian puritanical morality of Zaza's family. Of her own family, she says: "From ages seventeen to twenty, my parents' attitude caused me profound hurt without bringing any personal benefit."[6] Then she met the young Jean-Paul Sartre:

> How would I have developed if I had not met Sartre? Would I have got rid of my individualism, of the idealism and spiritualism that still encumbered my mind? I don't know. The fact is that I met him and that this was the capital event of my life.[7]

When one reads today Simone de Beauvoir's admirable *Cahiers de jeunesse* (*Notebooks of Youth*), one realises that she had already begun, before encountering Sartre, to get rid of the ideas that plagued her mind. If this encounter changed her life, it is also because she had prepared herself for it by her own liberation, which she could then pursue with him.

Beauvoir notes in *Tout compte fait*: "I had my eyes fixed on a promising future: I would become a writer. It is essentially the apprenticeship of writing that my freedom was engaged with."[8] Further on, she writes: "If I look at the general line of my life, I am struck by its continuity."[9] This continuity has the permanence of a place to live in: the city of Paris. This is followed by a reflexion on ageing: "I know and feel my finitude. Even if two or three volumes are added, my work will remain what it is now."[10] She notes her relative indifference towards death. Is it

chronologie; mais c'est autour de certains thèmes que j'organiserai mes souvenirs." (Beauvoir 1972, 9-10.)

[6] "De dix-sept à vingt ans, l'attitude de mes parents m'a profondément peinée sans que j'en tire aucun profit." (Ibid., 25.)

[7] "Comment aurais-je évolué si je n'avais pas rencontré Sartre? Me serais-je débarrassée plus tôt ou plus tard de mon individualisme, de l'idéalisme et du spiritualisme qui m'encombraient encore? Je ne le sais pas. Le fait est que je l'ai rencontré et que ce fut l'événement capital de mon existence." (Ibid., 28.)

[8] "J'avais les yeux fixés sur un avenir prometteur: je deviendrais écrivain. C'est dans mon apprentissage de l'écriture qu'essentiellement ma liberté était engagée." (Ibid., 30-31.)

[9] "Si je considère la ligne générale de ma vie, elle me frappe par sa continuité." (Ibid., 37.)

[10] "J'éprouve ma finitude. Même enrichie de deux ou trois volumes, mon œuvre restera ce qu'elle est." (Ibid., 44).

because death is still far away? She, who as a young woman experienced such terrible anxieties about death, notes soberly: "[I]t is not nothingness that repulses: it is to become nothing."[11]

Then she makes an inventory of her present friendships: Stépha, Claude Courchay (a young writer), Claire Etcherelli, the Canadian journalist and Professor Madeleine Gobeil, Tito Gerassi (son of her friends Fernand and Stépha Gerassi), and of course Sylvie Le Bon, whom she had adopted as her daughter. She tells at length the sad story of "Camille", Sartre's first love, who ended her life as a pitiful alcoholic, in terrible mental and physical distress. She also remembers Lise (Natalie Sorokine), her former pupil (and lover, but that is not acknowledged), who went to live in the USA and whom she met again in California—there is an account of their voyage together across the USA in *L'Amérique au jour le jour* (*America from Day to Day*) which is one of Beauvoir's best books. She narrates the last days of Alberto Giacometti and of Sartre's mother, Madame Mancy. These narratives are followed by a long and not very successful chapter on her dreams, with no attempt at interpretation.

In chapter two, she explains the genesis of her books: *La Force des choses* (*Force of Circumstance*), *Les Belles Images* (*The Pretty Pictures,* although translations have preferred to retain the French title), *La Vieillesse* (*Old Age*), *Une Mort très douce* (*A Very Easy Death*), her finest book, in my opinion. This is followed by a chapter about her readings, which is interesting at the beginning but grows rapidly tedious because of sheer enumerations. What she has to say about the novel *Belle du Seigneur*, by Albert Cohen, is worth reading.[12] But her lists of the books she read as a "book devourer", as she characterises herself, are mere inventories. The same can be said about the films she has seen in the decade 1962–1972, the plays and exhibitions. It is as if she thinks that any information about her tastes is interesting, without her having to offer any commentary.

Perhaps the most interesting chapter in the book is the one dealing with her travels, with special attention paid to her trip to Japan in 1966, which is recounted at length. Other trips often resemble the parody by Michel-Antoine Burnier, called "Voyage en Avanie populaire" ("Travels in the Land of Popular Humiliation"), in which the pastiche Beauvoir notes that she and Sartre have been greeted by charming bureaucrats: "I liked the

---

[11] "[C]e n'est pas le néant qui répugne: c'est de s'anéantir." (Ibid., 50.)

[12] Literally, *The Beautiful Woman of the Lord*, or *The Master's Mistress*, this title is not translated in the Penguin Twentieth Century Classics edition, 1997, but appears as *Her Lover (Belle du Seigneur)* on the cover of the Penguin Modern Classics edition, 2005. In both cases the translator is David Coward. (Eds.)

airport with its hangars and its planes".[13] The lengthy accounts of their many trips to the USSR, from 1962 to 1966—which was to be their last—give an interesting view on the years of liberalisation of Communist Russia under Khrushchev. Beauvoir also gives a portrait of Lena Zonina, their guide in Russia, but she does not say that Lena was Sartre's lover during all these years, and that she was the main reason for their trips there. The detailed account of the Russell Tribunal on American war crimes in Vietnam is a valuable firsthand testimony. Also interesting is the narration of their trip to Egypt and Israel in 1967, just before the Six Day War.

The last chapter is an analysis of the relationship that Beauvoir had with her own country. She says that, before 1968, she had no great interest in what was happening in France. The May 68 events were for her more than a juvenile explosion of romantic rebellion: they were a real crisis of society: "For the first time in thirty-five years [since 1936 and the Popular Front], the question was one of revolution, of the transition to socialism in an advanced capitalist country."[14] She gives an account of her and Sartre's commitment to the young French Maoists of the newspaper *La Cause du people* (*The People's Cause*), and of her own commitment to the radical Women's Liberation Front, which was her own specific commitment during the 1970s, the *gauchiste* years of the far left. She was less of a fellow traveller with the militants of *la Gauche prolétarienne* (the Proletarian Left), with whom she did not have the same personal relations as Sartre.

She ends with a reaffirmation of her atheism:

> I know what the faith of a child is: for him or her, to believe in God is to believe in the adults who speak to them of God. Once s/he has ceased to trust in them, faith remains only a doubtful compromise which consists of believing that one believes. By the age of fifteen, I was already too uncompromising to be satisfied with that. Later on, the study of philosophy made me understand that a being which exists simultaneously in the mode of the in-itself and that of the for-itself was unthinkable. There was never any question for me—and there never will be—of returning to the fairy-tales that charmed my early years.[15]

---

[13] "L'aéroport me plaisait, avec ses hangars et ses avions." (Burnier 1977, 12.)

[14] "Pour la première fois depuis trente-cinq ans [le Front Populaire de 1936] avait été posée la question de la révolution et du passage au socialisme dans un pays capitaliste avancé." (Beauvoir 1972, 477.)

[15] "Je sais ce qu'est la foi d'un enfant: croire en Dieu, pour lui, c'est croire aux adultes qui lui parlent de Dieu. Quand il a cessé de leur faire confiance, la foi n'est plus qu'un douteux compromis qui consiste à croire qu'on croit. A quinze ans,

Finally, she evokes her unrepentant "optimism", despite the various "demystifications" she has worked through, and she leaves the conclusion to the reader.

As we see, and as the title indicates, *Tout compte fait* is a book that tries to draw up an account. And is it a similar account that Beauvoir invites Sartre to draw up in the 1974 *Entretiens*. But the perspective that Sartre adopts is different, because he does not share the same conception of the autobiographical act. Beauvoir writes memoirs, a life narration in the form of a chronicle. She writes down a first draft, with no concern for form; then she reviews her manuscript using crafted, high-quality writing, a transformation into *bel écrit* (fine writing). So, an initial memorial narrative is then shaped into literary form. By contrast, Sartre proceeds in a *primarily* literary way: he has ideas about his own life in advance, then he seeks to make them multi-layered through style, that is to say to rediscover them altered by literary writing itself, in other words by a multiplicity of voices. *Les Mots* is written in this way: literature is in charge, style reveals on the surface those ambiguities, contradictions and equivocations that have *meaning*. To write one's autobiography is not to tell the story of one's life, but rather to disclose its meaning.

Let us take a look at the order of themes in the *Entretiens*. As Sartre had already dealt with his childhood in *Les Mots*, Beauvoir begins by questioning him about his adolescence, the period she had not covered in her memoirs. So, he tells her about his early writings and the transition from a form of romanticism to realism. He had the idea that he was a genius, even if his writings were not good—genius is an essence: "The mere fact of writing proved that I was a genius."[16] Then he narrates his apprenticeship of violence in La Rochelle: the bullying that he had to cope with, the thefts he committed in order to buy sweets for his classmates, and thereby their friendship.

Then back to Paris, boarding school at the Lycée Henri IV, and his friendship with Paul Nizan who also wanted to become a writer: "I wanted to gain immortality through literature, and philosophy was a means by

j'étais trop entière pour m'en contenter. Par la suite, l'étude de la philosophie m'a fait comprendre qu'un être existant à la fois sur le mode de l'en-soi et sur celui du pour-soi n'était pas pensable. Jamais il n'a été question pour moi—jamais il ne saurait être question—de revenir aux fables qui ont charmé mes premières années." (Ibid., 511.)

[16] "Le seul fait d'écrire prouvait que j'avais du génie." (Sartre, in Beauvoir 1981, 185.)

which to get there."[17] But he firmly believed that one has to write essential things, and that if one does not have this goal, there is no point in writing. Beauvoir reminds him of his early ambition "to be at the same time Spinoza and Stendhal".[18] And she reminds him also of what the young Hippias said, and which Sartre repeated—in all modesty!—on his own account: "I have never met a man of comparable worth to myself."[19] He wants to live his life as a future biography: to be at one and the same time a genius and *n'importe qui*, just anyone. He had this idea very early. Pride and modesty are compatible and rely upon self-confidence. To be a man is to be totally a man, totally free and totally creative. And everyone is capable of this: "Stupidity is a form of oppression."[20]

Then there is a reflexion on fame and glory. Glory would come only at the end, as the crowning of a work: "The fame that I acquired after the war prevented me from wanting anything else, but I never confused it with the glory that I would or would not have: that would come later."[21] The relationship with Simone de Beauvoir was mediated by literature, which was their common ambition: "You have been of great service to me: you gave me the confidence in myself that I would never have had without you."[22]

This is followed by a reflexion on his relationship to philosophy in his adult years, how he discovered Heidegger and, above all, his rapport with Marxism. Beauvoir then questions him on his relation to his self-image, and he insists that when he was writing his notebooks during the war, he considered this an inferior type of activity, for it was not literature. As for his letters, he considered them an inferior form of literature, but was also aware that they might be published one day since they partly fulfilled the function of a diary. He then proceeds to an inventory of the books he abandoned: *La Psyché*, *Le Tintoret*, *La Reine Albemarle*, *La Morale*, and his work on the French Revolution.[23] About his theatre, he has this to say:

---

[17] "Je souhaite obtenir l'immortalité par la littérature, la philosophie est un moyen d'y arriver." (Ibid., 201.)
[18] "[Ê]tre à la fois Spinoza et Stendhal." (Ibid., 206.)
[19] "Je n'ai jamais rencontré un homme qui me valût." (Ibid., 206.)
[20] "La bêtise est une forme d'oppression." (Ibid., 211.)
[21] "La renommée que j'ai eue après la guerre m'a empêché de désirer quoi que ce soit d'autre mais je ne l'ai jamais confondue avec la gloire que j'aurais ou que je n'aurais pas, qui vient après." (Ibid., 213.)
[22] "Vous m'avez rendu un grand service; vous m'avez donné une confiance en moi que je n'aurais pas eue seul." (Ibid., 218.)
[23] *The Psyche*, *Tintoretto*, *Queen Albemarle*, *Ethics*.

"There is an age when you lose interest in writing plays. Good plays are not written by old people."[24]

He divides his reading matter into "useful" and "disengaged": on the one hand, Proust, *La Nouvelle Revue française*[25] ("the very odour of literature"), and American novels read for their techniques, to which he had been alerted by Paul Nizan; on the other hand, the thrillers that he read on the train. He began to build up a personal library only in 1946, when he moved in to share an apartment with his mother. Next, he returns to *La Nausée*—"Without a doubt, the subject of *La Nausée* is the world, a metaphysical dimension of the world that is bound to reveal itself"[26]—and to his critical essays. They had to be elegant by respecting classical rules: lightness, clarity, necessity. Ideas must be expressed according to artistic standards. In literature, one has to "seduce the reader with the truth". Commitment does not in any way suppress this requirement. But it is true that in *Les Mots* he had tried, by raising the stakes on literary quality, to "inter literature" in some sense, an objective resulting from his "literary disenchantment", dating from about 1952.

I shall briefly enumerate the topics he touches upon: music, arts, travel, the moon ("the moon was my satellite, I wrote discourses on the moon"). Early on in life, he took sides against what he called *les salauds* (shits, bastards), that is to say the elite. His refusal of the Nobel Prize comes from that, the desire to be just anybody, *n'importe qui*: "I don't understand why others are not as proud as I."[27] The sense of "togetherness"—whether at the École Normale Supérieure, or in his prison camp—was rewarding because it meant recognition for what one is personally, for what one brings to the group. When he was a teacher, however, he had a very poor relationship with his colleagues, but a very good one with his pupils. He recalls friendships with Charles Dullin, Michel Leiris, Albert Camus ("we had a real friendship with Camus, yet a superficial one"), with Maurice Merleau-Ponty ("no intimacy there"), Giacometti, Jean Genet, Cocteau, Raymond Aron. He felt a kind of indifference towards men, and always preferred the company of women, although his friends from *Les Temps*

---

[24] "Il y a un âge où on se déprend du théâtre. Les bonnes pièces ne sont pas écrites par des vieux." (Sartre, in Beauvoir 1981, 243.)

[25] *The New French Review*, founded in 1909 by a group of intellectuals including André Gide, edited for a time by Gaston Gallimard, and the forerunner of the Gallimard *Collection blanche* editions, whose covers still bear the *nrf* logo. (Eds.)

[26] "Ce n'est pas douteux que le sujet de *La Nausée* c'est le monde. Une dimension métaphysique du monde qui doit se révéler." (Sartre, in Beauvoir 1981, 264.)

[27] "Je ne comprends pas que les autres hommes ne soient pas aussi orgueilleux que moi." (Ibid., 326.)

modernes[28] are Jean Pouillon, Jacques-Laurent Bost, Gérard Horst (known as André Gorz), and—much later on—Benny Lévy (formerly known as Pierre Victor).

Simone de Beauvoir suggests that he is macho, yet Sartre claims that "the male adult is profoundly disgusting to me".[29] His relationship to his own body produces a kind of stiffness in his relations with other people when he does not know them well. He feels ill-at-ease in his own skin when he is with others. But what of his relationship to women? His first sexual experience, aged eighteen, was with a married woman of thirty; she was not very pretty, says Sartre, and he never really understood why she went to bed with him, albeit only once. He recalls sex with nice and easily available girls from the Latin Quarter, and a fundamental occasion with Lisette Joiris when he was only twelve or thirteen. She was the prettiest girl in La Rochelle, daughter of a ship's chandler, with whom he tried to flirt and who rebuffed him as "an old fool with a silly hat". In those words, he heard the condemnation of his ugliness.

Sartre had an enduring fantasy, dating from childhood: to be the heroic saviour of a young damsel in distress, and Beauvoir concludes that "you wanted women to love you". To which Sartre replies philosophically that to appropriate a woman's affection is to feminise oneself through love. That is what he was looking for and, as a man who knew how to caress, he was "in other words, more a masturbator of women than a copulator"[30], as he puts it, characteristically calling a spade a spade. But he was also a Pygmalion figure with women. Beauvoir infers: "Women for you have always been the stuff of romance and adventure [*le romanesque*], in the Stendhalian sense of the term."[31] He speaks of the women he loved on his travels as the incarnations of a country: Dolorès is America, Christina is Brazil; but he does not mention the Russian, Lena Zonina, an omission due probably to censorship by Beauvoir.

He goes back to the question of the body, what it meant to be small, to be wall-eyed: "As a child, I very quickly conceived of my body as a centre of action, and I neglected the passive and sensitive side."[32] He adds that

---

[28] *Modern Times*, the review that Sartre and Beauvoir founded immediately after the war, named in homage to Chaplin's movie. (Eds.)

[29] "[L]'adulte mâle me dégoûte profondément." (Sartre, in Beauvoir 1981, 364.)

[30] "Autrement dit, j'étais plutôt un masturbateur de femmes qu'un coïteur." (Ibid., 385.)

[31] "La femme a toujours été pour vous le 'romanesque', au sens stendhalien." (Ibid.)

[32] "Très vite, quand j'étais enfant, j'ai conçu mon corps comme un centre d'action, en négligeant le côté sensation et passivité." (Ibid., 398.)

his "imaginary body" was that of a bold captain, a swashbuckling comic-book hero. Passivity—to abandon oneself to one's body, as his mother did—was profoundly disagreeable to him. He needed stimulation, speed, amphetamines, benzedrine, to make full use of himself. He also denied himself the right to suffer. One consents to illness as an alibi, he thought. He boxed as an amateur. This activism in his relationship to the body of others could go so far as to be a sort of sadism. And his hyperactivity went so far as nervous agitation—he wore out Beauvoir's rugs and the armrests of her easy chairs. But she insists on the positive side of this restlessness: his vivacity, his cheerfulness.

There is also a clever analysis of Sartre's relationship to money. He never really grasped what the (agreeable) work he was doing had to do with the money he got. Hence his generosity, the enormous tips he gave, and his habit of having large sums of cash about him so as to be constantly open to all his possibilities. He never had cause to worry about his financial future, and yet "now"—at the date of the interviews—he fears that he might not have enough to live beyond the next five years or so. In their exchange on this subject, Beauvoir does not conceal her contempt for the women around Sartre who are happy to be supported by him.

Then they return to the idea of freedom. First, Sartre had the feeling of his personal freedom, and philosophy came later. Beauvoir says:

> Your conception of freedom was basically the stoic idea of freedom: what does not depend on us is of no importance, and what does depend on us is freedom. Thus we are free in every situation, in every circumstance.[33]

This is the idea that philosophy helped to challenge and also to foster, whilst making it more complex, until he came to describe alienation as being constitutive of the historical being of the present, even though alienation cannot be understood, is really *unthinkable*, if freedom is not primary. It is this primal freedom that is the foundation of Sartre's hostility to fascism, and then his rallying socialism. It is the alliance of socialism and freedom that has always been his direction. I will skip his account of his political journey from rebellious anarchism to radical Maoism. This is well known, and deserves to be dealt with separately.

Beauvoir goes on to question him about his relationship to time. He continues to divide his time as he did when a teacher: nine months of work, three months of vacation. His relationship to time used to be a

[33] "Votre conception de la liberté, c'était au fond la liberté stoïcienne: ce qui ne dépend pas de nous n'a pas d'importance et ce qui dépend de nous c'est la liberté; donc on est libre en toute situation, en toute circonstance." (Beauvoir 1981, 445.)

relationship to the future. Now he has a real rapport with time, a rapport with age: only the present, no future. When he was thirty-five, he was a boy who pretended to be an adult. Now he feels like a 55-year-old man who has had an accident. He thinks that for his books to be read, he has a life-span of fifty years, maybe less. But he thinks that he will be forgotten, or relegated to literary history, and it is very moving to hear him speaking of a "chapter", as if he were really writing a book:

> I accept myself totally and I feel myself precisely as I wanted to be. And if I go back to my past, to my childhood, to my youth, certainly I realise *that I wanted less than what I have actually achieved* [emphasis added]. So, when I die, I shall die satisfied. Unhappy to die that very day, rather than ten years later, but satisfied. Death has never weighed on me hitherto, and probably it never will. I would like to end this chapter on that note.[34]

Beauvoir asks him about survival and the way Christians think of an afterlife: he says that something of that certainly persists. The conversation then goes back to the sudden disappearance of the idea of God in his life. He was eight or nine, waiting for the bus, and he said to himself: "It's funny, God does not exist." This was probably prepared by inner reflexions that were more or less unconscious, but it was a truism that he never questioned again, "an intuition that appeared suddenly and determined [his] whole life":

> I was not at all attached to the Catholic religion, I never went to church before and I never went afterwards. So it had nothing specific to do with my life at the time. I don't remember ever having complained or been surprised by the non-existence of God. I thought it was a joke I had been told, and that some people believed it, but I realised it was just a joke.[35]

---

[34] "Je m'accepte totalement, et je me sens avec précision tel que j'ai voulu être. Et certainement, si je me rapporte au passé, à mon enfance, à ma jeunesse, je voulais moins que je n'ai fait. [...] Donc, quand je mourrai, je mourrai satisfait. Mécontent de mourir ce jour-là, plutôt que dix ans plus tard, mais satisfait. Et jamais la mort n'a jusqu'ici et probablement ne le fera, jamais la mort n'a pesé sur ma vie. C'est là-dessus que je veux terminer ce chapitre." (Ibid., 544.)

[35] "Je n'étais pas du tout lié à la religion catholique, je n'allais pas à l'église avant, je n'y allais pas après. Ça n'avait aucun rapport précis avec ma vie du moment. Je ne me souviens pas de m'être jamais plaint ou étonné que Dieu n'existât pas. J'estimais que c'était une blague qu'on m'avait racontée, et dont les gens étaient persuadés, et moi j'avais compris que c'était faux." (Ibid., 546.)

We can see a parallel between this and what Simone de Beauvoir had to say about the "fables" of her early years.

Sartre goes on to say that it seemed to him that "a philosophy of man and of a world without God was a new undertaking", because he was not really "familiar with the works of the atheists":

> Besides, they have not written much philosophy, all the great philosophers are more or less believers. This has different meanings for different times. Spinoza's belief in God is not the same as that of Descartes or Kant. But it seemed to me that a great atheist philosophy, truly atheist, was missing from philosophy as a whole, and so it was in that direction that one should now strive to work.[36]

To build a philosophy of man in a material world is what he had tried to do, and yet "the transition from an idealist atheism to a materialist atheism is difficult". In *Les Mots*, Sartre speaks of atheism as a "cruel and lengthy undertaking [which he] thinks [he] has seen through to the end".[37] Here, he sums up:

> I do think there was a time when it was normal to believe in God, for example in the 17th century. Today, given the way we live, and the way that we become conscious of our own consciousness and of our perception that God eludes us, there is no more intuition of the divine. I think that in our time the notion of God is already going out of date, and I have always felt that there was something quaint, old-fashioned about people who spoke to me of God whilst actually believing in him. [...] To re-establish the old notion of a God conscious of everything, seeing the relations between everything, and establishing those relations—willing them, as well as their consequences—one has to turn one's back on the sciences, human as well as natural, and return to a universe completely contrary to the one we have subsequently established. In other words, one would have to preserve a notion which the natural and human sciences, without saying so or deliberately willing it so, have largely helped to dispel.[38]

---

[36] "Ils ont d'ailleurs peu fait de philosophie, tous les grands philosophes sont plus ou moins croyants. Ça signifie différentes choses pour les différentes époques. La croyance en Dieu de Spinoza n'est pas celle de Descartes ou de Kant. Mais ce qui me semblait, c'est qu'une grande philosophie athée, réellement athée, manquait dans la philosophie. Et c'était dans cette direction que l'on devait maintenant s'efforcer de travailler." (Ibid., 548.)

[37] "[L]'athéisme est une entreprise cruelle et de longue haleine: je crois l'avoir menée jusqu'au bout." (Sartre 1964, 210-11.)

[38] "Je pense qu'il y a eu un temps où il était normal de croire en Dieu, au XVIIe siècle, par exemple. A l'heure qu'il est, étant donné la manière dont on vit, la façon

And what about morality, asks Beauvoir? Sartre ripostes that he "has no need of God in order to love [his] neighbour", since it is a matter of "direct relations" from person to person, and there is "no need at all for the infinite":

> JPS:—You and I, for example, we have lived without worrying about this problem. I don't think many of our conversations have been concerned with it.
> SdB:—No, never.
> JPS:—And yet we have still lived, we feel that we have taken an interest in our world, that we have tried to *see* it [emphasis added].[39]

Those are the last words of the *Entretiens*. Thus, the culmination of this dialogue is a reaffirmation of Sartre's atheism as constitutive of his philosophy of freedom. In a certain sense, it was a book of militant atheist philosophy that Sartre and Beauvoir conceived together. This is an important issue because, under the influence of Benny Lévy[40] and of Bernard-Henri Lévy[41], the notion has been advanced of a "third" Sartre, a final Sartre, a Sartre who had supposedly renounced his atheism. In my opinion, it is quite clear that what we have here is an ideological assault, disguised beneath a philosophy and a metaphysics inspired by Levinas, to which I am completely opposed. And in that respect I am totally with Simone de Beauvoir. These 1974 *Entretiens* are, in a sense, a posthumous re-appropriation of Sartre by Beauvoir. She is defending her "ideological

---

dont on prend conscience de sa conscience et dont on s'aperçoit que Dieu se dérobe, il n'y a pas d'intuition du divin. Je pense qu'à ce moment-là, la notion de Dieu est une notion qui déjà date, et j'ai toujours senti quelque chose de périmé, de vieillot chez les gens qui m'ont parlé de Dieu en y croyant. [...] Pour rétablir la vieille notion de Dieu conscient de tout, et voyant les rapports entre tout, et établissant ces rapports, les voulant, ainsi que leurs conséquences, il faut tourner le dos à la science, aux sciences humaines aussi bien qu'aux sciences naturelles, il faut en revenir à un univers tout à fait contraire à celui que nous avons établi depuis. C'est-à-dire conserver une notion que les sciences de la nature et de l'homme ont, sans le dire, sans le vouloir expressément, largement contribué à expulser." (Sartre, in Beauvoir 1981, 556, 557.)

[39] "Nous avons vécu vous et moi par exemple, sans nous préoccuper de ce problème. Je ne pense pas qu'il y ait beaucoup de nos conversations qui aient porté là-dessus. / Non, jamais. / Et nous avons quand même vécu, nous avons l'impression de nous être intéressés à notre monde, d'avoir essayé de le voir." (Ibid., 559.)

[40] See Sartre 1991.

[41] See *Le Siècle de Sartre*.

interests", as Sartre would have said, and I am fully conscious of defending my own by taking sides with her. Nevertheless, this is a battle of ideas that is wholly justified, and even urgent, in this present time of mounting fundamentalist obscurantism.[42]

Works Cited

Astruc, Alexandre, and Michel Contat. *Sartre par lui-même*, 1976. (A documentary film: see under "Sartre", below.)

Beauvoir, Simone de. *L'Amérique au jour le jour*. Paris: Morihien, 1948.

—. *Les Belles Images*. Paris: Gallimard, 1966.

—. *Cahiers de jeunesse: 1926–1930* (ed. Sylvie Le Bon de Beauvoir). Paris: Gallimard, 2008.

—. *La Cérémonie des adieux*, suivi de *Entretiens avec Jean-Paul Sartre, août–septembre 1974*. Paris: Gallimard, 1981.

—. *Le Deuxième Sexe*. Paris: Gallimard, 1949.

—. *La Force de l'âge*. Paris: Gallimard, 1962.

—. *La Force des choses*. Paris: Gallimard, 1964.

—. *L'Invitée*. Paris: Gallimard, 1943.

—. *La Longue Marche*. Paris: Gallimard, 1957.

—. *Mémoires d'une jeune fille rangée*. Paris: Gallimard, 1958.

—. "Merleau-Ponty et le pseudo-sartrisme", *Les Temps modernes*, nos. 114-15, 1955 (2072-2122).

—. *Une Mort très douce*. Paris: Gallimard, 1964.

—. *Tout compte fait*. Paris: Gallimard, 1972.

—. *La Vieillesse*. Paris: Gallimard, 1970.

Burnier, Michel-Antoine. "Voyage en Avanie populaire", in Burnier and Patrick Rambaud, *La Farce des choses, et autres parodies*. Paris: Balland, 1977.

Cohen, Albert. *Belle du Seigneur*. Paris: Gallimard, 1968.

Contat, Michel, and Michel Rybalka. *Les Écrits de Sartre*. Paris: Gallimard, 1970.

Dos Passos, John. *The U.S.A. Trilogy* (1938): *The 42nd Parallel* (1930), *1919* (1932), *The Big Money* (1936). In print as: *U.S.A.* New York: The Library of America, 1996.

Lévy, Bernard-Henri. *Le Siècle de Sartre: enquête philosophique*. Paris: Bernard Grasset, 2000.

Merleau-Ponty, Maurice. "Sartre et l'ultra-bolchévisme", in *Les Aventures de la dialectique*. Paris: Gallimard, 1955.

---

[42] My thanks to Pascale Fautrier for having suggested the subject of this essay.

Sartre, Jean-Paul. *L'Age de raison*. Paris: Gallimard, 1945.
—. *Carnets de la drôle de guerre*. Paris: Gallimard, 1983.
—. *L'Espoir maintenant: les entretiens de 1980* (with Benny Lévy). Paris: Verdier, 1991.
—. *Les Mots*. Paris: Gallimard, 1964.
—. "Un Promeneur dans Paris insurgé". (A series of seven articles on the liberation of Paris, in *Combat*, edited by Albert Camus, 28 August–4 September, 1944: see Contat and Rybalka 1970, 103-106).
—. *Sartre par lui-même*. Transcript of the biographical movie published as *Sartre, un film,* réalisé par Alexandre Astruc et Michel Contat. Paris: Gallimard, 1977.

Part III:

Sartre:
Ideology and Politics

CHAPTER SEVEN

FRANCE AND CUBA, CASTRO AND DE GAULLE: REVISITING SARTRE'S "OURAGAN SUR LE SUCRE"

JOHN IRELAND

Sartre's visit to Cuba early in 1960—a roughly four-week stay from 22 February to 20 March, to view the transformation of the island following Fidel Castro's overthrow of Fulgencio Batista's dictatorial regime one year earlier—is well known and well documented. His own enthusiastic observations and reflections on that visit were published later that year in a series of sixteen detailed articles in the French daily, *France-Soir,* under the dramatic title: "Ouragan sur le sucre" (literally "Hurricane in the Sugarcane"), that ran from 28 June to 15 July. Surprisingly, these articles, after their intense but fleeting impact that summer in the most widely-read French daily of the time, never appeared again in print in French, although Sartre did not prevent translations of the series appearing in book form in both English and Spanish.[1] Given Sartre's clear support for Castro's revolution, it seems odd that he should have neglected to provide the same service for French readers. Whatever the reason, the point remained moot for almost fifty years until in 2007, a manuscript of over 1,000 pages of Sartre's writings on Cuba—including those from which the *France-Soir* articles were taken—was discovered in the Harry Ransom Research Center archives at the University of Texas in Austin.[2] On the eve of the fiftieth anniversary of the Cuban revolution, it was perhaps natural that

---

[1] In 1961, Ballantine Books brought out an English translation under the more laconic title *Sartre on Cuba*, and various translations were made available throughout the Spanish-speaking world, particularly in Latin America. For more details, see Contat and Rybalka, *Les Écrits de Sartre*, 351.

[2] It was transcribed and reconstituted over the course of the following year by the ITEM *Équipe Sartre* under the direction of Gilles Philippe and Jean Bourgault.

Claude Lanzmann, the current director of *Les Temps Modernes,* who had set up the original deal with *France-Soir* and even helped shape the sixteen articles from Sartre's first rough manuscript, should have agreed to republish "Ouragan sur le sucre" in the summer 2008 edition of *Les Temps Modernes*.[3]

There was however a second reason that made the publication of the Cuba manuscript even more compelling. In the final article of the "Ouragan sur le sucre" series, Sartre announced a forthcoming book on Cuba that never saw the light of day.[4] The manuscript discovered in Texas also contained a number of folio pages written (apparently) after the "Ouragan sur le sucre" articles that appear to be fragments of a draft of that book. After some hesitation, Lanzmann agreed that these should be published under the title "Ouragan sur le sucre, II" as an appendix to the published material of 1960. I found these pages of special interest in that they constitute a kind of French prologue to the Cuban adventure, reminding us that the lens through which Sartre viewed Cuba was forged in France and that the French context itself, notably the paralysis of French political life that precipitated De Gaulle's return to power in 1958 and the shameful quagmire of the Algerian war, shaped Sartre's vision of Cuba and his hopes for its new social order. Nobody has been able to date precisely the temporal lag between these two components of the Cuba manuscripts but it is virtually certain that the pages reconstituted as the appendix to "Ouragan sur le sucre" were also written in 1960, some months after Sartre's return from Cuba and that they post-date the manuscript from which the *France-Soir* articles were culled. Beyond contextualizing more precisely his Cuban adventure, the latter manuscript also develops Sartre's sense of Castro and the time they spent together. Castro had clearly made an enormous personal impression on Sartre. But finally—and for me this is perhaps their most intriguing aspect—these pages reflect a quandary for Sartre which sheds some light, I think, on why the projected book was finally abandoned.

This chapter will focus on three aspects of Sartre's involvement with Castro and the Cuban revolution. Concentrating essentially on what I will call "Ouragan II", the unpublished appendix to the sixteen *France-Soir* articles, I want to show how Sartre's account of his experience in Cuba was shaped by his disillusionment with France. I then want to sharpen that focus to suggest more particularly that his portrait of Castro as a political leader is fashioned in direct opposition to De Gaulle, that Castro is, in

[3] *Les Temps Modernes,* no. 649, 2008. All successive references to *TM* refer to this issue.
[4] See *TM,* 153.

Sartre's eyes, an anti-De Gaulle. He is of course other things as well, but that is a central conceptual and poetic component of the portrait. Finally, I hope to show that "Ouragan II" is quite fascinating for an unacknowledged confrontation that it stages between Sartre's hopes for the Cuban revolution, and a much more pessimistic prognosis formulated by the theorist of the *Critique of Dialectical Reason*, which just happened to be in press during Sartre's Cuban visit.

Sartre discovered Cuba in the heady days of the revolution's honeymoon. In February 1960, Castro had been in power for just over a year; the island and its population had thrown out Batista and his militia, Cuba's economic and social structure was changing day by day. The sixteen articles of "Ouragan sur le sucre", a dramatic title that brings together "hurricane" and "sugar cane", the basis of Cubas's economy read—and this is no coincidence—like the journalism of a foreign correspondent on assignment, anxious to impart to readers not only the dramatic and rapidly evolving events around him but the flavour of Cuba and its people at this unique juncture of its history. Although these articles contain a number of learned "asides"—in which Sartre proposes summaries of Cuba's colonial history in order to highlight the central importance of its sugar crop and, as a result of that history, its crippling economic dependency on the United States that the revolution is now committed to severing—Sartre's writing is unusually vivid and at times almost deliberately unpolished. Much of the writing seems to have been done in snatches, when Sartre was in transit or in transitory spaces, hotel rooms or vestibules, before his next appointment. As a result, these pages have at times an almost "breathless" quality, Sartre hastily sketching urban and rural landscapes, profiles and personalities as he rapidly absorbs information and impressions and proposes on-the-spot commentaries. For Sartre, this is unusually visceral journalistic writing. Initially on his guard, Sartre is rapidly won over by what he sees and hears: the growing excitement that attends his discoveries vies with the fatigue induced by the many late-night appointments and interviews with Castro and his ministers—all of them absurdly young—who appear (to Sartre's eyes) never to sleep. Gradually, one realizes that Sartre has put his pen in the service of a revolution that has captivated him, just as he is awed by its leader, Castro. Sartre wants his written testimony to help the Cuban revolution consolidate its victory.[5]

[5] While these pages remind us inevitably of the series of seven articles Sartre wrote for Camus's *Combat* (published between 28 August and 4 September 1944) under the collective title: "Un promeneur dans Paris insurgé", the larger point is probably that they conform perfectly to a central aspect of committed literature as Sartre had

France and Cuba: two countries on opposing paths

At first glance—and this was certainly Sartre's intention—the recently discovered manuscript pages we are calling "Ouragan II", published in the same issue of *Les Temps modernes,* appear (sometimes even more fervently) to serve the same cause as the articles published in *France-Soir.* These fragments cover some of the same ground—notably in their depiction of Castro—in even more depth and offer a prologue to Sartre's Cuban adventure by relating more precisely the circumstances and context in which the invitation to visit Cuba first presented itself. Sartre begins by reminding us that he had visited Cuba after a more extensive trip to Haiti in 1949, and that the comparison did not favour Cuba. Pre-revolutionary Havana, underneath its glitz and neon, was principally a playground for American businessmen and tourists. The social inequalities were striking, but even worse was the unacknowledged racism. Sartre saw Cuban society as corrupt and consumed by bad faith, unable to look at its situation with either honesty or clarity and when, four years later, Batista seized power in the face of no opposition whatsoever, Sartre was cuttingly dismissive:

> Pas une barricade! Pas un coup de fusil! […] la démocratie les appelait à son secours et ils l'ont laissé crever la gueule ouverte plutôt que de risquer un seul cheveu de leur tête pour leurs élus. Je conclus: "Ces gens-là n'ont que ce qu'ils méritent", et je tirais le trait.[6]

This is how Sartre sets the scene ten years later as he sits in his Paris apartment awaiting the visit of Carlos Franqui, director of the Cuban daily *Revolución,* who had come to Paris to invite Sartre to visit the Caribbean island and witness the revolution for himself. Pondering the changes since his initial visit, Sartre reflects ruefully on the differences a decade has made. If Cuba has asserted and transformed itself out of all recognition, France has moved from disaster to disaster, colonially and politically and is now mired in shame. The debacle of Indochina, the collapse of the

---

conceived it in the years that followed the liberation of France in 1944–45 (see, in particular, "Écrire pour son époque" ("Writing for one's time", *Les Temps modernes,* no. 33, 1948). Committed literature is current and active; it addresses the burning issues of an era, it is about the present. The first article of the "Ouragan" series, published on 28 June, is headed: "La Havane … juin", no doubt to reinforce the immediacy of the present that Sartre is anxious to impart.

[6] "Not a barricade! Not a rifle shot! […] democracy cried out for help and they let it die in the gutter rather than risk a single hair of their heads. I concluded: 'These people got what they deserved', and left it there." (*TM,* 178. Unless otherwise indicated, all translations from cited French editions are my own.)

Fourth Republic, De Gaulle's manipulative return to power and the revelations of the dirty war in Algeria have depressed Sartre beyond measure:

> [...] je pensais à mes anciens amis cubains: "Que sont-ils devenus? Remonteront-ils la pente? L'ont-ils remontée déjà?" me disais-je. Au fond de moi je souhaitais vaguement et criminellement qu'ils fussent restés dans leurs marécages. "Parce que s'ils la remontaient la pente, ils nous croiseraient sûrement, vu que nous sommes en train de la descendre." Tiré bien malgré moi vers le plus bas, je n'avais aucune envie de me retourner un instant sur cette cordée d'alpinistes et de m'extasier de leur ascension.[7]

The "mountaineering" metaphor underscores the extent to which Sartre now sees Cuba and France as countries on opposing paths. The *singes résignés* (literally, resigned monkeys) that Sartre remembers from his 1949 trip have since found their dignity, and Sartre speculates that Cuba's unexpected transformation occurred because nobody realized how powerful a revolutionary force shame could become. In 1959, Sartre acknowledges, "les singes résignés c'est nous" ("*we* are the resigned monkeys"), but he is much less hopeful about his country's own future:

> On peut donc tomber si bas et remonter si haut? Pour nous ce sera difficile: nous sommes beaucoup plus bas qu'ils n'étaient; voilà cinq ans qu'on torture et les travailleurs ni les ménagères ne semblent très incommodés.[8]

Whereas the *France-Soir* articles made almost no reference to France, these unpublished sheets remind us that the portrait of Cuba put together by the reporter abroad is half of a diptych which has as its counterpart a largely invisible and entirely negative view of Sartre's native land. "Ouragan II" helps us to appreciate the extent to which Sartre's sense of

---

[7] "[...] I thought of my old Cuban friends: 'What's become of them? Will they get back on their feet and scale the mountain? Have they already done so?' I wondered. Deep down, quite criminally, I wanted them to remain down and out in their swamp of bad faith. 'Because if they do manage to ascend that slope to human dignity, they'll pass us, since we're tumbling down it rapidly.' Pulled down with the rest in spite of myself, I had no desire to turn and gaze in admiration at the ascending mountaineers." (*TM,* 180.)

[8] "Can one fall so far and yet still climb back so high again? For us it will be difficult. We've fallen so much farther than they ever did. We have given ourselves over to torture for the last five years and our housewives and workers don't seem troubled in the least." (*TM,* 190.)

Cuba is shaped by the rage and frustration that his own country inspires in him.

Sartre begins by noting that the French media can make no sense of Cuba's evolution. While the right-wing press lambastes the communist regime that has seized power with Castro, the French communist press deplores the "blind virulence of its anti-communism".[9] But France's inability to provide a coherent account of Cuba's situation is not only the result of divergent ideological prisms. France has become, in Sartre's eyes, so entrenched and weighted down by its moribund political institutions that it simply is no longer capable of evaluating the social transformation underway in Cuba. It is this structural and cultural incomprehension that is made manifest in Sartre's first question to the visiting Cuban journalist: "Démocratie, dictature [...] Est-ce qu'on essaye d'y répondre? Ou sont-ce de vieux soucis scolastiques qui nous tourmentent encore ici mais qui n'inquiètent personne chez vous?"[10] Maybe this revolution, he suggests, just did not want to define itself, or perhaps it had precipitated ideas so new that we had no terms with which to understand them.[11]

But Cuba is above all else a reminder of the frustration and shame that Sartre feels as a French citizen in 1959. Castro's victory cannot but bring up the situation in Algeria, a conflict analogous in some respects to Cuba's struggle, but with no end in sight.[12] In one of the most dramatic sequences

---

[9] See *TM,* 182.

[10] "Democracy, dictatorship [...] how do we sort it out? Or are these merely scholastic concerns that still torment us here but don't worry any of you?" (*TM,* 183.)

[11] Sartre extends this idea into the more general realm of culture and the comparison does not favour France: "Il y a un peuple, une culture à Cuba, et nous venons d'un pays cloisonné où la culture a depuis longtemps fait place aux départements culturels [...] la tâche de la Révolution sera de maintenir une culture afro-cubaine et, dans bien des cas, de la créer. Ils n'en sont qu'aux semailles mais la récolte peut être bonne; chez nous la récolte est faite: elle ne vaut rien du tout." ("There is a people, a culture in Cuba; we come from a parcelled country whose culture has long since given way to the culture of its *départements* [...] the task of the Revolution will be to maintain an Afro-Cuban culture, and in many cases, to create it. They are only sowing seed at the moment but the harvest may be good; our harvest is already in: it is quite worthless." *TM,* 187.) One notes in passing the attack on Malraux who, as French Minister of Culture under De Gaulle, had instituted the new domestic cultural policy.

[12] It should be remembered that Sartre first read Fanon's *Les Damnés de la terre* (*The Wretched of the Earth*) during his Cuban visit. It is tempting to speculate that the violent tone of the preface, for which he was strongly criticized, was influenced by what he saw as the direct achievement of Cuba's armed revolutionary struggle.

in "Ouragan II", Sartre, unable to sleep on the long flight from Madrid to Havana, uncharacteristically admits to something resembling depression: "Je me sens le cœur plein de suie",[13] he reveals at one moment, as he reviews his country's situation: "Il y a la journée des Mères, bientôt celle des Pères, celle de l'Armistice ou de la Victoire: à quand la journée de Honte nationale?"[14] It is this national shame that explains to some extent the speed with which Sartre's initial scepticism gives way to the unbridled enthusiasm that permeates his whole visit: Cuba quickly becomes in Sartre's mind the antithesis of the sad country he is forced to call home. But Cuba is also living proof that national shame can be overcome. As Sartre prepares to set foot on Cuban soil, he concludes quite simply: "Je viens chercher à Cuba la preuve que nous avons encore une chance [...] que pour nous aussi, le temps du mépris prendra fin."[15]

Castro and De Gaulle

If France emerges in the unpublished appendix to "Ouragan sur le sucre" as the hidden but indispensable complement to Sartre's portrait of the Cuban Spring, a similar and unacknowledged comparison is even more evident in Sartre's compelling portrait of Castro. Although the entire Cuban manuscript contains only one brief mention of France's President, De Gaulle, there are a number of indications that Sartre saw in Castro first and foremost a counterpoint to De Gaulle. The single reference to the French President comes during a passage in which Sartre is meticulously constructing what he sees as the single most important aspect of Castro as a revolutionary leader: his determination to abolish any distinction between himself as an individual and his existence as the embodiment of the island and its people as a whole. If Sartre sees Castro like Aristotle's God as the "prime mover" of the revolution, the revolution could only succeed, he says, because the Cuban people gradually came to see in Castro's individual features the incarnation of their own collective aspirations. Much of "Ouragan II" is devoted to this symbiosis as Sartre takes enormous pains to indicate all of Castro's strategies to abolish any sense of separation between himself and the Cuban people. Castro, says Sartre, does not lead or rule. He has consistently refused any initiative that would constitute power over his countrymen. Fighting for the revolution,

[13] Literally, "My heart is full of soot" (*TM,* 184).
[14] "There is a Mother's Day and soon a Father's Day, an Armistice Day and a Victory Day: when will we hold a National Day of Shame?" (*TM*, 190.)
[15] "I have come to Cuba for proof that we still have a chance [...] that for us too, the days of shame will come to an end." (*TM,* 191.)

he has always sought equals in the struggle, other men and women realizing themselves as the Cuban people—like himself—through action undertaken with others. He does not want subordinates. In the same way, argues Sartre, Castro's many speeches are not lectures: their principal aim is not to inform but to initiate exchanges that will put him on the same plane as his audience and make manifest "la pensée même de la Nation" ("the very thought of the Nation"). Abruptly, Sartre introduces De Gaulle:

> Une fois le Président de notre Vème République a dit, à la fin d'un discours: "Et maintenant vous en savez autant que moi sur le problème algérien." Après l'avoir entendu, il fallait choisir: si ce n'était pas vrai, il méprisait le peuple français; si c'était vrai, il fallait mépriser le gouvernement. Mais Castro, s'il disait un jour, après avoir examiné devant le peuple un problème: "Vous en savez autant que moi", ce serait vrai: pour faire et maintenir l'unité d'un peuple, il ne daigne compter que sur la vérité.[16]

In this fascinating example, two identical speech acts have entirely different meanings. Note that this argument, made chiefly through affirmation, depends entirely on accepting Sartre's contextual demonstration. But this brief glimpse of De Gaulle is compelling, because it helps to establish the two leaders as polar opposites, by extending the same logic that Sartre had brought to bear eighteen months earlier on the De Gaulle referendum, in a series of articles that followed the constitutional crisis of 1958 and De Gaulle's return to power. The titles of those articles: "Le Prétendant" ("The Pretender"), "La Constitution du mépris" ("The Constitution of contempt"), and "Les Grenouilles qui demandent un roi" ("The Frogs that demanded a king"), all showcase Sartre's disgust at the abject abdication on the part of France's political institutions, and its electorate, that De Gaulle shamelessly manipulated to found what Sartre would always see as a tainted Republic. In Sartre's eyes, De Gaulle always remained the "Pretender" to a virtual "throne". As the Fourth Republic collapsed, De Gaulle positioned himself tactically behind a veil of silence and secrecy that further fuelled the anxiety paralyzing France: "Cette montagne de silence tirait sa force de toutes nos faiblesses,

[16] "De Gaulle once said at the end of a speech: 'And now you know as much as I do about the Algerian problem.' After hearing him, one had to decide: if it was not true, it was the French people he was disparaging; if true, the government. But if Castro, after examining a problem in front of a Cuban audience, said: 'You now know as much as I do', it would be true. To effect and maintain the people's unity, Castro relies solely on the truth." (*TM,* 204.)

c'était le lieu géométrique de toutes nos impuissances […]."[17] It was, notes Sartre, the first move of a manipulative strategy designed to create a need for his return that would frame the debate in personal and not political terms: "De Gaulle ne veut pas qu'on le plébiscite sur un programme, mais sur sa personne […]. Notre adhésion, s'il nous la réclame […] ce n'est pas malgré notre ignorance de ses desseins mais à cause d'elle."[18] De Gaulle, says Sartre, hopes to supersede the tawdry domain of politics to return again as a Saviour of France, reprising the role he had played so effectively in 1944. His ambition is to reframe the present moment as the providential return of his heroic past. But Sartre's indictment of De Gaulle's machinations extended well beyond De Gaulle. By refusing to demand that he present a political agenda that could be rationally evaluated, France's voters colluded in the disappearance of their civic rights. By demanding only that De Gaulle save them from the paralysis and potential chaos around them, the French voters who voted "Yes" to the referendum abdicated their responsibilities as citizens to accept instead a more archaic and apolitical relationship to their Saviour, that of "vassals". This is the argument at the core of "Les Grenouilles qui demandent un roi": "[Les électeurs français] se démettent du soin de la chose publique entre les mains d'un homme qui fera tout pour eux […] on leur montre une muselière; ils votent pour qu'on la leur mette au plus vite […]."[19] As Sartre concludes, dismissively: "Les voilà simplifiés: ils demeurent époux, fils, employés, champions de billard—mais ils ne seront plus citoyens."[20]

In short, Sartre blames De Gaulle for having exploited the panic and turmoil that precipitated the collapse of the Fourth Republic to reframe a political debate as something quite different, recasting himself in the process as a messianic agent, the chosen individual who will save France from the degraded dealings of men. It is, says Sartre, a transmutation that sets him apart and reconfigures him as a *surhomme* (superman) on a quite

[17] "This mountain of silence drew its strength from our impotence. It was the geometrical intersection of all our weaknesses […]." ("Le Prétendant", in *Situations, V,* 95.)
[18] "De Gaulle does not want our votes in response to a political programme but because of who he is […]. He is not asking for our support *in spite* of our ignorance as to his intentions; he is *counting on* that ignorance." (Ibid., 99.)
[19] "[French voters] abandon civic issues and leave them in the hands of a man who will do everything for them. They are shown a muzzle and ask that it be placed on them as quickly as possible." (Ibid., 137.)
[20] "This simplifies their situation. They remain husbands, sons, employees, snooker champions—but they are no longer citizens." (Ibid., 137.)

different plane from the rest of humanity; it is this *supériorité d'espèce* (innate superiority) that consecrates his sense of leadership, fuels his vocation as a leader and seals the legitimacy of his rule. But this rule, the triumph of De Gaulle's new executive powers, can only be built on the ruins of French republicanism.

Castro: a new messianic model

The snapshot comparison between De Gaulle and Castro in "Ouragan sur le sucre" is emblematic of their different conceptions of leadership, and also helps us to understand better Sartre's implacable and enduring hostility to De Gaulle. In every way, De Gaulle serves as a negative counterpart for the portrait of the Cuban leader that Sartre painstakingly details. In place of the mystery and sense of solitude carefully cultivated by De Gaulle to enhancc his mystique, Castro works relentlessly to break down any barrier that would separate him or distinguish him (in both senses of the term) from the Cuban people. But Castro's example also supplies a corrective to one of the most tenacious mythic models in Sartre's thinking and imagination that is particularly prevalent in his political theatre: the separation of his dramatic protagonists, cast in a heroic mould, from the groups whose causes they espouse and attempt to embody. From Sartre's first play, *Bariona*—a "Nativity" in which the eponymous hero lays down his life so that the infant Jesus, together with his parents, can escape the Roman soldiers sent to kill him—to the theatrical project outlined in Sartre's final interview months before his death—which would have featured the last revolutionary to die for the revolution expiring on "une sorte de croix" ("a sort of cross")—it is as if Sartre's dramatic protagonists find themselves caught in a bind that associates action with tragic heroism and self-sacrifice. Michel Contat has effectively summarized the idiosyncratic messianic strain in much of Sartre's theatre:

> Tout le théâtre de Sartre peut ainsi être lu comme un parcours christique—critiqué, contredit, réaffirmé en douce—à la condition de garder à l'esprit que, dans cette perspective, le Christ est un suicidé qui offre sa vie pour sauver les hommes, comble d'orgueil et de narcissisme.[21]

---

[21] "In that sense, all of Sartre's theatre can be read as a variant of Christ's passion—criticized, denied, surreptitiously reaffirmed—as long as one bears in mind that from that perspective, Christ is a suicide who sacrifices his life for mankind in a gesture where pride and narcissism are pushed to their limits."

Sartre actually explored the divide tragically separating activist leaders from the masses they lead in a preface to Roger Stéphane's 1950 book, *Portrait de l'aventurier* (*Portrait of the Adventurer*). Class is the central component of the barrier between the two. Unlike the working-class militant whose class allegiance to revolutionary struggle is determined at birth, just as his personal identity is subsumed by the collective goal of mass liberation, their well-intentioned leaders—Stéphane's book focuses on three examples: André Malraux, T. E. Lawrence and Ernst von Salomon—are often born into the middle class; individual subjectivity is the cornerstone of their bourgeois identity. "N'est pas militant qui veut", warns Sartre: "Si le Moi vient d'abord, on est séparé pour toujours. Dans la classe bourgeoise, il naît de bonne heure."[22] In Sartre's eyes, the working-class militant is one among many comrades whose personal identity is subsumed by the revolutionary goal of mass liberation that unites and defines them. In contrast, a bourgeois is first and foremost an individual who defines himself in opposition to his friends and associates: he is above all "an original". It follows, continues Sartre, that bourgeois society is a "civilization of solitudes".

How does one escape that separation from others? Some look to love as a bridge; others, more resolute, attempt to escape their isolation through radical political action. By allying themselves with a revolutionary or national liberation movement, these young bourgeois activists (Stéphane calls them "adventurers") attempt to break out of the confines of bourgeois individualism and change themselves as they try to change the world. But the separation that defines the bourgeoisie is as inescapable as original sin. However committed to the cause of his working-class comrades, the young bourgeois activist can never become one of them. He is forever condemned to seek recognition from those for whom individuality has no constructive meaning: "S'il veut qu'ils acceptent sa nature singulière, il faut qu'il la leur donne. Et comme ils n'en ont que faire, il la détruira en grande cérémonie et les rendra témoins de son sacrifice."[23] His individual worth can only be redeemed through self-sacrifice, as the most spectacular form of gift he can conceive. That redemption is only conceivable in the

(Contat, "Sartre et la gloire", 33.) See also John Ireland, "Freedom as Passion: Sartre's Mystery Plays".

[22] "Not everyone can be a militant. […] If your ego is already formed, you are separated forever. In the bourgeoisie, that happens early on." ("Préface", in *Portrait de l'aventurier*, 14.)

[23] "If he wants them to accept his singular nature, he must make a gift of it for them. And since they have no use for it, he must destroy it with great pomp and make them witnesses of his sacrifice." (Ibid., 19.)

form of individual heroism and glory, which suggest in turn a hidden core of narcissism. For Sartre, the bourgeois *aventurier*, however outwardly humble, is always secretly anticipating his own heroic death, composing in advance the obituary that will embalm his glory:

> La gloire: voilà le mot. Ce n'est pas dans la fraternité, où l'on abandonne toujours un peu de soi-même à l'autre, qu'ils [les aventuriers] cherchent la communication mais dans la gloire, où l'on existe pour tous sans rien retrancher de soi. Le moment de la mort sera le sommet de leur vie, ils l'attendent "*avec extase*".[24]

This obsessive quest for glory, which Sartre would subsequently condemn in the strongest terms, is a drive he understands only too well.[25] As *Les Mots* (*Words*) makes clear, individual glory was the value that fuelled the early evolution of the writer, before Sartre's political conversion precipitated a violent revolt against the values of his class.

Sartre's portrait of Castro in "Ouragan II" thus simultaneously details a new model of direct democracy and shared social responsibility—correcting the degraded relationship between De Gaulle and the French electorate—while revising a vexing syndrome undermining revolutionary struggle. Castro is the living refutation that revolutionary leaders must be messianic heroes, consecrated only by their martyrdom. Sartre takes pains to specify that "Castro […] ne s'est jamais présenté comme le héros qui vient délivrer les pauvres hommes."[26] While he had to take risks to launch the revolution, particularly in the early days of the fighting, he was "trop lucide pour se donner à l'île en holocauste".[27] On the contrary, says Sartre,

---

[24] "Glory, that's the word. It is not in a spirit of brotherhood, where one always gives up part of oneself to the other, that they [adventurers] look to communicate but in a blaze of glory, where one exists for everyone without giving up anything of oneself. The moment of death will be the crowning point of their lives; they await it '*in ecstasy*'." (Ibid., 20.)

[25] That condemnation is already apparent in *Portrait de l'aventurier* when Sartre describes heroes as "parasites" (22) of the working-class militants. It is reiterated even more forcefully twenty years later in his exchanges with his Maoist comrades: "The guy who is into self-sacrifice can't see beyond himself […]. He doesn't understand others. Wrapped up in his own sacrifice, he listens to nobody. All my life, I've never stopped hammering away at the idea of self-sacrifice." (See *On a raison de se révolter* (*We Are Right to Rebel*), 183.)

[26] "Castro […] never presents himself as the hero who has come to liberate his poor countrymen." (*TM,* 206.)

[27] "[…] too clear-sighted to offer himself in spectacular self-immolation to the island." (*TM,* 197.)

Castro's tactics were designed to encourage *equals*, activists like himself who saw themselves becoming, through their efforts and shared goals, the embodiment of a new sovereign people.

These are the nuances that help us appreciate the detail and imagination that Sartre brings to fashioning a portrait of Castro which does justice to the paradoxical, multi-faceted existential project whereby Castro "undoes" or dispossesses himself as an individual in order to reinvent himself on the scale of a nation and a people. At a basic level, this dispossession is material. Castro does not have a hectare of land that belongs to him, no residence, no personal fortune, not a nickel. Sartre even remembers witnessing Castro, on the road, being asked to contribute spare change to a local relief fund. Patting his pockets and finding nothing, Castro unabashedly borrows from the first passer-by to make his contribution. Castro, says Sartre, refuses all possessions; he chooses to be and to act, not to have. This refusal to possess is the secret of his power. His supreme power is the refusal of all powers: "Castro *n'a pas* le pouvoir: son orgueil est de *l'être*."[28]

A religious model of popular union

The refusal of all possessions is matched by Castro's drive—which Sartre dates from his young adulthood and the beginnings of a revolutionary consciousness—to rid himself progressively of his sense of self as an individual. For Sartre, there is an intense ascetic quality at work, as Castro embarks on a determining existential project to abolish within himself the notions of personal distinction, achievement and prestige that are the hallmarks of "success" in bourgeois, middle-class society. But Castro, continues Sartre, saw them not only as empty markers of questionable values, but as barriers that could only reinforce his isolation. In what is certainly the most intellectually "daring" development of the "Ouragan II" appendix, Sartre adopts a religious model of self-abnegation, that he locates in the mysticism of the Spanish Counter-reformation, to illustrate the process by which Fidel, the young revolutionary activist, begins the depersonalization of himself as a privileged individual in order to see himself instead as the instrument of a perfect national union. To save their Church, reeling under the attacks and charges levelled by the Reformation, a woman in a convent and a man, working with the sick in a hospital in Medina, strove to give it back its unity "par l'union de tous en Dieu" ("through the union of everyone in God"). Sartre proceeds to

28 "Castro does not *possess* power: his aspiration is to *embody it.*" (*TM,* 203.)

summarize the mystical process by which Saint Theresa of Avila and Saint John of the Cross aim to achieve this unity:

> Le mystique s'abolissait devant tous pour montrer publiquement la réunification, en lui, de l'Eglise par l'Être pur et sans parties, par la présence de l'âme à Dieu. Il supprimait en lui la multiplicité des désirs parce qu'elle témoignait des divisions religieuses. Il se dépossédait pour arracher en même temps les traits individuels et l'impuissance; il prouvait qu'on passe par l'anéantissement mais qu'on n'y reste pas: il faut être un atome ou tout.[29]

At first glance, it is quite startling to see a religious model of this intensity invoked to showcase what we would be more inclined to categorize as a political relationship. But Sartre's vision of Castro and the Cuban people as communicating vessels in perfect equilibrium has no established political model. Constantly reaffirmed and highlighted using italics—"Il était *déjà* l'île entière [...] il *était* le peuple"[30]—Sartre needed a model transcending political consensus, no matter how unanimous, to arrive at a more absolute notion of union. The mysterious logic of religious mysticism allows Sartre to put the understanding between Castro and the Cuban people on a plane of total symbiosis, far from any political negotiation or calculation. The invocation of John of the Cross reinforces the point. For the Spanish mystic, the terrestrial domain, the political sphere, are of little consequence. As Sartre remarks: "Jamais Jean de la Croix n'eût daigné se soumettre aux élections pontificales: commander à l'Église en vertu d'un mandat contesté souvent, pourquoi faire?"[31] For Castro, as for John of the Cross—and the analogy is breathtakingly daring—Sartre establishes a radical alternative that posits the necessity of a cohesive unity beyond any political order: "[...] il faut être un atome ou tout" ("one must be either an atom or everything").

---

[29] "The mystic abolishes himself to demonstrate publicly the reunification within him of the Church by pure indivisible being, by the openness of the soul to God. He suppresses within himself the multiplicity of his desires because they betray religious difference. He depersonalizes himself, tearing out both individual traits and impotence. He proves that one passes through annihilation [literally, the reduction to nothingness] but one does not remain there. One is either an atom or everything." (*TM,* 200.)

[30] "He was *already* the whole island [...] he *was* the people". (*TM*, 192, 197.)

[31] "John of the Cross would never stoop to submitting his candidacy in any papal election. To command the Church by virtue of a mandate that would be contested regularly, whatever for?" (*TM,* 201.)

The problem of revolutionary terror

One is either an atom or everything. Sartre's dizzying intellectual detour by way of the Spanish Counter-reformation and its mystical philosophy is also grounded and tactical: it allows him to tackle obliquely a particularly thorny issue that he is reluctant to formulate in political terms. Throughout his stay on the island, Sartre, initially sceptical, has come to embrace Cuba's "direct democracy": he has seen Castro, without bodyguards or escorts tour the island, picking up peasants and giving them a lift along the road to their villages, talking to Cubans from every walk of life on an equal footing, interacting in every setting imaginable, many of them impromptu encounters. One senses that Castro is one of very few individuals to have awed and subjugated Sartre, with the force both of his biography and of his personality. But how long can this direct democracy last, with no democratic safeguards, without political parties or elections, or functioning assemblies?

Throughout the *France-Soir* articles, Sartre insists that the economic imperatives are so overwhelming that Cubans are happy to defer the whole question of democratic representation. In any case, he adds, everyone agrees that Castro would receive 95% of the vote on any ballot. But Sartre is not naïve. And more importantly, he is the author of the *Critique of Dialectical Reason,* in press during his visit to Cuba, whose comprehensive analyses of social revolution indicate strongly that Cuba's Terror is still to come. In the early months of 1960, Cuba still appeared to be living the first, spontaneous and optimistic phase of revolutionary activity that corresponds to what the theorist of the *Critique* called *le groupe-en-fusion* (the group-in-formation), a stage which, according to the theses of the *Critique*, gradually congeals into what he calls *la fraternité-terreur* (fraternity-terror), a process of institutionalization that hardens in turn into dictatorship, suspicion and repression. Sartre's models are the French and Russian revolutions. Will Cuba too be condemned to experience repression and terror, like its predecessors?

Reading them today, I find real drama, even poignancy, in these unpublished manuscript pages. Unlike the French and Russian revolutions, where Sartre's intellect could range clearly and dispassionately, Cuba's revolution was real and vibrantly alive and full of hope for the dispirited and frustrated Frenchman. The *France-Soir* articles are a paean to those hopes for the new social order that Sartre experienced directly in Cuba. But for me, incomplete though it is, the appendix, "Ouragan II", is an absolutely fascinating coda to Sartre's published text, inasmuch as these pages gradually reveal the unstated but very perceptible tension generated by an unacknowledged confrontation between Sartre's hopes for the first socialist utopia of the 1960s, and the more dispassionate analyses of the *Critique* and their much less hopeful diagnoses. Back in France, as the weeks and months go by, increasingly distanced from the Cuba that had so charmed him—and just as the theses of the *Critique* are receiving their first public airing—one senses the first stirrings of doubt, if only in the fervour with which Sartre affirms and reaffirms what he wants to believe but cannot prove: the perfect union of leader and people. In that regard, Sartre's detour through the mysticism of the Spanish Counter-reformation allows him a sinuous approach to the political question of Cuba's direct democracy, which he does not want to tackle too directly. The religious analogy ("the union of everyone in God") is invoked to suggest that Castro would never permit Terror because Terror would be divisive; it would be the end of Castro's perfect union: "Précisément parce qu'il ne peut plus vivre sans être le Tout au milieu du Tout, Castro ne peut vouloir la Terreur en aucun cas."[32]

Does Sartre believe what he is formulating? I think it is fair to say that "Ouragan II" mobilizes all of Sartre's inventive genius to ward off the intellectual conclusions he himself had formulated before Cuba ever intruded on his horizons. In the wake of what was for him, for all the reasons we have detailed, a transformative experience, it is as if Sartre feels that he owes it to the Cuban people to make the best case imaginable that Castro's Cuban revolution might somehow be different. The last sentence of the final "Ouragan sur le sucre" article reads: "Il faut que les Cubains gagnent ou que nous perdions tout, même l'espoir."[33] As we now know, the Cuban spring could not be sustained. Toward the end of the same year 1960, Sartre passed briefly again through Cuba on his way home from a trip to Brazil. The difference in atmosphere was already perceptible. Castro's regime had hardened. Russian aid and Soviet influence were helping Castro counter the American blockade; the Bay of Pigs, the missile crisis and the Khrushchev–Kennedy confrontation were looming. All things considered, it is probably no great surprise that Sartre's projected book on Cuba faded quietly away and that Sartre, after 1960, would only offer brief commentaries on Cuba, before Castro's harsher treatment of Cuban dissidents finally provoked a written denunciation at the time of the Padilla affair in 1971. Sartre's break with Castro was thereafter definitive.

---

[32] "Precisely because he cannot live without being the whole at the centre of everything, Castro cannot want Terror under any circumstances." (*TM,* 207.)

[33] "The Cubans must win, or we must lose everything, even hope." (*TM,* 155.)

Castro and Sartre

But if Castro's place in Sartre's personal pantheon would also fade, the model of perfect leadership that Sartre crafted in his ambitious, idealized portrait of Castro—the perfect counterpoint to Gaullism—would find echoes in Sartre's work and most strikingly in his own autobiography, *Les Mots* (*Words*), which also uses a religious framework to revisit the notion of the messianic hero, albeit comically undermined by parody in Sartre's case. As Lanzmann has pointed out, Sartre cannot but wishfully identify with some of the traits he ascribes to Castro. And what attracts him most is the paradox at the heart of his portrait. Sartre is fascinated less by a man seen as an individual than as a project: in Castro's case, as the movement away from the contours that contain and define individuality. At the heart of Sartre's political philosophy is the notion that individuality is a prison. For Sartre, Castro's founding insight was the recognition that his only chance of realizing himself as a revolutionary leader entailed a radical process of self-dispossession. It is only when the boundaries of individuality have been breached, if not destroyed, that a man can legitimately pretend to be "Un homme, fait de tous les hommes" ("A man, made of all men"), as the last sentence of *Les Mots* memorably puts it.[34]

Here, a form of identification becomes very clear: Castro's revolutionary project to depersonalize himself doubled in Sartre's eyes as a critique of bourgeois elitism and, within those parameters, his determination to rid himself of any form of individual attribute, distinction or prestige, is also one that Sartre aspired to and indeed tried to appropriate as his own legacy in the famous final sentence of *Les Mots*. But, while that aspiration remains something of an abstraction in Sartre's own case—a rejection of castes and hierarchies, a refusal to see any human being as worth more than any other—it describes very precisely the scope of Castro's existential project, whilst fully articulating its political dimension, which Sartre could never integrate so satisfactorily into his own biographical narratives.[35]

---

[34] Sartre, *Les Mots*, 206.

[35] For a fuller version of this article, originally written in French, see John Ireland, "'Ouragan sur le sucre': Sartre, Castro et la révolution cubaine".

Works cited

Contat, Michel. "Sartre et la gloire", in Ingrid Galster (ed.), *La Naissance du phénomène Sartre: raisons d'un succès, 1938–1945*. Paris: Seuil, 2001.

Contat, Michel, and Michel Rybalka. *Les Écrits de Sartre*. Paris: Gallimard, 1970.

Ireland, John. "'Ouragan sur le sucre': Sartre, Castro et la révolution cubaine", *Les Temps Modernes,* no. 656, 2009 (9-37).

—. "Freedom as Passion: Sartre's Mystery Plays", *Theatre Journal,* no. 50, 1998 (335-48).

Sartre, Jean-Paul. "Écrire pour son époque", *Les Temps modernes,* no. 33, 1948.

—. *Les Mots*. Paris: Gallimard, 1964.

—. *On a raison de se révolter. Entretiens avec Philippe Gavi et Pierre Victor*. Paris: Gallimard, 1974.

—. "Ouragan sur le sucre, II", *Les Temps Modernes,* no. 649, 2008.

—. "Préface", in Frantz Fanon, *Les Damnés de la terre*. Paris: Maspero, 1961. (Also in *Situations, V*. Paris: Gallimard, 1964.)

—. "Préface", in Roger Stéphane, *Portrait de l'aventurier*. Paris: Grasset, 1950. (Also in *Situations, VI*. Paris : Gallimard, 1964.)

—. "Le Prétendant", in *Situations, V*. Paris: Gallimard, 1964.

CHAPTER EIGHT

WHAT CAN PHILOSOPHERS TEACH POLITICIANS?

JEAN-PIERRE BOULÉ

"Ensemble, tout devient possible"[1]

When I thought about the relevance of Jean-Paul Sartre today, I was struck by a recent speech made by Nicholas Sarkozy on the subject of May 1968.[2] May 68 is, of course, a milestone in Sartre's own intellectual life[3], and so I decided to investigate "Sartre, Sarkozy and May 68". At first sight, it seems strange to have associated these two names in a chapter on May 68. The impact of May 68 on Jean-Paul Sartre initially appeared to be non-existent; however in retrospect it exerted a profound influence upon him. Nicolas Sarkozy, the French President, was thirteen in 1968. Allegedly, he wanted to attend the 30 May pro-De Gaulle demonstration, but his mother ensured that he was kept in school to prevent him from going.[4] Another association with the events is the fact that he was a law student in the mid 1970s at Nanterre University, where the student movement had begun and where Daniel Cohn-Bendit had been a sociology student. And yet again, many will remember the (in)famous speech that Sarkozy gave at Bercy in April 2007, prior to the second round of voting in the French presidential elections, when he launched into a virulent attack on May 68, concluding that he wanted once and for all to dispose of

[1] "Together, anything becomes possible." This political slogan appeared on the website of Nicolas Sarkozy's party, the UMP (Union pour un Mouvement Populaire; Union for a Popular Movement). See www.u-m-p.org/site (accessed 13 September 2010).

[2] My thanks go to David Drake for his judicious comments on this chapter. An earlier version of this text first appeared as an article: see Boulé 2009.

[3] See Boulé 1995.

[4] See Nivelle and Karlin.

the spirit of May 68.[5] My argument is that, whilst taking this standpoint, Sarkozy has appropriated left-wing rhetoric in order to convince his audience, and this is what I aim to demonstrate in this chapter; I am not at any point arguing that Sarkozy has been influenced by Sartre, merely that he is using left-wing rhetoric to pursue a right-wing agenda.

There are a number of parallels between Sarkozy's actions as Minister of the Interior and presidential candidate, and the lessons Sartre drew from May 68. Both men saw the need to reach out to a wider public; both men understood the value of praxis (political action), and both men interrogated themselves on how to make people feel solidarity amongst disparate groups, what Sartre will call a "group-in-fusion". Whereas Sartre saw the emergence of the "new intellectual", the parallel with Sarkozy is "the new politician". I will start by examining the influence of May 68 on Sartre before turning my attention to Sarkozy. I will then highlight the differences between them before concluding with a discussion of what lies behind Sarkozy's attack on May 68.

By the mid-1940s, Sartre was well aware that he was essentially a bourgeois writer, writing for a bourgeois public. In "Qu'est-ce que la littérature?" ("What is Literature?"), published in *Les Temps Modernes* in 1946, Sartre was something of a trail-blazer when he decided to use the mass media (radio, newspapers and periodicals) in order to communicate with a wider public. He no longer wanted to write exclusively for a bourgeois audience, but to reach out to the masses. On the one hand, this can be analyzed as Sartre breaking away from the sacrosanct status of the novel, a tradition embodied by nineteenth-century writers such as Flaubert. On the other hand, the rationale for Sartre's attitude remained very traditional: "It is not acceptable to lower our standards to seduce our audience, but on the contrary, to reveal to the public its own demands and to raise these gradually, until it has a *need* to read."[6] In other words, Sartre's commitment to using the mass media in 1946 reflected the wish to preserve the status of the written work. He wanted to conquer a public of non-readers and entice them to start reading his novels. In practice, as he admitted in 1972 when reflecting on the post-war period, Sartre was obliged to revise his assumption according to which he could widen his public and reach out to the masses by using the mass media alone.[7] Immediately after the Liberation, the elections revealed the French

[5] For a comprehensive overview of this remark, see Gordon.

[6] "Il ne convient pas de s'abaisser pour plaire, mais au contraire, de révéler au public ses exigences propres et de l'élever, petit à petit, jusqu'à ce qu'il ait *besoin de* lire." (Sartre 1948, 292.) All translations from the French are my own.

[7] See Astruc, Contat, 85.

Communist Party to be the party of the workers, and Sartre needed their support to widen his public. Thus, in 1946, he realized that unless he joined the French Communist Party (PCF), and therefore could communicate with the masses, he would be condemned to write primarily for a bourgeois public.[8] Sartre being distrustful of the mass media, the way to reach out to them was to be endorsed by the PCF.

From 1952, when he wrote "Les Communistes et la paix" ("The Communists and Peace"[9]), Sartre became, according to his own expression, a fellow-traveller of the Communist Party until the Soviet invasion of Hungary four years later, which he condemned in an interview. But whether he ever did, even when he was a fellow traveller, "communicate with the workers through the PCF" is another matter. Following the Soviet invasion of Hungary, he wrote "Le Fantôme de Staline" ("The Phantom of Stalin"[10]) where he explicitly dissociated himself from the Communist party. In so doing, Sartre felt that he had isolated himself from the workers (and had to abandon the idea of communicating with them through the Communist Party), even though by 1956, especially after the invasion of Hungary, the PCF was no longer the "party of the working class" in the way that it could, justifiably, have been called in 1945 and 1946.

There then followed a period of reflection about Marxism. Sartre started to write *Critique de la raison dialectique* (*Critique of Dialectical Reason,* published in 1960[11]), in which he redefined his position on communism and the Soviet Union. He also reflected upon notions of group action by looking at past historical events, notably the French Revolution, defining a group-in-fusion as a group in the process of being constituted by the dissolution of seriality (which he calls "Apocalypse"), under the pressure of an opposing praxis. Through this concept, Sartre developed the theoretical concept of reciprocity.

It is only in *Critique of Dialectical Reason* that reciprocity appears in Sartre's theoretical work. The notion of reciprocity is explicitly denied in *L'Être et le néant* (*Being and Nothingness*, published in 1943), where Sartre's "being-for-others" (*être-pour-autrui*) is first and foremost an object; hence there can be no reciprocity between two subjects: "From the moment I exist, I establish *de facto* a limit to the freedom of the Other."[12] In *Being and Nothingness* in 1943, Sartre was convinced that two subjects

---

[8] Ibid.
[9] Sartre 1964.
[10] Sartre 1965.
[11] Sartre 1960.
[12] "Dès lors que j'existe, j'établis une limite de fait à la liberté d'Autrui." (Sartre 1943, 292.)

could have only a relation of subject and object, hence his theory of objectifying someone (*la chosification*). The Other was an obstacle to one's freedom; now, in 1960 in the *Critique*, *autrui* becomes necessary to the realisation of this freedom, made possible by the concept of reciprocity. The Other becomes a means to an end and not "*my* end" because s/he is "praxis". Human relations (positive or negative) are reciprocal, because the *praxis* of one individual (his or her organising project transformed into action) recognizes the *praxis* of the other.[13] The concept of *praxis* is a cornerstone to Sartre's understanding of reciprocity, as well as the concept of dialectics. The philosophical question is initially how one passes from a quasi-object to an object-subject and to a subject-object.[14] Sartre can allow himself to commit through language since "the human voice is given as *praxis* and the listener becomes the object of that *praxis* [...] it is a univocal relation of interiority".[15]

In 1965 Sartre gave a series of conferences in Japan where he reflected upon the role, not of the writer, but of the intellectual, employing his recent reflection on Marxist analysis.[16] He claimed that the intellectual had become a "technician of practical knowledge" whose goal was to facilitate the "proletarian awakening", but who must also be wary of the distinction between the particular and the universal. If the intellectual claims to be the guardian of the universal, he or she thus reduces him/herself to representing a specific class, falling into the old illusion of the bourgeoisie thinking that it represents a universal class.[17] The events of May 68 were going to make Sartre revise once more his definition of the intellectual.

The *Critique of Dialectical Reason* was an important reference work for the actors of May 68. Epistémon, pseudonym for a professor of psychology, declared that the *Critique of Dialectical Reason* was a premonitory work which allowed one to *think* the revolution of May, in particular Sartre's theories on alienated freedom, the practico-inert, the concepts of the group and of creative freedom.[18] Cohn-Bendit himself acknowledged that the great majority of the militants taking part in the Movement of 22 March had read Sartre.[19]

Using periodicals, newspapers and radio, Sartre is readily applying the

---

[13] See Sartre 1960, 207.
[14] See Sartre 1972, 88.
[15] "La voix humaine se donne comme *praxis* et constitue l'auditeur comme l'objet de la *praxis* [...] c'est une relation univoque d'intériorité." (Sartre 1960, 321.)
[16] Sartre 1972.
[17] See ibid., 387, 420, 421.
[18] See "Entretien avec Epistémon".
[19] See Contat and Rybalka, 462.

theoretical concepts of the *Critique of Dialectical Reason*: "[...] the only possible means of communication *with the Others,* as they are already serialized, is the serial unity of the mass media."[20] There is one major difference with his declaration of 1946: Sartre is no longer trying to preserve the status of the written work, nor is he speaking in the name of the universal class, the ruling class. He pledged his public support for the students' movement.[21] He spoke to the students who occupied the Sorbonne. He granted an interview to Radio-Luxembourg where he stated that, regardless of the political affiliation of any government, violence was the only option for the students who wanted radical change. He justified the violence of the students in the name of the violence perpetrated against them. For him, the only rapport they could have with the university was to destroy it, and in order to do so, they had to take to the streets.[22] Sartre provided Cohn-Bendit with a political platform by interviewing him; the interview was later published in *Le Nouvel Observateur*.[23] Sartre no longer spoke in the name of the oppressed—for example, in favour of the people of Vietnam fighting against the American oppressor—but he was facilitating the accession of the oppressed to the media so that they could express themselves.

Sarkozy is a member of the centre-right "Union pour un Mouvement Populaire" (Union for a Popular Movement). Nationally, Sarkozy first created a sensation as a twenty-year-old youth delegate at a Gaullist rally in Nice in June 1975. According to Daniel Gordon's analysis, "his 1975 speech was powerful because it attempted to appropriate the language of youth and revolution away from the *gauchistes*", for example: "To belong to the Gaullist youth is to be a revolutionary, but not like those who are professional demonstrators."[24] This Sarkozian strategy of appropriating the language of youth and revolution will be repeated again and again.[25] He co-opts concepts and language from left-wing politicians, but manipulates them to his ideological advantage. Whilst Sarkozy was Minister of the Interior, a polemic ensued in November 2005 with film director Mathieu Kassovitz (*La Haine*, 1995) over the crisis in the *banlieues* (working-class suburbs comprising *cités*, or estates inhabited by a high proportion of

---

[20] "[…] le seul moyen de communication possible *avec les Autres,* en tant qu'ils sont déjà sérialisés, c'est l'unité sérielle des mass media." (Sartre 1960, 582.)

[21] See Contat and Rybalka, 462-63.

[22] Ibid., 463-64.

[23] "L'Imagination au pouvoir".

[24] "Etre jeune gaulliste, c'est être révolutionnaire, révolutionnaire pas à la manière de ceux qui sont des professionnels de la manif." (See Nivelle and Karlin.)

[25] See the penetrating articles by Giorgione on Sarkozy's political rhetoric.

people from ethnic minorities, that replaced shanty-towns).[26] In this instance, I believe that more can be gleaned from the medium than from the argument itself. Sarkozy responded to Kassovitz's internet blog which blamed the government, the police, and also Sarkozy as Minister of the Interior, for recent crises in the *banlieues*. Sarkozy's response to Kassovitz's blog is an illustration of what Sartre had said about using all means of communication possible in order to reach the serialized masses: language as praxis. It was pioneering for Sartre to use radio and newspapers in the late 1940s; in the twenty-first century, the internet is the equivalent medium.

There is a general consensus, both in France and abroad, that a French politician has never figured in the media as much as Sarkozy. His opening statement in his blog's response is that he believes in the virtue of debates and exchanges, and his closing statement invites Kassovitz to pursue their verbal exchange. He claims to be against "political cant" (*la langue de bois*) which he blames partly for the rise of extremism in France. May 68 activists were also in favour of the democratisation of language, so that it would not remain an elitist domain. In engaging with a young French filmmaker recognised for his sympathies with the Left, Sarkozy is also trying to reach out to a younger, more marginal audience, as opposed to the one traditionally associated with right-wing politicians. He is widening his net, not as a new intellectual, but as a new kind of politician. This is underpinned in the details of his argument. He introduces the concept of positive discrimination, something that previous French governments, including Socialist ones, have always shunned. He is also in favour of the right of foreigners to vote in local elections, and he promotes a heterogeneous France encapsulated in his trademark slogan: "Plural France" (*la France plurielle*). In the piece, we see him denouncing the supposed "equality" in France, which is only window-dressing. Inequality was a value at the heart of the May 68 opposition. Exclusion and discrimination on the grounds of race were to become important post-68.[27]

---

[26] See the website: u-m-p.org[...]/nicolas_sarkozyrepond_a_mathieu_kassovitz. Kassovitz's original article and his response are to be found at: www.mathieukassovitz.com (accessed 13 September 2010).

[27] I should make it clear at this point that I am not arguing that Sarkozy is a closet May 68 exponent; I would agree with Philipp Knee's formulation that there is an echo of May 68 values in Sarkozy's responses. Philipp Knee was the commentator for the first version of this paper, delivered at the conference of the society for "Existential and Phenomenological Theory and Culture", on 3-6 June 2008, at the University of British Columbia, and I would like to thank him for his attentive reading of my paper. A further version of this paper was delivered under the

In order to differentiate between Sartre and Sarkozy, it is necessary to return once again to Sartre. As reported in Cohen-Solal's biography of Sartre, Alain Geismar, one of the student leaders, later said that when he went with some comrades to meet Sartre and Beauvoir at the beginning of the riots, they did not truly have an exchange that day. He had the feeling that they listened to them, but that they did not understand.[28] This concurs with Sartre's own analysis in *On a raison de se révolter* (*We Are Right to Rebel*), published in 1974. He acknowledges that he supported the students' movement but, in actual fact, he did not understand it.[29] Whereas May 68 seemed to be temporarily forgotten by French society when traditional summer holidays took over, Sartre was one of the few intellectuals who continued to reflect upon May 68. The first lesson he drew from these events was the betrayal of the French Communist Party, writing in July 1968 that the PCF had betrayed the revolution, was objectively on the same side as De Gaulle, and accusing the Communist-dominated CGT trades union (*Confédération générale des travailleurs*) of doing everything it could to prevent contact between workers and students.[30] Simone de Beauvoir wrote in her memoirs that the Communists had been quick to condemn, in the pages of the Communist daily *L'Humanité*, the "German anarchist", Daniel Cohn-Bendit.[31]

When Soviet tanks invaded Czechoslovakia in August 1968, Sartre condemned both this invasion and the PCF (*Parti communiste français*). This final breakdown of Sartre's relationship with the French Communist Party opened new possibilities for him. Until then, he had always believed that the Communist Party was the party of the workers. In order to communicate with the workers, one had to use the mediation of the Communist Party. The students were testimony that one could dialogue with the workers without passing through the mediation of the PCF. Convinced that the Communist Party did not want a revolution, Sartre endeavoured to conquer the two audiences which had always eluded him, namely youth and workers. Sartre started to grant more and more

---

auspices of the Arts and Humanities Research Council, Research Networks and Workshops Scheme: "The Relevance of Jean-Paul Sartre Today", hosted by the *Association japonaise d'études sartriennes* (Japanese Society for Sartre Studies), at Rikkyô University, Tokyo, in July 2009. The research for this paper was supported by the AHRC.

[28] See Cohen-Solal, 86.

[29] See Sartre, Victor, Gavi, 63.

[30] See "M. J.-P. Sartre: le parti communiste a trahi la révolution de mai".

[31] Beauvoir 1972, 50.

interviews to young people[32], and he himself remembered the moment when he began to make sense of May 68[33], during a discussion with young people in Italy during the summer of 1968.[34]

An important incident took place in February 1969 when Sartre was one of the speakers during a debate organized by students. As he was about to speak, he found a note on his desk which read: "Sartre, be clear, keep it short: we want to discuss the tactics."[35] In *On a raison de se révolter*, a record of discussions between Sartre, Pierre Victor and Philippe Gavi recorded in 1972 and published in 1974, Sartre analyses how this event was the starting point of his own evolution. He says he did not have anything to say in this meeting called to discuss practical matters. His presence was "scandalous" because, since he was neither a professor nor a student, his intervention could only be constructed as that of a star; he had spoken as a traditional intellectual, opposing the universal to the particular.[36]

Subsequently, Sartre began to question his status as a traditional intellectual. In her memoirs, Beauvoir testified that he thought about the role of the intellectual to the point of "breaking bones in his head".[37] To the traditional intellectual, he opposed the "new intellectual" who denies in himself the intellectual moment to try to find a new *popular* status; the new intellectual seeks to blend with the masses so that true universality can triumph.[38] Over the next few years, Sartre would support and facilitate the publication of the newspapers *La Cause du peuple* and *Libération*, so that the masses could express themselves. As he explained in an interview: "Henceforth I consider myself available for all politically appropriate tasks that will be asked of me."[39] Nevertheless, everything was not clear-cut as we learn in "Autoportrait à soixante-dix ans" (Self Portrait at Seventy). Sartre admitted that almost two years after May 68, he was still thinking about what had happened, which he had not really understood. What did these young people want, and what role could "old schmucks" (*vieux cons*)

---

[32] See Boulé 1992.
[33] See Sartre, Victor, Gavi, 63.
[34] See "I Communisti hanno paura della rivoluzione".
[35] "Sartre, sois clair, sois bref: nous voulons discuter des consignes à adopter." (Sartre 1972, 240.)
[36] See Sartre, Victor, Gavi, 66.
[37] Beauvoir 1985, 5.
[38] See ibid., 16-17.
[39] "Maintenant je me considère comme disponible pour toutes tâches politiquement justes qui me seront demandées." (Sartre 1972, 470).

such as himself have?[40] In 1971, during one of the popular tribunals held by the Maoists, Sartre insisted on the role of the masses, from object (spectator) to subject (actor).[41] In his foreword to Michèle Manceaux's *Les Maos en France,* Sartre pointed out that the workers, up until then objects of capitalist authoritarianism, had become, even for one moment, the subjects of their own history.[42] Sartre subsequently pushed his analysis further in an interview with Leo Fretz, where he spoke about a society without power becoming an ethical society because a new form of freedom is established, which is the freedom of the reciprocal relations of persons in the form of an "us" (*nous*).[43] This "us" Sartre endeavoured to put into practice with Victor and Gavi by recording their discussions and publishing the result as a book.

Sartre was to develop further the notion of "us" in the context of writing. He devoted the last five years of his life to writing a book of dialogues with Pierre Victor—real name, Benny Lévy—*Pouvoir et liberté* (*Power and Freedom*), where he continued to draw lessons from May 68: "Those who made May 68 happen […] demanded everything: freedom. They did not ask for power [...] because [...] it is the very social structure which allows the exercise of power which we need to do away with."[44]

May 68 has long been the subject of revisionist politics. As Reynolds demonstrates, respected intellectuals—from both sides of the political spectrum, such as Régis Debray, Luc Ferry and Gilles Lipovetsky—have all drawn attention to some negative aspects of May 68, from furthering the dominance of capitalism to being responsible for the (narcissistic) individualism of the 1980s.[45] The headlines following Sarkozy's speech at Bercy on 29 April 2007 concentrated on one particular phrase: "I want to turn the page on May 68."[46] Sarkozy's speech—in fact written by Henri Guaino, an economist[47]—needs only a cursory glance to illustrate that

---

[40] Sartre 1976, 185.

[41] See "Pourquoi un tribunal populaire contre la police?".

[42] See Sartre 1976, 45.

[43] See Leo Fretz, "An interview with Jean-Paul Sartre", in Silvermann and Elliston, 233.

[44] "Ceux qui ont fait Mai 68 […] demandaient tout: la liberté. Ils ne demandaient pas le pouvoir [...] car [...] c'est la structure sociale même, permettant l'exercice du pouvoir qu'il s'agit de supprimer." (Sartre 1976, 184.) For Sartre in May 68, a good starting point would be Aronson, to be complemented by Drake. For May 68, see Hamon and Rotman, Ross, Touraine, and Weber.

[45] See Reynolds, and also Badiou, Debray, Ferry and Renaut, and Lipovetsky.

[46] "Je veux tourner la page de Mai 68."

[47] See Aeschimann. In a polemical piece, Cohn-Bendit and Geismar, two of the main actors of May 68, point the finger at André Glucksmann, "the chief thinker of

some of the values of May 68, and some of the lessons Sartre learned from that event, are still being promoted in Sarkozy's discourse. The context surrounding his speech is important: he was making a direct appeal to voters on the eve of the second round of the presidential elections, where he was opposed by Ségolène Royal, the Socialist candidate. He wanted to widen his public (potential voters) and to be inclusive of all French people, even those who in the past had never been his supporters.

The Bercy speech is a typical illustration of Sarkozy co-opting left-wing political tools and concepts, but then twisting them for his own ideological ends. Sarkozy is widely acknowledged as someone who does not adhere to boundaries, and not only between public and private spheres. This can be seen in a positive light, as a new type of politician, or a negative one, as someone unprincipled and disingenuous. One of his leitmotivs is that he wants to be "the candidate of the people". Politics is there to give the people hope, so that they can become again *actors* in their own history. Sarkozy has realised that politics must once more reflect the wishes of those who have lost the strength to want things. One can almost hear Sartre talking about reciprocity and the fact that the masses are no longer objects (spectators) but subjects (actors).[48] During his campaign, Sarkozy went to meet the masses (*le peuple*). He argues that everyone always pretends to speak in their name when this is not the case, that no-one ever really speaks to them, and that no-one ever does anything for them, as if the masses should be forever sidelined, excluded from power and decision-making. He mentions that, during his campaign, he went to meet and talk with as many French people as possible, from all possible walks of life. Again, this is an illustration of language as praxis. He singles out young people, condemned to have a worse standard of living than their parents, and whose qualifications are not enough to get a job. He acknowledges that they are resentful of being discriminated against, be it for the colour of their skin or the milieu they come from. He says he has also heard the voices of those who are angry against a Republic that does not keep its promises of equality and fraternity. This rhetoric is consonant with May 68 aspirations. Again, I am not claiming that Sarkozy is a May 68 revolutionary, but that he has exploited May 68 to serve his own aspirations.

Sarkozy has met all these anonymous and ordinary people that nobody pays any attention to, that nobody listens to, that nobody wants to hear.

Sarkozy's cultural revolution". See also Glucksmann, and Geismar, especially 9-21. For information on Guaino, go to http://notre.republique.free.fr/bioguaino.htm (accessed 13 September 2010).

[48] See "Pourquoi un tribunal populaire contre la police?".

Unlike Sartre, whose ultimate aim was to blend with the masses, Sarkozy wants to speak *for* them, to be their spokesperson, using "us" *twenty-two times* during his speech. This quest for power directly contradicts Sartre's line of enquiry in the project that was *Power and Freedom*, which consisted in eradicating the very social structures which allowed the exercise of power. In his polemic with Kassovitz, Sarkozy had already argued that he spoke for the majority of French people, claiming to represent the majority of families and young people. Sartre had warned of the need to be wary of the distinction between the particular and the universal. Sarkozy projects himself as a new politician who tries to find a new *popular* status. The future President is at pains to stress that he is not interested in meeting those who do not want to share, who seize all the benefits and who feel they owe nothing to their country. Again, this is akin to criticising the very social structures that Sartre wanted to eliminate after May 68, but this is where Sarkozy is dangerous. Whilst it may appear that Sarkozy is attacking the rich, he is in fact using this rhetoric to attack people on social benefits, people at the margins of society, and people who, he claims, have no sense of civic duty.

Sarkozy speaks about an identity crisis in France. He even goes so far as to claim that people's doubt is "existential", an unwitting echo of Sartrean existentialism, when human beings realise that their life is contingent. As part of Sartre's theoretical reflections in *Critique of Dialectical Reason*, the philosopher, now strongly influenced by Marxism, was asking himself what unites people, introducing the concepts of seriality, praxis, and alienation. Against the practico-inert and seriality was the group, where reciprocity appeared, and which became a group-in-fusion under certain circumstances such as to counteract adversity[49], the essential characteristic of the group-in-fusion being the resurgence of freedom.[50] Sarkozy is rhetorically asking himself the same questions, but without the philosopher's rigour and method. What is a people? What does the future hold? What unites (French) people? How can they build together? How can they live together? But his answer precedes his questioning and lies in his political project.

One of the cornerstones of May 68, of the Maoist movement in France, and of the *Gauche Prolétarienne*, is the discovery of the power of the masses. In the midst of the above interrogations, Sarkozy evokes the power of the masses. According to him, this power can be used for better or for worse and, in order to use this power for the better, he introduces the

---

[49] See Sartre 1960, 154.
[50] Ibid., 425.

notion of ethics in politics. This will be the platform from which he will launch his attack on May 68.

Sarkozy proceeds to argue that ethics disappeared with May 68, that all values were the same and that there were to be no differences between right and wrong. This is a staggering misinterpretation of May 68 and Sarkozy yet again blurs boundaries. He stretches somewhat the definition of ethics since, later on in his speech, it becomes clear that the value he wants to promote is that of work; the crisis of work is a *moral* crisis due mostly to May 68 and Sarkozy wants to rehabilitate work. If we go back to the *Critique of Dialectical Reason*, Sartre describes work as a free *praxis* interacting with the surrounding matter.[51] It is only because of the capitalist system and because of material scarcity that work is a cause of alienation and exploitation. Sarkozy's argument has a logic of its own. With ethics come authority, work and nation; duty over rights. This is not dissimilar to the Pétainist discourse of the Vichy government in France: *Travail, famille, patrie* (Work, Family, Fatherland). Knee is surprised by this comparison between Sarkozy and Pétain and objects that there is nothing wrong with work as a value. I make this very point above, using Sartre, but the context of Vichy France was quite different. Pétain argued that France had become too preoccupied with workers' rights during the Popular Front (*Front populaire*) in the late 1930s, and that, instead of rights, one had to go back to duties. "Work, Family, Fatherland" is a triptych that denies the rights of the individual for the greater good of the (Catholic) country. And the most powerful argument is that during World War II, the French economy became a vital part of the German war machine, with a large proportion of the French gross domestic product being given to Nazi Germany, rising from 20% to 50% of official GDP between 1940 and 1943.[52] Sarkozy denigrates the May 68 movement by scorning workers' rights and wanting to replace rights with work. One can trace the same sacrifice of the individual for the greater good of the nation. "Work" is never defined but, presumably, Sarkozy means paid work or employment, in which case he is denying all unpaid labour, including that of mothers. Finally, whilst stopping short of calling his political manifesto a revolution, Sarkozy calls it "a moral and intellectual reform".[53]

---

[51] Ibid., 369.

[52] See Occhino, et al.

[53] In a thought-provoking article, Alain Badiou argues that beyond the attack on May 68, the spectre of communism haunts Sarkozy. He also compares Sarkozy's political discourse to neo-Pétainism on four counts: the alliance of fear and war; the displacement of politics by morality; the paradigmatic function of foreign experience; the source of the crisis lying in a disastrous past event (Badiou, 32-34).

Economy of space prevents me from going into intricate details, but many of the criticisms levelled at May 68 are unjustified[54], including when he reproached May 68 for having disposed of the school system of Jules Ferry—compulsory primary education, instituted in 1881—concluding that, between Jules Ferry and May 68, the left had chosen May 68. What provoked the biggest reaction in the French press was Sarkozy's claiming that May 68 introduced cynicism into French society and politics, that it was to blame for the cult of money, short-term profit, speculation, and all the pitfalls of financial capitalism. In an extraordinary leap, May 68 was said to be responsible for the immorality of capitalism such as golden handshakes.[55] As Dhombres pointed out, May 68 demonstrators went to the Stock Exchange in Paris to burn it down, not to buy "hedge funds".[56] By then in full flight, Sarkozy lambasted all the politicians who claim the heritage of May 68.[57] Finally, he moved on to attacking the left, which he presents as the bedrock of May 68 values. Sarkozy claimed that the left had paralysed France, and the poorest workers were its main victims (and by implication Sarkozy was their defender). Not unlike Sartre after May 68, Sarkozy is trying to appeal both to young people, and to disadvantaged classes. Jean-Pierre Le Goff, a sociologist and author of *Mai 68: L'Héritage impossible* (*The Impossible Heritage*), reacted to the Bercy speech by pointing out that France had been wavering between fascination and rejection of May 68 for thirty years.[58] Sarkozy plays on both tendencies; he uses and promotes through distortion many of the values associated with the events, whilst trying to leave behind its heritage.

In the middle of the Algerian war, Sartre had said that the greatness of a nation is measured not by how much blood it sheds, but by how many humanitarian problems it solves.[59] The final part of Sarkozy's speech bears a further connection with May 68, but with another twist. According to Sarkozy, once his reforms are accomplished, France will be reconstructed

---

[54] For a systematic rebuttal of Sarkozy's argument, see Bensaid and Krivine, 22.

[55] See the interview with Cohn-Bendit by Werly; and, in the same issue, "Référence de la gauche, un héritage qui épouvante à droite", for the reactions of François Hollande and Ségolène Royal. See also: "Mai 68: Sarkozy provoque l'ire de la gauche", for the reactions of Cohn-Bendit, Lang, Royal and Weber.

[56] See Dhombres.

[57] Within weeks of his speech, Sarkozy would appoint, as Minister for Foreign and European Affairs, Bernard Kouchner, one of the symbols of May 68 and, at the time, leader of the French Communist students' union. For good measure, he would welcome support from ex-PCF member, the philosopher André Glucksmann (see Glucksmann, 98).

[58] Le Goff on Radio France-Culture, 30 April 2007.

[59] See Sartre 1964, 127.

as a "fraternal Republic". (This expression introduces a gender bias: where is the sorority?). It represents a dream never realised since the first day that France became conscious of its existence as a nation. One could point out that France is not a nation: it is a country or a state. The French are a nation. Sarkozy has used "Equality and Fraternity" before but not "Liberty". He now uses the concept, not in a *national* context but in a *global* context. He wants to be President of a country that defends freedom at home but also in the whole world. He justifies this by saying that it is France's vocation and destiny. In fact, he wants to be the President of Human Rights. So that there is no equivocation, he states that every time a woman or a child is abused or battered (*martyrisé*) in the world, he wants France to be by their side. He then proceeds to give five examples of women's oppression before pledging that he wants every "martyred woman" in the world to be given France's protection, by offering her the possibility of becoming French. Quite a number of commentators observed that Sarkozy had never acknowledged the positive impact of May 68 on women's liberation.[60] Now, he wants to be the knight in shining armour defending oppressed women worldwide. Sartre would see the fault line in his argument: Sarkozy, not content with speaking for all French people, now claiming to embody the entire French nation as a global President of Human Rights, with France promoted as a global Justice Minister. In 1958, when De Gaulle called a referendum, Sartre explained that if God existed and if he had to choose between God and De Gaulle when casting his vote, he would vote for God, as He is more modest than De Gaulle.[61] My guess is that he would have used the same logic with Sarkozy.

Sarkozy, pursuing his line of reasoning, tries to define the nation, and once more this is done within a global context. For Sarkozy, "France" is more than a territory; "France" is an ideal, indefatigably pursued by its great people, who, from the outset, have believed in the conviction of its ideas, in their capacity to transform the world and to create happiness for the whole of humanity. Sarkozy sees himself as the catalyst for France to recover its universal values, which should form the basis for its *internal* and *external* politics.

Before concluding, Sarkozy condemns those who have criticised him, and in the process he reveals his true motive. His detractors are the same as those who demonstrated against De Gaulle in 1958, shouting: "Fascism will not win!"[62] It is timely to remember that some of these De Gaulle supporters—as members of the OAS (*Organisation de l'armée secrète*:

---

[60] See, for instance, Cohn-Bendit and Royal.
[61] See Sartre 1964, 107.
[62] "Le fascisme ne passera pas!".

Organization of the secret army)—were also shouting "Shoot Sartre!"[63] Indirectly, Sarkozy is claiming De Gaulle's heritage, which is a direct appeal to another particular group of voters. 1958 was a time of political crisis in France, mostly due to events in Algeria, then constitutionally part of France. De Gaulle was recalled to power, on the understanding that he would keep Algeria French. It is no coincidence that Sarkozy compares himself to De Gaulle because the role he proposes for France, as detailed in the final part of his speech, is tainted by a colonialist discourse. Le Goff rightly qualifies this last manoeuvre as "pure nostalgia", made in order to claim that what was in place before May 68 was preferable.[64] Analysts of May 68 have long established that the students' movement is to be understood in a long line of various protest movements in the 1960s such as decolonisation, the Vietnam War, sexual liberation and so forth.[65] Sarkozy wants to dispose of May 68 because he craves for a "golden age" of colonialism, or rather a nostalgic hankering for a colonial rule.[66] He wants France to "transform the world and to create happiness in the whole of humanity" whilst giving lessons on human rights.[67] In his first blog on the *banlieues*, Kassovitz referred to Sarkozy as a "puny, would-be Napoléon"[68]; he thus anticipated the Bercy speech and the front covers of both *Stern* and *The Economist* in 2007.

If one contrasts the rhetoric used by Sarkozy as Minister of the Interior and during the presidential campaign with his record as President, differences start to open up. The "us" has been largely replaced by the "I". Sarkozy is often seen in the media mixing with the rich and powerful. He has given himself a 170% pay increase and, having promised that he would raise people's standard of living—"I will be the President of purchasing power"[69]—he has in fact told them: "The coffers are empty."[70] At the same time, he has been giving tax concessions to the very rich. How could one explain such discrepancies? What can philosophers teach politicians? Sarkozy should have heeded Sartre's own warning in the project of *Power and Freedom,* about the corrupting effect of power and

63 "Fusillez Sartre!".
64 See Aeschimann.
65 See for instance Brown, and also Singer.
66 See website u-m-p.org/[...]sarkozy_a_bercy (accessed 13 September 2010).
67 Ibid.: "[…] transformer le monde et [à] faire le bonheur de l'humanité."
68 "Petit Napoléon en devenir". http://www.mathieukassovitz.com/blog/2005/11/la-france-den-bas.html (accessed 13 September 2010).
69 "Je serai le Président du pouvoir d'achat."
70 "Les caisses sont vides."

its antithetical relationship to freedom: philosophers *can* teach politicians about ethics.[71]

I want to conclude with an extract from the book by Yasmina Reza, *L'Aube, le soir ou la nuit* (*Dawn, Evening or Night*):

> NICOLAS (*repeating a phrase from his Bercy speech*):—Between Jules Ferry and 68, they chose 68… Well, it verges on bad faith…
> YASMINA:—I am glad to hear you say it…
> NICOLAS (*laughing*):—Yes. It's even terrifyingly in bad faith, but in the end, you have to go for it![72]

Works Cited

Aeschimann, Eric. "Mai 68. Retour acide". *Libération,* 4 May 2007 (30).

Aronson, Ronald. *Jean-Paul Sartre, Philosophy in the World.* London: Verso, 1980.

Astruc, Alexandre and Michel Contat. *Sartre, un film.* Paris: Gallimard, 1977.

Badiou, Alain. "The Communist Hypothesis", *New Left Review*, no. 49, Jan-Feb 2008 (29-42).

—. *De quoi Sarkozy est-il le nom?* Paris: Editions Lignes, 2007.

Beauvoir, Simone de. *Tout compte fait.* Paris: Gallimard, 1972.

—. *La Cérémonie des adieux*, suivi de *Entretiens avec Jean-Paul Sartre.* Paris: Gallimard, 1981.

Bensaid, Daniel and Alain Krivine. "La haine de 68", *Libération, "Rebonds"*, 3 May 2007.

Boulé, Jean-Pierre. *Sartre médiatique. La place de l'interview dans son œuvre.* Paris: Minard, 1992.

—. "L'influence de Mai 68 sur Sartre", *Romanistische Zeitschrift für Literaturgeschichte* (*Cahiers d'histoire des littératures romanes*), vol. 19, no. 1/2, 1995 (33-49).

—. "May 1968, Sartre and Sarkozy", *PhaenEx: Journal of Existential and Phenomenological Theory and Culture*, vol. 4, no. 2, 2009. Special

[71] I would agree with Knee that one cannot make a straightforward comparison between a politician involved in pragmatics and a philosopher involved in theoretical ruminations, which Knee qualifies as "imaginary politics", using the May 68 slogan: "Power to the imagination!" (*L'Imagination au pouvoir!*).

[72] "N. (*répétant une phrase de son discours de Bercy*): Entre Jules Ferry et 68, ils ont choisi 68… Bon, c'est à la limite mauvaise foi… [*another Sartrean concept*]. / Y.: Je suis contente de te l'entendre dire … / N. (*il rit*): Oui. C'est même terrifiant de mauvaise foi, mais enfin, il faut y aller!" (Reza, 159.)

issue (ed. Kevin W. Gray): "Rethinking 1968" (1-25), @ www.phaenex.uwindsor.ca/ojs/leddy/index.php/phaenex/issue/current/showToc (accessed 13 September 2010).

Brown, Bernard E. *Protest in Paris: Anatomy of a Revolt*. London: General Learning Press, 1974.

Cohen-Solal, Annie. *Sartre 1905-1980*. Paris: Gallimard, 1985.

Cohn-Bendit, Daniel. "L'imagination au pouvoir: entretien de Jean-Paul Sartre avec Daniel Cohn-Bendit", *Le Nouvel Observateur,* 20 May 1968.

Cohn-Bendit, Daniel and Alain Geismar, "Nous sommes coupables...", *Libération*, *"Rebonds",* 2 May 2007.

Cohn-Bendit, Daniel and Ségolène Royal. *Journal de midi*, "Présidentielle: la campagne de l'entre-deux tours sur thème de confrontation et de débat". @ http://web2.radio-france.fr/chaines/franceculture/information/accueil/fiche.php?diffusionid=52554&index=5 (accessed 13 September 2010).

Contat, Michel and Michel Rybalka. *Les Écrits de Sartre*. Paris: Gallimard, 1970.

Debray, Régis. *Modeste Contribution aux discours et cérémonies officielles du Xe anniversaire*. Paris: Maspero, 1978.

Dhombres, Dominique. "Une victime cachée de Mai 68", *Le Monde,* 2 May 2007.

Drake, David. *Intellectuals and Politics in Post-War France*. Basingstoke: Palgrave, 2002.

"Entretien avec Epistémon." *Le Monde*, supplement to issue no. 7428, 30 November 1986 (iv).

Ferry, Luc and Alain Renaut. *La Pensée 68. Essai sur l'anti-humanisme contemporain*. Paris: Gallimard, 1988.

Fretz, Leo. "An interview with Jean-Paul Sartre", in Hugh J. Silvermann and Frederick A. Elliston (eds.), *Jean-Paul Sartre. Contemporary Approaches to his Philosophy*. Pittsburgh: Duquesne University Press, 1980.

Geismar, Alain. *Mon Mai 1968*. Paris: Perrin, 2008.

Giorgione. www.philosophie.blogs.liberation.fr/noudelmann/rhetorique/ (accessed 13 September 2010).

Glucksmann, André and Raphaël Glucksmann. *Mai 68 expliqué à Nicolas Sarkozy*. Paris: Denoël, 2008.

Gordon, Daniel. "Liquidating May 68? Generational Trajectories of the 2007 Presidential Candidates", *Modern and Contemporary France*, vol. 16, no. 2, May 2008 (143-59).

Hamon, Hervé and Patrick Rotman. *Génération. 1. Les Années de rêve.* Paris: Seuil, 1987.

Le Goff, Jean-Pierre. *Mai 68, l'héritage impossible*. Paris: La Découverte, 1998.

Lipovetsky, Gilles. *L'Ère du vide. Essais sur l'individualisme contemporain.* Paris: Gallimard, 1983.

"Mai 68: Sarkozy provoque l'ire de la gauche", *Le Figaro,* 30 April 2007.

Nivelle, P. and E. Karlin. "Nicolas Sarkozy: secrets de jeunesse", *L'Express,* 5 October 2006.

Occhino, Filippo, Kim Oosterlinck and Eugene N. White. "How Occupied France Financed Its Own Exploitation in World War II", *American Economic Review*, vol. 97, no. 2, May 2007 (295-99).

"Pourquoi un tribunal populaire contre la police?", *La Cause du peuple—J'accuse*, no. 6, 21 June 1971.

"Référence de la gauche, un héritage qui épouvante à droite, réactions de François Hollande et Ségolène Royal", *Le Figaro,* 30 April 2007.

Reynolds, Chris. "May 68: A Contested History", *Sens Public*, October 2007. @ http://www.senspublic.org/article.php3?id_article=472. (accessed 13 September 2010).

Reza, Yasmina. *L'Aube, le soir ou la nuit*. Paris: Flammarion, 2007.

Ross, Kristin. *Mai 68 et ses vies ultérieures.* Paris: Complexe, 2005.

Sartre, Jean-Paul. *L'Être et le néant.* Paris: Gallimard. 1943.

—. "Qu'est-ce que la littérature ?", *Les Temps Modernes*, nos. 17-22, 1946, and in *Situations, II*. Paris: Gallimard, 1948 (55-330).

—. *Critique de la raison dialectique*. Paris: Gallimard, 1960.

—. "La constitution du mépris", in *Situations, V*. Paris: Gallimard, 1964 (102-112).

—. "Les communistes et la paix", in *Situations, VI*. Paris: Gallimard, 1964 (80-384).

—. "Les grenouilles qui demandent un roi.", in *Situations, V*. Paris: Gallimard, 1964 (113-44).

—. "Le fantôme de Staline", in *Situations, VII*. Paris: Gallimard, 1965 (144-307).

—. "L'anthropologie", in *Situations, IX*. Paris: Gallimard, 1972 (83-98).

—. "Plaidoyer pour les intellectuels", in *Situations, VIII*. Paris: Gallimard, 1972 (375-455).

—. "Les Maos en France", in *Situations, X*. Paris: Gallimard, 1976 (38-47).

—. "Autoportrait à soixante-dix ans" (entretien avec Michel Contat), in *Situations, X*. Paris: Gallimard, 1976 (133-226).

—. "M. J.-P. Sartre: le parti communiste a trahi la révolution de mai", *Le Monde*, 16 July 1968 (7).

Sartre, Jean-Paul, Pierre Victor and Philippe Gavi. *On a raison de se révolter*. Paris: Gallimard, 1974.

Silvermann, Hugh J. and Frederick A. Elliston (eds.). *Jean-Paul Sartre: Contemporary Approaches to his Philosophy*. Pittsburgh: Duquesne University Press, 1980.

Singer, Daniel. *Prelude to a Revolution*. London: Jonathan Cape, 1970.

Touraine, Alain. *Le Mouvement de mai ou le communisme utopique*. Paris: Seuil, 1968.

Weber, Henri. *Que reste-t-il de mai 68? Essai sur les interprétations des "événements"*. Paris: Seuil, 1988.

Werly, Richard. "Par rapport à Mai 68, Nicolas Sarkozy se comporte en pur stalinien". *Le Monde*, 1 May 2007.

CHAPTER NINE

SARTRE'S CONCEPT OF MAN: EXISTENTIALISM AND FEMINISM

SAWADA NAO

In 1945 Sartre declared in his famous lecture entitled *L'Existentialisme est un humanisme* (*Existentialism and Humanism*), in reply to criticisms made by Catholics and Marxists, that existentialism belonged within the philosophical tradition of humanism.[1] In this text, Sartre emphasises that the starting point for existentialism is primarily the situation of the "forlorn" or "abandoned" man:

> Everything is indeed permitted if God does not exist, and man is in consequence forlorn, for he cannot find anything to depend upon either within or outside himself. He discovers forthwith that he is without excuse. For if indeed existence precedes essence, one will never be able to explain one's action by reference to a given and specific human nature; in other words, there is no determinism—man is free, man is freedom.[2]

What we need to note in this extract are the two central tenets of Sartre's thought. The first is that there is no such thing as a given and immutable human nature. In other words, there is no human essence. Second, a corollary of the first, is that man is free, man *is* freedom or, if you prefer, "Man is condemned to be free". From these two statements Sartre insisted that existentialism (a word he had not chosen to describe his philosophy, but one which he accepted) can be a humanism because it can indicate new ethical directives for people. It is clear that the humanism which

---

[1] This chapter was written in French and the editors wish to thank Dr David Drake, Emeritus Reader at Middlesex University, for the translation into English. A previous draft was given as a paper at the conference of the UK Sartre Society at the Institut Français, South Kensington, in September 2009.

[2] *L'Existentialisme est un humanisme,* 37.

Sartre is proposing is very different from the classical forms of humanism that he criticises because of their essentialism. Existential humanism, while rejecting the notion of human nature, considers that man is always to be fashioned and is only what he makes himself to be.

Although Sartre's relationship with humanism is full of complexities and ambiguities, we can say at the very least that he shows a constant interest in man (*l'homme*). It is well known that Sartre's notion of man came under strong attack from the structuralists, in particular Michel Foucault, in the conclusion of *Les Mots et les choses* (*The Order of Things*).[3] But I do not intend to go into the arguments that have been aired so many times in the clashes between existentialism and structuralism. Nor do I intend to examine Sartre's ambiguous relations with humanism. Rather, I am choosing to analyse the different ways in which Sartre uses the term "man". Or, to put it another way, what I am interested in here is the concept of "man" as presented by Sartre in several of his texts. Indeed, as we have seen, and whether we accept the label of humanism or not, man is one of the central notions for Sartre's existentialism. And yet, when we look more carefully, we can see that this central concept of "man" is neither as clear nor as unambiguous as it might appear. What exactly does the term "man" signify? Which "man" are we talking about? Who is the "man"? Or, rather, who is *not* the "man"? It is difficult to reply to these questions because, on the one hand, given that there is no fixed human essence, we cannot define what we mean by "man". On the other hand, there is also a linguistic ambiguity. And it is on this second point that I wish to focus.

When Sartre says that man is free, it seems obvious that he is talking about men and women—in other words, human beings or humanity. At any rate, that is what we may think. But is it really so straightforward? While it is true that in the philosophical texts the word "man" is almost always unequivocal, in the literary texts it is used in several different ways. It was while I was translating *Les Chemins de la liberté* (*The Roads to Freedom*) into Japanese that this question, which might perhaps appear a somewhat minor point, particularly struck me. This was because in Japanese we have two different words for man: one used to refer to the male of the human species, and another used to refer to men and women,

[3] "One thing is certain: that is that man is no longer the old problem or the old constant which faced human knowledge. Man is an invention which the archaeology of our thought clearly reveals to have been a recent invention, and which will soon disappear [...] we can probably bet that man will fade away, a little like the sea washes away a face in the sand." (Foucault, *Les Mots et les choses*—literally, *Words and Things*— 398.)

that is to say humanity; whereas in French, as in English, the word "man" is ambiguous. It may simultaneously refer to several things at the same time.

I propose therefore to revisit Sartre's concept of "man". This concept is well-known, has been sufficiently clarified and explained, not to say discussed at enormous length, but I shall be analysing Sartre's *use* of the term "man". However, as I cannot draw up an exhaustive list, I will restrict myself to referring mainly to *The Roads to Freedom* and, where necessary, to other literary and theoretical texts such as *L'Être et le néant* (*Being and Nothingness*). In the course of this brief survey, I will try both to tease out a number of aspects of this concept which are not well known, and to reveal its current significance and importance.

1. The Problematic

Let us first of all recall that the word *l'homme* (man) in French has at least two meanings:

(a) A being (male or female) belonging to the human race: *homo sapiens*; *anthropos* in Greek.

(b) A male of the human species: *aner* in Greek.

Furthermore, the second sense has at least two subdivisions: a male of the human species of any age; a male of the human species who is an adult.

The ambiguity of the word *homme* in French, and the sexism linked to it, have frequently been the target of feminist criticism. One has only to remember the "Declaration of the Rights of the Woman and the Female Citizen" (*Déclaration des droits de la femme et de la citoyenne*), drawn up in 1791 by Olympe de Gouges. This text, which demanded the full legal, political and social integration of women, is not only the first document to demand that women should have the same legal rights as men, but also the first important text to denounce, from the point of view of gender, the false universalism which lay hidden behind the word *homme*. The text of Olympe de Gouges is a critical pastiche of the "Declaration of the Rights of Man and of the Citizen" (*Déclaration des Droits de l'Homme et du Citoyen*), which sets out rights which apply only to men, that is to say, to males of the species. Indeed, at that time, women had neither the right to vote, nor to gain access to public bodies or the liberal professions, nor were they allowed to own property. Thus, Olympe de Gouges reveals the sexism hidden behind the mask of universalism of "man", the male. In fact, the rights of "man" are far from being universal, since they exclude half of humanity. The first article of the *Rights of Man*, which reads: "Men are born free and remain free and equal in rights", is modified to read: "Women are born free and remain equal in rights with men".

Following Olympe de Gouges, we may ask ourselves whether women are "condemned to be free" in the same way as men. Common sense suggests that we should respond in the affirmative. When Sartre writes *l'homme* (man, the man), it is simply because the linguistic choice that exists in Japanese, for example, to which I referred above, is missing in French. We should read and understand *l'homme* each time as meaning "men and women". But common sense sometimes flows from conventional wisdom, prejudices of the time, or linguistic structures.

2. "Man" in philosophical texts

In fact, in his major text, *L'Être et le néant* (*Being and Nothingness*), Sartre hardly uses the word *homme* at all. He prefers a more technical term, namely "human reality" (*la réalité humaine*), a neologism coined by Henri Corbin to translate Heidegger's *Dasein* (literally, "there being").[4]

All the way through *Being and Nothingness* we find this term, of which "man" is the common equivalent. Let us take for example a famous passage which appears at the end of the fourth part of this work:

> Every human reality is a passion in that it projects losing itself so as to found being and by the same stroke to constitute the in-itself which escapes contingency by being its own foundation, the *Ens causa sui*, which religions call God. Thus the passion of man is the reverse of that of Christ, for man loses himself as man in order that God may be born. But the idea of God is contradictory and we lose ourselves in vain. Man is a useless passion.[5]

Here, "man" is synonymous with human reality and does not signify "to be male" but "to be male and female", in other words "to be human". In this work, the use of the word *homme* (rarely, incidentally, written with a capital letter) is actually rather limited. It is either "man" in opposition to or in relation to God—as, for example, when Sartre writes: "to be man means to reach toward being God"[6]—or in opposition to animals and to things, unless it is in those passages where he describes a scene as an example of a point he is making. It is crystal clear that the phrase "human

---

[4] See Henri Corbin, "Avant-propos", in Martin Heidegger, *Qu'est-ce que la métaphysique?*, 13.

[5] *L'Être et le néant*, 708 / *Being and Nothingness*, 784.

[6] *L'Être et le néant*, 653 / *Being and Nothingness*, 724.

reality" is used unambiguously to refer to men *and* to women. However, the *pour-soi* (for-itself) in Sartre, unlike Heidegger's *Dasein*, is not a neutral being but has a sexual dimension. Sartre himself criticises the German philosopher on this point: "Existential philosophies did not believe they had to concern themselves with sexuality. Heidegger in particular makes not the slightest allusion in his existential analysis, with the result that his *Dasein* is presented to us as asexual."[7]

Sartre, on the other hand, attempts to take into account the sexual dimension of human reality, especially in the third part of *Being and Nothingness* devoted to "Being-for-others". Given this fact, should we think in terms of two types of human reality: feminine reality and masculine reality? No, not exactly. For, if Sartre's "for-itself" has a sexual body, this does not mean that the "for-itself" is conditioned by its gender, at least not by its biology (*sexe biologique*). In other words, the word "sexual" here does not seem to be applicable to a male "for-itself" or a female "for-itself", given that Sartre does not include sex in the realm of facticity and that sexuality is not just a simple psychological corollary of a biological given. We should instead consider that "sexual" is one form of the grasping of an object by consciousness. In other words, there is not a male nature or a female nature, any more than there is a human essence. Indeed, it is for this reason that Simone de Beauvoir was able to draw on this theory of Sartre's to write *The Second Sex*. There is therefore, theoretically, no sexism in Sartre's philosophical thought.

3. The representation of "man" in the literary texts

I shall now turn to examine the use of the term "man" in Sartre's literary texts. First, let us note that the structure of the world of Sartre's novels is as dichotomous as his philosophy. In addition, as far as gender is concerned, there seem to be two hierarchical categories and a clear dissymmetry between male and female characters. The men are defined by their actions and the choices that these actions express, while the freedom of action of the women is very limited. The men do, act, look, choose, whilst the women are, react, are watched and are chosen. On occasions it is almost a stereotypical view. Furthermore, the main characters are often men: Antoine Roquentin, Mathieu Delarue—who are both to some extent copies of Sartre himself—Goetz, Kean, Frantz, etc. On the other hand, the female characters, however attractive they may be, remain secondary

---

[7] *L'Être et le néant,* 451 / *Being and Nothingness*, 498.

characters: Anny in *Nausea*, Marcelle, Ivich or Lola in *The Roads to Freedom*.

Sartre's world remains dominated by males; the portrayal of the female characters is more often than not stereotypical. One could even say that the development of the novel is shaped by a somewhat essentialist framework. In general terms, the woman is there, as it were, to be won and seduced, or else she is a maternal figure. But that is only how it seems. I shall return to this later. For the moment, let us look more closely at the case of *The Roads to Freedom*, where the dichotomous structure is more marked than in the other writings: bourgeois / proletarian; intellectuals / members of the popular classes; normal / abnormal; young / old; good / bad; strong / weak; brave / cowardly; and the dichotomy of man / woman, where the men are active and the women are passive. This split between active and passive is particularly obvious in the first volume, *L'Age de raison* (*The Age of Reason*), where the story is told from the point of view of different characters in turn. Throughout the eighteen chapters, Mathieu Delarue, Sartre's alter ego, is the main character, but other men, such as Boris and Daniel, also occupy at times the central position of narrator. Through Sartre's presentation of a variety of viewpoints, the male characters are often seen from the inside, as it were, whereas the female characters are only ever seen from the outside, like objects; they are *en-soi*, "in-themselves". The only chapter offering a female perspective is number five, which is told from Marcelle's point of view. But this takes the form of a monologue.

Thus, the word "man" in this series of novels most frequently signifies "being male", in the strongest sense of the term. Let us take for example the discussion between Mathieu and his communist friend Brunet, who suggests that Mathieu should join the PCF (French Communist Party). Mathieu is of the opinion that Brunet, who is politically committed, is in fact freer than he, Mathieu, who has chosen not to commit himself politically in order to retain his freedom. He says suddenly:

> "You are a man."
>
> "A man?" asked Brunet, surprised. "It would be a bit worrying if I wasn't. What do you mean?"
>
> "Just what I say. You have chosen to be a man."
>
> A man with powerful and slightly knotted muscles who thinks in short harsh truths, a man who stands tall and who gives little away, who is sure of himself, a man with both feet firmly on the ground, impervious to the unworldly temptations of art, psychology, politics—a complete man and nothing but a man. And Mathieu was there facing him, undecided, half his

> life gone, yet still not really mature and assailed by all the temptations of inhumanity. He thought: "I don't even look like a man."[8]

Brunet is surprised by Mathieu's comment because he does not understand exactly what Mathieu means by the sentence: "You are a man". It is blindingly obvious, since Brunet is not a woman, nor an animal, nor an object—just like Mathieu, in fact (Brunet would doubtless think). For the reader, however, the subtext of this phrase is easily understood. Mathieu is thinking of the adult man, a man who is autonomous and responsible. Brunet is such a man, while Mathieu is not. Despite his age (mid-thirties), Mathieu acts the young man; he prefers to spend time with young people and he does not assume responsibility. Although his mistress Marcelle is pregnant, he wants at all costs to avoid getting married. But, at the same time, deep down he feels his age; he knows that he is no longer a young man, that he is a *monsieur*.[9]

So the word "man" in the novel is very often used as the opposite of "woman". Does this mean that Sartre has a sexist or discriminatory view of the world? Certainly not. It is more a question of the structure of the novel. *The Age of Reason* presents us with Mathieu's personal story but the underlying theme is that of imminent war, and it is this imminence of war that emphasises the sexual segregation. In fact, if the dichotomy man / woman is still present in the second volume, *Le Sursis* (*The Reprieve*), there the hierarchy male / female breaks down because of the portent of war. There is a shift in the focalisation of the narrative as well. The main characters in the first novel no longer have the same importance, and the domination of the male point of view is less strong and this gradually creates space for a female perspective. We even find Mathieu, the hero of the first volume, described as he is seen by Odette, his sister-in-law. Indeed it is in this scene at the beach that Odette thinks about men and women:

> "I'd like to be a man", said Odette.
> Mathieu replied: "So you can play at being a soldier?"
> Odette blushed. "Oh no", she said sharply. "But I'm finding it stupid being a woman at the moment."
> "It can't be very easy", he admitted.[10]

[8] Sartre, *Œuvres romanesques* (henceforth *OR*), 522.
[9] *OR*, 633.
[10] *OR*, 750.

So, Odette felt excluded from the war, from the world of the war. But the men are not so sure of themselves either. She wanted to say to Mathieu that:

> […] the men always made her feel ill-at-ease when they talked about the war in front of her. They weren't natural, they showed too much self-confidence, as if they had wanted to make her realise that it was men's business and yet, at the same time, they always seemed to be expecting something from her: a sort of arbitration, because she was a woman and would not be going off to war and would remain above the fray.[11]

Once war has broken out, it will be the women's turn to look at the men and judge them. But it is the men, the adults—or "the upright ones", as Charles, the young paralytic confined to bed calls them—who decided to go to war. The men may be courageous and heroic, but they are also nasty. Sarah, a Jewess, remarks on this to her husband, an artist-turned-colonel during the Spanish Civil War: "Gomez […] do you know what I've learned lately: that men are nasty."[12] Here, "men" could refer to human beings in general, but from the context it means more "male", since it is an observation made by Sarah as she watches her little son Pablo playing with a toy gun given him by his father, Gomez.

The men and women do not agree on this issue. The men get ready for war, while the women try to maintain peace. Brunet thinks: "The women should just leave us alone. This is not the time to come bothering the men with their nonsense."[13] If the difference between men and women is so marked, it is because *The Age of Reason* and *The Reprieve* are still only a catalogue of false freedoms.

Let us consider another example, set this time in Marrakesh, involving Maud and Pierre, a couple who met by chance during a visit to Morocco. Pierre is a young provincial bourgeois, and the son of a general, who is playing the young Adonis in front of Maud, a violinist in a female quartet called *l'Orchestre Baby's*. Maud asks Pierre:

> "Aren't you afraid of the war then?"
> He felt an unpleasant shiver run down his spine.
> "My dear girl. No, I'm not afraid. A man is not frightened of war."
> "Well I can assure you that Lucien was!" she said. "It's precisely that which turned me off him. He was really too much of a scaredy-cat."[14]

---

[11] *OR*, 750.
[12] *OR*, 823.
[13] *OR*, 750.
[14] *OR*, 779.

Pierre is as proud as he can be, but deep down he is frightened—although, for the time being, he is not aware of it:

> "Firstly", she continued, "how can a man possibly protect a woman if he spends all his time being afraid?"
> "He wasn't a man", he said softly. "*I* am a man."[15]

This episode represents a real caricature of "virility": the man has to be strong in order to protect the woman. Sartre describes all this in order, later on, to reveal another side to this character. I shall return to this point.

I have said that the world of Sartre's novels is a world of the segregation of the sexes. But alongside these "normal" heterosexual characters, we find homosexuals who frequently play an extremely important part in the development of the "homosexual" dimension of the story.

4. The homosexual

All through his works, be it in his literary texts—theatre, novels and short stories—or in his philosophical writings, Sartre is constantly addressing the theme of homosexuality. In *Nausea*, there is that strange character whom Roquentin nicknames the "Autodidact", who is presented as a homosexual if not a paedophile. The theme of homosexuality is also to be found in two of the collected short stories published as *Le Mur* (*The Wall*, 1939), namely in "Intimité" ("Intimacy", implicit in Lulu's and Rirette's sexual fantasies), and in "L'Enfance d'un chef" ("The Childhood of a Leader"), in which the young Lucien Fleurier, while experiencing ambivalent feelings of attraction and repulsion, allows himself to be seduced by the "pederast" Bergère, and ends up sleeping with him. In *Huis clos* (*No Exit*), it is a lesbian who takes the lead in the drawing-room hell, where she is imprisoned for eternity with Garcin and Estelle, a man and a woman who are both thoroughly heterosexual.

But it is particularly in *The Roads to Freedom* that the theme of homosexuality is developed more explicitly around the demonic character of Daniel Sereno. (Strangely, his surname resembles that of the lesbian in *No Exit*, Inès Serano).[16] Possibly with a certain delight, Sartre uses Daniel Sereno to describe the world and the psychology of the homosexual. The

---

[15] *OR*, 779.

[16] Sartre liked to play games with names, and it seems probable that in both these cases he was punning ironically upon the adjective *serein(e)*, meaning "serene", since these two characters are highly neurotic and anything but "serene". (Eds.)

whole of chapter nine revolves around Daniel's homosexuality, from the initial description of the pick-up at the fair on the Boulevard Sebastopol—where the young tearaways "were strutting their stuff in front of the slot machines, waiting for a customer"—up until the point where Daniel makes a hesitant attempt to pick up Boris. In this novel, not only do we find several homosexuals who make no secret of their sexual orientation—like Bobby and his friend Ralph—but we also find people who have homosexual leanings, such as the pacifist Piteaux. We also meet Lucien Fleurier's double, a certain Philippe Grésigne, the young bourgeois son of a general who, in the third volume, allows himself to be seduced by Daniel.

Given that, throughout the book, Daniel is in fact as important a character as Mathieu, the theme of homosexuality is far from incidental. We could say that Daniel was both Mathieu's twin brother and his rival. This angelic and diabolical character is the champion of "bad faith", while Mathieu believes himself to be the champion of lucidity and transparency, and therefore of authenticity. In point of fact, both Daniel's and Mathieu's identities are inconsistent and contradictory. Daniel leads a double life as a pederast in denial, whereas Mathieu is a liberal heterosexual whose beliefs are at odds with the life he leads. Both of them have a fear of being judged by others, and neither manages completely to affirm his freedom. Very often in the parts of the novel which consist of internal monologues, each one splits his personality in two in order to judge himself with complete lucidity. Basically, they hate themselves and each other. Each man reproaches himself, but not in the same way as the other. It is therefore very significant that Sartre describes Daniel's feelings of self-hatred which lead him to marry Mathieu's mistress, Marcelle.

The issue of sexuality for Sartre is intimately linked to that of lucidity, and thus to authenticity. Let us take, for example, a famous passage from *Being and Nothingness*. Right in the middle of the chapter on "bad faith", we find a few pages on the homosexual who is torn between the refusal of self and the demand to be sincere:

> A homosexual often experiences an unbearable feeling of guilt and his whole existence is determined in relation to this feeling. One can easily see from this that he is in bad faith. In fact, it often happens that this man, while recognising his homosexual leanings, while admitting each and every single mistake he has made, refuses with all his might to consider himself "*a pederast*".[17]

---

[17] *L'Être et le néant,* 103 / *Being and Nothingness,* 107.

Is this a statement of fact or a personal opinion? These observations on the tension which exists between, on the one hand, the alienating nature of "identity" conceived as an essence and therefore as fate and, on the other hand, those lies we tell about ourselves which are part of the non-acceptance of who we are, in many ways constitute a foretaste of later discussions about the notion of identity and the affirmation of self. They pave the way for an affirmation of self as an act of freedom. Sartre is consciously describing our need to "tell" somebody what we are, which results in Daniel's "confession" to Mathieu. Mathieu, good liberal heterosexual that he is, here reveals his tolerance while at the same time remaining incapable of understanding that Daniel feels the need to *raconter* (narrate or recount) in this way. He is even less able to understand how Daniel can be "ashamed" of what he is. But at the same time, Mathieu can see in Daniel's confession a genuine manifestation of freedom, since it would now be impossible for him to return to where he had been, and he understands that this gesture will turn Daniel's life upside down: "'It's true', thought Mathieu, 'he's gone the whole way this time.' Suddenly a heart-rending thought struck him. 'He's free'."[18]

5. Homosexuality and femininity

Nonetheless Sartre has, it seems to me, a very stereotypical view of homosexuality which assimilates homosexuality and femininity. Sartre shows that Daniel is an attractive man with irresistible charm, but whose virile exterior conceals his femininity, namely his passivity, his sensitivity, his cowardliness, etc. Daniel is ashamed of his femininity: he is often irritated by the femininity which homosexuals generally display, or the phoney virility which they exhibit in order to conceal their femininity. The affinity between femininity and homosexuality is also expressed from another angle in Sartre's article, "Qu'est-ce qu'un collaborateur?" ("What is a collaborator?"), originally published 1945 in New York, in *La République française*. In this text, whilst arguing that collaboration was a social phenomenon, Sartre also paints a psychological portrait of the collaborator and considers that collaboration marks a return to feudal relations. According to him, the collaborator has a feminine personality: "He recognises [therefore] his weakness and this preacher of virility and masculine virtues takes up the weapons of the weak, of the woman."[19] Sartre identifies, in the writings of the collaborators, "strange metaphors

[18] *OR*, 727.
[19] "Qu'est-ce qu'un collaborateur?", in *Situations, III*, 43-62 (58).

which present the relations between France and Germany in the form of a sexual union, where France plays the part of the woman."[20] From this, Sartre concludes that "the feudal relationship between the collaborator and his master has a sexual dimension. Inasmuch as we can conceive the state of mind of collaboration, we can detect a climate (so to speak) of femininity."[21] It is clear that Sartre here is using the notion of "femininity" as a negative value, at least as far as "femininity and men" is concerned. Sartre claims to discern "a strange mixture of masochism and homosexuality" amongst the collaborators, and adds: "Moreover, the homosexual circles in Paris provided numerous and brilliant recruits."[22]

There is something indisputably homophobic about this statement, and we find the same view of homosexuals and collaborators in *The Roads to Freedom*. In the third volume, *La Mort dans l'âme* (translated as *Iron in the Soul*, but literally *Death in the Soul*), Daniel is thrilled by the German troops marching into Paris, and by the humiliating blow that the defeat of France will inflict on traditional conservative morality. And in the extant fragments of the fourth volume, *La Dernière Chance* (*The Last Chance*), we find that Daniel has become a collaborator. Thus, homosexuals are often represented as negative characters.

It seems to me that homophobia and misogyny go together. Sartre has frequently been described as a sexist and a misogynist, and there are reasons for this. We know that there are a large number of negative comments and observations in *Being and Nothingness*—"the obscenity of the female sex organs"[23], for example, or elsewhere the frigid woman, and the woman who allows herself to be seduced on a first date—which are given as examples of bad faith. That said, however, this view of misogyny needs to be qualified. In the passages devoted to analysing sado-masochistic relations, it is certain that Sartre explicitly associates activity with the man and passivity with the woman, and he has been criticised by more than one feminist critic for doing so. But Sartre does not believe that there is a male essence or a female essence as such. There exists only the "male" and the "female". In other words, these terms placed in opposition do not really describe sexual relations because male-activity is no more the prerogative of the biological male than female-passivity is of the biological female.

---

[20] Ibid.
[21] Ibid.
[22] Ibid.
[23] *L'Être et le néant,* 706 / *Being and Nothingness*, 782 .

6. Cowardice

Actually if the "masculine" and the "feminine" are not derived from biology, they nevertheless have a powerful existential, not to say ethical, value for Sartre. I will address this question from another perspective, this time by invoking the theme of "cowardice". Whether they are presented as idiots, as nasty types, or as crooks, Sartre's male characters in *The Roads to Freedom* are described in different ways, but not as *lâches*, cowards. The "coward" is almost an obsession for Sartre, along with *le salaud*, and indeed they form a linked concept.[24] From a masculine point of view, to call someone *lâche* is much more insulting than to call him *salaud*. Both imply serious failings, but there is a key difference: a "coward" is linked to passivity which is a feminine trait, whereas a "bastard" belongs with activity and thus virility. We have already seen how Daniel suffers because he is a coward. Here is another example: Daniel is unable to kill his cats. He reproaches himself and says to himself: "A coward. A guy who loved his cats and didn't want to chuck them in the water."[25]

As for Mathieu, he is willing to recognise that he has been and is a *salaud* (even if basically he does not much like it), whereas, had he been taken for a coward, he would have been shocked and outraged.[26] Let us take another example: this time, Pierre, the young Adonis proud of his virility. We have already read his conversation with Maud, now here is what happens next. In the *souk* in Marrakesh, Pierre comes across a book by a certain Colonel Pico, full of pictures of disfigured soldiers, and suddenly becomes very subdued. Maud asks:

> "Oh Pierre", she said gently, "are you frightened after all then?"
>
> "[…] Every man is frightened. Every man. Anyone who isn't frightened isn't normal. It's got nothing to do with courage. And as for you, you have no right to judge me. You don't have to go off and fight."
>
> They continued their walk in silence. She thought: "He's a coward."[27]

---

[24] *Un salaud* is a bastard or a shit. Note that cowardice is the besetting sin of the man condemned to eternal torment in *Huis clos*, Garcin, and that this name is a masculinisation of the pejorative feminine noun *garce*, meaning bitch or tart. (Eds.)

[25] *OR*, 490.

[26] Similarly, Garcin is unmoved by accusations that, as a promiscuous although married philanderer, he is / was *un salaud* because, if anything, these sexual peccadilloes flatter his self-image as a real man. (Eds.)

[27] *OR*, 789.

Here, the word "man" clearly refers to males, and Maud is not in this category because she will not be going off to fight.

In *No Exit*, what bothers Garcin is that he will still be thought of as a coward. So, he needs someone to reassure him that he is not a coward, and asks Estelle whether she loves him, but she turns on him:

> ESTELLE:—Idiot! My dear idiot. Do you think I could love a coward?
> GARCIN:—But you were saying…
> ESTELLE:—I was having you on. I like men, Garcin, real men, with rough skin and strong hands.[28]

However, Garcin is not fundamentally seeking the approval of Estelle because what matters most for him is how other *men* see him; he does not want to be treated as a coward by his former colleagues. In fact, in Sartre, we can find evidence both of homophobia and of expressions of non-sexual warmth and intimacy between men—or, more precisely, the dream of a male community. As Eve Kosofky Sedgwick has argued in *Epistemology of the Closet*, homophobia can conceal a homosexual tendency or, at least, a dream of a male community with male values. Without attempting to embark upon a psychological analysis, I just want to note in passing this "homophile" tendency that we find in Sartre. We can observe that, in his novels, the men often seem more relaxed when there are no women around. Even the heterosexual Boris Serguine, a disciple of Mathieu and the lover of Lola, a nightclub singer in her fifties, says that he prefers men. After making love with Lola, Mathieu's face appears in his mind and Boris thinks: "That's funny […] I prefer guys to women. When I'm with a woman I'm not half as happy as I am when I'm with a guy. But nothing in the world would induce me to sleep with a guy."[29]

We can find numerous examples of this atmosphere of a community of males, or a "homosocial" *milieu* in Sartre's writings. I have already referred to the case of Garcin in *No Exit*, whose main concern is how he is perceived by his former colleagues. He says: "There's a smell of men and cigars. I liked living among men in shirt-sleeves."[30]

The same goes for Mathieu and Brunet, for whom women do not fundamentally matter. Brunet meets Maurice, the Communist worker, and his wife. Reflecting afterwards that Maurice, unlike his wife, is *sympathique*, he says to himself: "I suppose not all the comrades can be

---

[28] Sartre, *Huis clos* (premiered May 1944, published 1945), in *Théâtre complet*, 91-128 (123).
[29] *OR*, 429-30.
[30] *Huis clos*, 100.

bachelors."[31] In the second half of the third volume, *Iron in the Soul*, the environment is totally male, as we have the story of soldiers who have been captured and are waiting to be transferred to a camp in Germany. It is a world of friendship and fraternity, from which not only the enemy but also women are excluded.

But to return to the notion of "cowardice", which seems to me to be particularly linked to virility: who is going to criticise the cowardice of a woman? If this idea appeared only in the world of Sartre's novels, there would not be a problem, but it appears also in the philosophical texts. The word "coward" is also a key word linked to "authenticity". After the passage on the homosexual in *Being and Nothingness*, which I quoted earlier, we come back to the theme of cowardice:

> I am only able to try and capture myself as "*not being cowardly*", when I am cowardly, if this "being cowardly" is itself in question at the very moment when it exists. Only if it is itself a question. Only if at the very moment when I want to capture it, it slips away in all directions and destroys itself.[32]

Another example is to be found in *Reflections on the Jewish Question* (*Réflexions sur la question juive*) where, in his analysis of the anti-Semite, Sartre writes:

> He is a man who is afraid. Not of Jews, to be sure, but of himself, of his own consciousness, his freedom, his instincts, his responsibilities, of his being alone in the world, of change, of society and of the world. Of everything except the Jews. He is a coward who is unwilling to recognise his cowardice.[33]

So, that cowardice, over and above being a failing, represents a moral value. But of course this does not mean that Sartre considers cowardice to be an essence: not at all. In *Existentialism and Humanism* he writes:

> When the existentialist describes a coward, he says that the coward is responsible for his cowardice. He is not the way he is because he has a cowardly heart, or a cowardly lung or cowardly brain. He is not the way he is because of some physiological configuration. He is like that because he has made himself a coward through his actions. There is no such thing as a cowardly temperament. There are nervous temperaments; there is what

---

[31] *OR*, 747.
[32] *L'Être et le néant*, 107 / *Being and Nothingness*, 112.
[33] *Réflexions sur la question juive*, 62-63.

> people call impoverished blood, and there are also rich temperaments. But this does not mean that someone with poor blood is a coward. What produces cowardice is the act of giving up or backing down. A temperament is not an action. A coward is defined by the deed he has done. What people vaguely feel and what frightens them is that the coward that we present to the world is guilty of being a coward.[34]

As this is the way things are, it is clear that cowardice is a negative value and the opposite of heroism. Furthermore, it would seem that the negative value of cowardice has a distinctly and peculiarly male, not to say macho, character. Indeed, when we consider the examples given by Sartre to illustrate the moments when a decision is taken to exercise human freedom, we find that they very often have a heroic dimension. According to Sartre, one is neither a hero nor a coward—one becomes a hero, one becomes a coward: "One is not born, but rather one becomes a coward", to paraphrase Beauvoir. But what is this "one" which lacks any human qualities? Is this what Sartre means by "human reality"? But it's a huge vacuum. Everyone knows the story: human essence does not exist, only the human condition exists, or to be more exact, the situation from which you project yourself. So far, so good: but are there not both a female and a male condition, even if these do not have a pre-figured essence? Sartre's presentation and representation of the image of the male is most frequently accompanied by grandeur and heroism. To put it briefly, man in Sartre's work is still too human, that is to say too male.

Conclusion

Thus far I have examined the various ways in which the term "man" appears in Sartre's writings. We have seen that one use of the word "man", despite its apparent neutrality, actually has clear overtones of gender, and that this even impacts upon Sartre's theoretical and philosophical concept of "man". Just after the Second World War, Sartre wrote:

> After the death of God, now people are talking about the death of Man [...]. And if the whole of humanity continues to live, it will not simply be because it has been born but because it has chosen to carry on living. There is no longer a human species. The community which has placed itself in charge of the atomic bomb is above the natural order since it has power over its life and death. Every minute of every day, it has to make the choice to live.[35]

---

[34] *L'Existentialisme est un humanisme,* 60.
[35] *Situations, III*, 69.

Sartre's position is clear: human existence no longer exists, man is dead but at the same time man remains to be made because man is freedom. When Sartre declares that man is freedom, he is not just talking about men as in "males" but also and equally about women. But it is still true that his concept of man is too male. Henceforth, should the portrayal of "man" not become more female—or at least less male?

In order to continue living or surviving on our planet, which is threatened not only by weapons of mass destruction but also by global warming and other disasters for which humanity is totally responsible, we need to adopt other values and notions, besides those which are too male like heroism, exertion, struggle, conquest, development, etc. Humanity should be able to envisage "softer" notions which are less tough and more inspired by what have traditionally been considered feminine values. Can there be a feminine Sartrean existentialism? Yes certainly, since it was on the basis of Sartrean existentialism that Beauvoir constructed *The Second Sex*. But a few male prejudices should be expunged from Sartre's concept of man which is rooted in freedom: those of exertion and heroism for example. The clarity of existentialism remains important and it prompts us to think about the notion of man, whose essence is not fixed but who is always in the process of becoming.

Works Cited

Foucault, Michel. *Les Mots et les choses*. Paris: Gallimard, 1966.

Heidegger, Martin. *Qu'est-ce que la métaphysique?* Paris: Gallimard, 1938.

Kosofky Sedgwick, Eve. *Epistemology of the Closet*. Berkeley: University of California Press, 1990.

Sartre, Jean-Paul. *L'Age de raison* (*Les Chemins de la liberté, I*). Paris: Gallimard, 1945.

—. *L'Être et le néant*. Paris: Gallimard, 1943 (translated as *Being and Nothingness*, by Hazel E. Barnes, New York: Washington Square Press, 1984).

—. *L'Existentialisme est un humanisme*. Paris: Nagel, 1946.

—. *Huis clos*. Paris: Gallimard, 1945, in *Théâtre complet* (ed. Michel Contat). Paris: Gallimard, Bibliothèque de la Pléiade, 2005.

—. *La Mort dans l'âme* (*Les Chemins de la liberté, III*). Paris: Gallimard, 1949.

—. *Le Mur*. Paris: Gallimard, 1939.

—. *La Nausée*. Paris: Gallimard, 1938.

—. *Œuvres romanesques* (eds. Michel Contat and Michel Rybalka). Paris: Gallimard, Bibliothèque de la Pléiade, 1981.
—. *Réflexions sur la question juive.* Paris: Gallimard, 1946.
—. *Situations, III*. Paris: Gallimard, 1972.
—. *Le Sursis* (*Les Chemins de la liberté, II*). Paris: Gallimard, 1945.

CHAPTER TEN

MURAKAMI, OBAMA, SARKOZY: WHAT *IS* AN INTELLECTUAL?

BENEDICT O'DONOHOE

Preface: Why Murakami?

In Sartre's centenary year, 2005, I attended a long conference on him in northern France, *La Décade de Cerisy*, at the historic Château de Cerisy-la-Salle on the Cherbourg peninsula. On that occasion, I was invited by Professor Sawada Nao, Chair of the Japanese Sartre Society (*Association japonaise d'études sartriennes*: AJES) to give a paper at the forthcoming Tokyo centenary conference in November 2005, which I gladly did. Given in French, my paper, as requested, concerned the status of Sartre as a public intellectual in the United Kingdom, with some commentary also on the state of "Sartre studies" in British universities, and it was subsequently published in the acts of the conference.[1]

During this (my first) visit to Japan, I was very struck by the extent of Sartre's fame in Japan, and this sent me to Asabuki Tomiko's book on his tour of Japan, with Simone de Beauvoir, in September–October 1966.[2] I was impressed also by his legacy and how vibrant it appeared to be. In particular, I became aware that Murakami Haruki was discussed as an "existentialist" writer, with a debt to Sartre, amongst other European authors, and this prompted me to read some of his work, for the first time.[3]

---

[1] See O'Donohoe, "Sartre en Grande Bretagne".

[2] See Asabuki, *Vingt-huit Jours au Japon*, henceforth cited *AT*.

[3] In keeping with other chapters in this volume, we respect the Japanese practice of placing surname before forename—Asabuki Tomiko, Sawada Nao—although Murakami Haruki is, of course, better known in the Anglophone world as Haruki Murakami.

This in turn led me to give a paper on his short story "Nausea 1979" at the London conference of the UK Sartre Society in 2006.[4]

A second visit to Japan was occasioned by my colleague and co-editor, Jean-Pierre Boulé, who secured AHRC (Arts and Humanities Research Council) funding for seminars on Sartre in Tokyo and London in 2009, with an exchange of British and Japanese scholars and postgraduate students. Once more, then, I was prompted to reflect on Sartre's 1966 visit, and on the impression he left behind through the lectures he delivered during his stay. These were subsequently published as "Plaidoyer pour les intellectuels"[5]—in English: "Apologia for the Intellectual".[6]

Sartre and Beauvoir in Japan

At the time of his visit with Beauvoir in the fall of 1966, Sartre was at the height of his celebrity in Japan, although his star was already in decline in France, where existentialism's long hegemony was coming under attack from the structuralists, Roland Barthes, Michel Foucault, and especially Claude Lévi-Strauss.[7] Nevertheless, as President of the Russell Tribunal, conceived by the aristocratic English philosopher, Bertrand Russell, to "try" the Americans for war crimes in Vietnam; and as a notorious *refusenik* of the Nobel Prize for Literature in 1964, which he declined because he refused to be domesticated by and associated with the West European political establishment—to become a "public monument" in his own lifetime—Sartre took advantage of his stay in Japan to analyse the vocation (his vocation) of the intellectual. What kind of creature was this? Where did it come from? What were the tasks, the duties, the capacities of the intellectual in the public sphere? And where, therefore was s/he to be located within that sphere? With whom could s/he establish and maintain relations—the proletariat or the bourgeoisie, or both, or neither? Or

---

[4] See O'Donohoe, "Contemporary perspectives".

[5] In Sartre, *Situations, VIII*, 375-455, hereafter cited *S,VIII*. Page references are to this edition, and translations from the French are my own.

[6] Earlier drafts of this chapter were given (in French) at the AJES conference at Rikkyô University, Tokyo, in July 2009, and again (in English, by invitation of Dr Simone Müller) at the *Ostasiatisches Seminar der Universität Zürich, Abteilung Japanologie* (East Asia Seminar of the University of Zürich Department of Japanology) in November 2009.

[7] A fascinating eye-witness account of Sartre's visit is given by Professor Suzuki Michihiko, interviewed by Sawada Nao, in the final chapter of this volume.

possibly and inevitably, only with other intellectuals? And what could s/he therefore hope to accomplish in the world?[8]

Without claiming to be able to answer any, let alone all, of these questions, I intend to approach them (in emulation of Sartre) by dividing my chapter into three unequal parts: (i) What was the critical reception of these lectures in Japan in 1966? Here, I shall rely upon Asabuki's book, *Vingt-huit Jours au Japon avec Jean-Paul Sartre et Simone de Beauvoir.*[9] (ii) Can an intellectual also be a politician, and vice-versa? Here, I shall refer in particular to Barack Obama, 44th President of the United States and (so far as I can observe) one of the few intellectuals to have succeeded in American politics in my lifetime. (iii) Can a writer be an intellectual and, if so, in what sense? Here, in the light of Sartre's analyses, I shall consider the role of the contemporary Japanese writer, Murakami Haruki, one of the most prominent writers in Japan itself, and almost certainly the Japanese writer best known in Europe today. Murakami could be seen as a 21st-century incarnation of the intellectualist contradiction which Sartre evoked: a "technician of practical knowledge", to use Sartre's terms (in this case, a "technician" of writing) who singularises the universal, or indeed who universalises singularity in his works, without that singularisation necessarily flowing back upon the universal, transporting anything of practical use into the public domain.

Sartre's reception

Asabuki Tomiko reports that the essayist Kato Shuichi cited, amongst the reasons that had made Sartre "popular in Japan", "the question of death as treated by Sartrean existentialism", which concerned the younger generation, following the Second World War, and his "atheism", which made his thought "more accessible to a Japanese public" than that of the "French Catholic philosophers" such as Emanuel Mounier or Gabriel Marcel.[10] Whereas these assertions may be true in general terms, it happens that neither death nor atheism, as problems *per se*, figures explicitly in Sartre's Japan lectures of 1966. Where these are concerned, their appeal might reside in the fact that Sartre had talked about "the role of intellectuals, the Vietnam War, nuclear weapons [...]; in short, about

---

[8] Whilst acutely aware that Simone de Beauvoir, no less an intellectual than Sartre, accompanied him on this trip, I shall henceforth, for simplicity, refer to the intellectual as "he".

[9] For a comprehensively detailed account of that reception, see the following chapter in the present volume by Suzuki Masamichi.

[10] See *AT*, 50.

contemporary subjects of interest to the Japanese public".[11] No doubt this is the case, but if these lectures were nothing more than reflections on subjects of contemporary journalism, they would have no enduring value other than as specific elements of the philosophic history of the period—and that would tend to deny them any useful role in a discussion focused on contemporary ideology, whereas I intend to show that they are still relevant today.

Moreover, Sartre, for his part, was posing absolute and transcendental questions, as well as some that were relative and contemporary. By asking himself initially: "What is an intellectual?"; and then what is the "Function of the intellectual"?; and finally, "Is the writer an intellectual?", Sartre was surely not intending to confine his thinking only to the field of 1960s' actuality. Even if, as Asabuki Tomiko notes, "his protests against the bombing of Hanoi [and his] consequent refusal to go to the United States had a definite impact."[12]

According to Asabuki, Sartre's "Apologia" was to provoke lively polemics amongst Japanese intellectuals:

> For the adherents of realism, [Sartre's ideas] were an abstract, arbitrary and old-fashioned theory. From the point of view of the idealists [however], it was felt that here was a master-work, explaining the primordial mission of the intellectual.[13]

I am struck by this dichotomy between "realists" on the one hand and "idealists" on the other. I wonder whether, in Europe at that time, this would no longer have been recognised as a philosophically valid distinction, unless one were to cast existentialists as realists and structuralists as idealists? However, in the public mind—and possibly no less so in Japan than in Europe?—these categories were meaningful. After all, youthful idealism—contesting the Vietnam War and striving for civil rights in the US, or preparing to ignite the spark of May 68 across Europe—was beginning to challenge the realist status quo of the post-war world bequeathed by the older generation.

---

[11] "[Sartre avait parlé] du rôle des intellectuels, de la guerre au Vietnam, des armes nucléaires [...]; bref, de sujets actuels qui intéressaient le public japonais." (Ibid.)

[12] "[S]es protestations contre le bombardement de Hanoï [et son] refus d'aller aux États-Unis qui s'ensuivit eurent un impact certain." (*AT*, 51.)

[13] "Pour les tenants du réalisme, il s'agit d'une théorie abstraite, arbitraire et dépassée. Du point de vue des idéalistes, on estime avoir affaire à une œuvre maîtresse explicitant la mission primordiale des intellectuels." (Ibid.)

It seems to me that we rejoin Sartre here in the context of his lectures on the situation, the function and the identity of the intellectual—not only in 1966, but in general. Because, according to Sartre, this is the very challenge that is faced by the intellectual: that of making the transition from a certain idealism (the disinterested search for truth undertaken by what he calls "the technician of practical knowledge") to a certain kind of realism (that of putting his knowledge at the service of society, whether to support it or to contest it). In a sense, he has to do the reverse as well: his status as a "technician of practical knowledge" implies already a realist perspective—he asks himself the question: "What is *realistically possible* in this particular domain of knowledge?"—a realism, in other words, which he will put at the service *either* of the dominant ideology, *or* of the ideological challenge to the dominant orthodoxy. This specialist is not yet an intellectual, according to Sartre, but rather an intellectual in embryo, a latent intellectual: "Taken as a whole, these technicians of practical knowledge are not yet intellectuals but it is amongst them—and nowhere else—that intellectuals are recruited."[14]

This is to say that, originally, the intellectual is a realistic idealist, and vice-versa. He approaches the questions that humanity asks itself on the practical level—insofar as he is in search of the truth—but he is nevertheless, *in his body*, the master of certain activities which enable him to subscribe to, or to mediate, or even to transmit (possibly unwittingly) the dominant ideology, of which he becomes the guardian. Sartre cites the clerics of the medieval church who alone knew how to deploy the practical aptitudes of reading and writing. Technicians of the practical skill of literacy, they became *de facto* guardians of the hegemonic ideology, Christianity.[15] They were potential intellectuals ahead of their time, but their potential would never surpass the stage of latency:

> [The cleric] conserves dogma, transmits and adapts tradition. As a man of the Church, he would not know how to be a specialist of knowledge. He offers a mythical image of the world, a totalitarian myth which [...] defines the place and the destiny of man.[16]

---

[14] "L'ensemble de ces techniciens du savoir pratique ne sont pas encore des intellectuels mais c'est parmi eux—et nulle part ailleurs—que ceux-ci se recrutent." (*S, VIII*, 381.)

[15] Ibid.

[16] "[Le clerc] conserve les dogmes, transmet la tradition et l'adapte. En tant qu'homme d'Église, il ne saurait être un spécialiste du savoir. Il offre une image mythique du monde, un mythe totalitaire qui [...] définit la place et le destin de l'homme." (*S, VIII*, 382.)

But it is with the advent of the bourgeoisie, says Sartre, a class of merchants with their own ideology of commercial capitalism, that one sees the arrival as well of the authentic "technician of practical knowledge". Through the Protestant Reformation, he asserts, and the Counter-Reformation of the Jesuits, we witness a gradual process which he calls the "*desanctification of all practical sectors*"[17], leading to "what has been called 'the crisis of thought in western Europe'"[18]:

> [Henceforth] it is no longer the clerics who will lead [the dominant ideology], but the specialists of practical knowledge: lawyers (Montesquieu), men of letters (Voltaire, Diderot, Rousseau), mathematicians (d'Alembert), a tax-collector general (Helvétius), doctors, etc. They take the place of the clerics and call themselves *philosophes*, that is to say "lovers of Wisdom". Wisdom, that is Reason. Besides their specialised labours, they are concerned to create a rational conception of the Universe which embraces and justifies the *actions* and the *claims* of the bourgeoisie.[19]

So, it is from the point of the Enlightenment that our specialist becomes capable of deciding *either*: to work exclusively in his field of technical knowledge (whether it be law, literature, mathematics, economics, medicine, etc.), towards the elaboration and, by implication, the defence of the dominant ideology; *or*: to undertake that back-and-forth movement that would lead him from his particular domain to the contestation of that ideology, to his becoming that locus of inherent contradiction and permanent dialectic which is the intellectual. In spite of himself, he will become that unfortunate person to whom this fundamental reproach will forever be made, namely that he is "*someone who meddles in things that do not concern him*".[20]

---

17 "[...] *désacralisation de tous les secteurs pratiques*" (ibid., Sartre's emphasis).
18 "[...] ce qu'on a appelé 'la crise de la pensée dans l'Europe occidentale'" (ibid.).
19 "[C]e ne sont plus les clercs qui conduiront [cette nouvelle idéologie bourgeoise], mais les spécialistes du savoir pratique: des hommes de loi (Montesquieu), des hommes de lettres (Voltaire, Diderot, Rousseau), des mathématiciens (d'Alembert), un fermier général (Helvétius), des médecins, etc. Ils prennent la place des clercs et se nomment *philosophes*, c'est-à-dire 'amants de la Sagesse'. La Sagesse, c'est la Raison. Outre leurs travaux spécialisés, il s'agit de créer une conception rationnelle de l'Univers qui embrasse et justifie les *actions* et les *revendications* de la bourgeoisie." (*S, VIII*, 383-84, Sartre's emphases.)
20 "[...] *quelqu'un qui se mêle de ce qui ne le regarde pas*" (*S, VIII*, 377, Sartre's emphasis). At the date of final edit, *precisely* this reproach is being made against France's leading public intellectual, Bernard-Henri Lévy, for his part in persuading

Certain damaging consequences follow. The intellectual necessarily tries to tear himself away from his class of origin, insofar as he rises above the community of his peers in order the better to observe them, whether at the same time supporting or denouncing them. One result of this for him is isolation and loneliness. He stands out against the background of his contemporary colleagues, all of them "technicians of practical knowledge", but who, unlike him, do not transcend their specificity in order to "*meddle in things that do not concern them*"—these are what Sartre calls "false intellectuals". Another result is the intrinsic and permanent fissure at the heart of the intellectual at war with himself. By trying to pass from a practical specialism (a realistic idealism) inculcated by an education rooted in and determined by the dominant ideology, to a universalism (a theoretical idealism) which is contestatory of that same ideology, the intellectual is doubly trapped. First, by his class of origin, from which he will never quite manage to escape altogether; next, by the contradiction inherent in his attempt to transcend his "practical knowledge" in order to attack the particularism of the hegemonic orthodoxy in the name of a new universalism, *different* from that which it derives from. A third consequence is the impossibility, therefore, of retranslating that contestation into practical terms, for it would have to be re-particularised by realistic means in order to accomplish anything useful in the real contemporary world.

The intellectual is therefore the man who becomes aware of the opposition, in himself and in society, between the search for the practical truth (with all the norms it implies) and the dominant ideology (with its system of traditional values). This awareness—although it must, *in order to be real*, take place in the intellectual *first* at the level of his professional activities and functions—is nothing other than the unveiling of the fundamental contradictions of the society, that is to say of class conflicts and, at the heart of the dominant class itself, of an organic conflict between the truth that it lays claim to for its project, and the myths, values and traditions that it maintains and with which it seeks to infect the other classes in order to guarantee its hegemony.[21]

President Nicolas Sarkozy to press at the UN for a "no-fly zone" in Libya (see, for example, *The Observer*, 27 March 2011, 13).

[21] See *S, VIII*, 399.

Intellectuals and politicians

Now, the question arises: given the apparent impossibility of achieving this transition, or coming to awareness, and then of translating it into practical action in the world, could an intellectual ever become a radically reforming politician, a person for whom any ideology would be above all a pretext for changing the world on a practical level? I think that the 44th President of the United States is an interesting case study here. Already established as a capable writer by the success of his memoir, *Dreams from My Father*, and acknowledged for more than ten years as an exceptional "technician of practical knowledge" in the domain of the law, Senator Barack Obama burst onto the national scene of North American politics thanks to four exceptional attributes which not only distinguished him from his presidential competitors, but also made him unique in the field of bilateral politics operated by Democrats and Republicans.

First, his class of origin—and arguably even his *race*—are not obvious. Is his background poor or comfortable, working or middle class? Is he black or white?[22] Are his religious roots Moslem or Christian? If he is imbued with a particular ideology, which is it? Presumably it is not the dominant neo-conservatism of the Bush administration, which he promised so forcefully and repeatedly to change. In the case of Obama, the terrible internal contradiction which haunts and handicaps the classic intellectual, as evoked by Sartre, is cast into doubt, if not completely disproved. The contingent facticity of Obama would appear to have equipped him with a chameleon-like adaptability, enabling him to approach the very centre and pinnacle of American power, from a starting point lying outside the normal margins of the American Dream.[23]

Second, Obama had already acquired a certain practical experience in the sector of housing for the homeless in downtown Chicago. So he had already effected, with success, a transition from his expert specialism (the law) to the particularism of a specific ideology (evangelical Christianity), and the putting into practice of that ideology in the form of charitable work: so, a realistic and practical work whose objective is to improve the real lives of real people in contemporary society. This represents a remarkable trajectory which most men and women in politics (seeing

---

[22] In his 2004 preface to the new edition, Obama memorably describes himself as a "a black man with a funny name" (*Dreams*, viii).

[23] At the time of editing (March 2011), it is universally acknowledged that Obama's attributes made him a much better candidate than President, but that is not the issue here.

themselves as intellectuals or not) would be unlikely to achieve over a long career, much less by the age of forty.

Third: Obama deployed his rhetoric—a professional skill, a practical tool—not only as a means of defeating his opponents (much less gifted than him in their powers of speech), but also—and more importantly—as a way of reaching his millions of potential supporters: those African Americans descended from slaves (like his own wife, indeed), although he personally is not actually one of their number. "Style is everything!" declared the writer Louis-Ferdinand Céline, whom President Nicolas Sarkozy is fond of quoting.[24]

Finally, Obama exploited all the new technologies of the mass media, inseparable, we were endlessly reminded, from his Blackberry. This was a matter of instrumentalising technical knowledge in order to assure his penetration into the virtual world of cyber-space, colonised chiefly by men and women who resemble him, despite his culturally hybrid background: namely, young professionals educated, like him, in the leading American universities, equally "technicians of practical knowledge", and on their way to becoming, like him, intellectuals. Perhaps Obama knew instinctively this axiom of democratic politics, recently enunciated by his French counterpart and admirer, Nicolas Sarkozy: "You don't win with the intellectuals alone, but you also don't win if they are against you."[25]

Indeed, during summer 2009 the French media got all excited about their President's belated conversion to intellectual life, a surprising metamorphosis largely credited to his wife: actress, model and pop-singer, Carla Bruni. It seemed she was responsible for recommending classic movies and great French literature, from Apollinaire to Zola, going (alphabetically, one supposes) via Sartre, amongst others:

> One day, [Sarkozy] took out of his briefcase a copy of Sartre's *Words*, with a succession of passages underlined in highlighter pen. "Progress, that long hard road that leads right to me..." He read the phrase to some journalists and remarked: "Imagine being able to write that... Amazing, isn't it?"[26]

---

[24] "Le style, c'est final." (See *L'Express (International)*, no. 3024, 28.)

[25] "On ne gagne pas avec les intellectuels, mais on ne gagne pas si on les a contre soi." (Ibid., 26.)

[26] "Un jour, [Sarkozy] sort de sa sacoche un exemplaire des *Mots* de Jean-Paul Sartre, avec une succession de passages soulignés au Stabilo. 'Le progrès, ce long chemin ardu qui mène jusqu'à moi...' Il lit la phrase à quelques journalistes et commente : 'Quelqu'un qui est capable d'écrire ça... C'est formidable, non?'" (Ibid., 25.)

This naïve comment may not be the height of literary criticism, but it would seem that Sarkozy is determined to pose our (and Sartre's) question in reverse, thus not: "Can an intellectual become a politician?", but rather: "Can a politician become an intellectual?"

Writer as intellectual: Murakami

To the best of my knowledge, history has not yet recorded whether Sarkozy's intellectual aspirations have encompassed Murakami. But whether they have or not, it is in relation to him that I want to consider the third and last question that Sartre asked in his 1966 Japan lectures, viz.: "Is the writer an intellectual?"—a question which Sartre posed about himself as much as any other writer, the danger no doubt being that he might otherwise stand to be condemned, out of his own mouth, as what he had called "a false intellectual":

> We have defined the situation of the intellectual by a contradiction within him between practical knowledge (truth, universality) and ideology (particularism). This definition can apply to teachers, scholars, doctors, etc. But in that case, is the writer an intellectual?[27]

I propose to apply this question in particular to Murakami's book, *Underground*, precisely because this is a work of non-fiction by an author whose reputation rests upon his works of fiction. *Underground* is a case of novelist-turned-journalist and so, on the face of it, of a writer "meddling in things that do not concern him"—which is for Sartre a trademark of the intellectual.

Sub-titled in English, *The Tokyo Gas Attack and the Japanese Psyche*, Murakami's book is a meditation upon the terrorist acts carried out by members of the cult *Aum Shinrikyo* in the Tokyo underground in March 1995. The volume, as published in English in 2000, brings together two sets of interviews published in Japan in 1997 and 1998. The first is a series of interviews with thirty-four survivors of the attacks on 20 March 1995. The second is a collection of interviews with eight former members—one might equally say "survivors"—of the *Aum Shinrikyo* sect. There is thereby a sort of implicit dialectic between the two parts. Moreover, each part has its own preface *and* postface, in which Murakami dialogues with

---

[27] "Nous avons défini la situation de l'intellectuel par la contradiction, en lui, du savoir pratique (vérité, universalité) et de l'idéologie (particularisme). Cette définition s'applique aux enseignants, aux savants, aux médecins, etc. Mais à ce compte, l'écrivain est-il un intellectuel?" (*S, VIII*, 430.)

himself about his rather peculiar project of recounting in detail—thereby seeking to understand—this terrible event, from numerous perspectives gathered under two headings: that of the victims and that of the assailants.

Occurring shortly after the Kobé earthquake in January 1995, these attacks in the Tokyo metro appear to have had a similarly phenomenal impact upon the Japanese psyche as the atrocities of "9/11" had upon the psychology of the citizens of the United States:

> It is no exaggeration to say that there was a marked change in the Japanese consciousness "before" and "after" these events. These twin catastrophes will remain embedded in our psyche as two milestones in our life as a people.[28]

Let us note, in passing, the echo of Sartre recalling how the Second World War had "divided [his] life in two", how it was for him "the real turning-point, before and after".[29] And let us note also how similar is Murakami's reaction to that of Sartre. Both writers—both *novelists* at their respective times—feel driven by these catastrophic interruptions to their life (and to the life of the nation) to become "engaged" with their collective time, *committed* to making new and different kinds of texts whose very strangeness would draw attention to the newness of their mission.

In his first preface, Murakami admits that he wanted initially to understand why a traumatised survivor had been dismissed from his employment on account of his subsequent nervous anxiety: "Personally, I wanted to probe deeper into how Japanese society could perpetrate such a double violence."[30] However, he is careful not to tumble into the trap that Sartre espied ahead of him, namely that of becoming "an amateur psychologist [or] an amateur sociologist".[31] On the contrary, he is intent on remaining conscious of his vocation as a novelist: as such, writes Murakami, "I am less interested in the 'big picture' as it were, than in the concrete, irreducible humanity of each individual."[32] But it is only *after* the thirty-four interviews that he begins to analyse his own "concrete, irreducible humanity", and that analysis is fascinating.

---

[28] *Underground*, 206.

[29] "La guerre a vraiment divisé ma vie en deux. [...] C'est ça le vrai tournant de ma vie: avant, après." (Sartre, "Autoportrait", 180.)

[30] *Underground*, 4.

[31] *S, VIII*, 445.

[32] *Underground*, 6. This focus of interest is very much the same as Sartre's in his existential biographies of Baudelaire, Genet, or Flaubert.

First, there is Murakami's own "sense of estrangement or displacement"[33], which remained with him throughout the day, and which in a sense made real the "period of self-imposed exile"[34] which he had deliberately chosen, first in Europe, then in the United States, precisely in order to "understand Japan at a deeper level". A period at the end of which, he notes—with a clear but unacknowledged reference to Nietzsche—he "could feel the change inside [himself], an ongoing 'revaluation' of [his] values." And then there is his impatience with the stupid Manicheanism of the mass media which reduced the whole affair to "'good' versus 'evil', 'sanity' versus 'madness', 'health' versus 'disease'. [...] an obvious exercise in opposites."[35] With a dialectical and thoroughly Sartrean lucidity, Murakami realises that he must strive to integrate, to some extent, this otherness of the cult into the ordinary run of Japanese society:

> My conjecture is this. The Aum "phenomenon" disturbs precisely because it is not *someone else's affair*. It shows us a distorted image of ourselves in a manner none of us could have foreseen. [...] Or rather, "they" are the mirror of "us".[36]

Here, then, is another Sartrean echo—most obviously, perhaps, of the play *Huis clos*, whose characters bemoan the lack of real mirrors in their hellish drawing-room, and deplore each other's past conduct as it is revealed through their coerced confessions, only to appreciate gradually that they are, in fact, the mirrors of each other. This reference is reinforced when, as he describes the situation and the ambience in the criminal court during the trial of the terrorists, Murakami writes:

> What I found there was a dismal, gloomy, hopeless scene. The court was like a room with no exit. There must have been a way out in the beginning, but now it had become a nightmarish chamber from which there was no escape.[37]

The allusion to Sartre's best-known play—often translated as *No Exit*—is overt and probably deliberate: the hopeless nightmare is hell, and "Hell is other people".

I have shown elsewhere that Murakami is clearly influenced by Sartre, both explicitly and implicitly. Yet such references, however self-conscious

[33] Ibid., 195.
[34] Ibid., 204.
[35] Ibid., 196.
[36] Ibid., 198-99.
[37] Ibid., 305.

and knowing, do not of themselves demonstrate that his project in *Underground* necessarily makes of him the writer-*qua*-intellectual that Sartre interrogates in his last and most personal Japan lecture, his apologia for the writer as intellectual. Nevertheless, by "meddling in things that do not [rightly] concern him" as a novelist, in this extraordinary and unclassifiable text which is certainly not a novel, Murakami appears to respond affirmatively to Sartre's third rhetorical question. Indeed, one might even say that *Underground* is the product of the intellectual writer *par excellence*, according to the definition Sartre gives us in his concluding remarks:

> In this sense, [the writer] is not an intellectual *by accident*, like [other intellectuals], but *in his essence*. Precisely for that reason, the work demands of itself that he place himself *outside it*, on the theoretico-practical plane where the other intellectuals already are: for it is, on the one hand, a restitution—on the level of not knowing—of being in a world that crushes us and, on the other hand, a lived affirmation of life as an absolute value and a demand of freedom addressed to all other freedoms.[38]

It seems to me that, consciously or otherwise, Murakami produced in *Underground* a hybrid work that corresponds closely to this Sartrean description of the project of the writer-as-intellectual—a description which Sartre had, fittingly enough, enunciated in Japan when the young Murakami was a seventeen-year-old student.

Postface: Whither Murakami?

Whether or not *Underground* is therefore a "good work of literature"—whatever that might be—is, of course, a completely different question. Quite by chance, during my second visit to Tokyo in July 2009, I came across this paragraph in a free magazine called *Metropolis*, published in Tokyo and claiming to be *Japan's N° 1 English Magazine*:

> Simply put, Haruki Murakami [*sic*] is a great read, but awful literature. Literature has the power to change the way readers think and feel... When

---

[38] "En ce sens, [l'écrivain] n'est pas intellectuel *par accident*, comme [les autres intellectuels], mais *par essence*. Précisément par cette raison, l'œuvre exige par elle-même qu'il se place *hors d'elle* sur le plan théorico-pratique où sont déjà les autres intellectuels: car elle est d'une part restitution—sur le plan du non-savoir—de l'être dans un monde qui nous écrase et, d'autre part, affirmation vécue de la vie comme valeur absolue et exigence d'une liberté qui s'adresse à toutes les autres." (*S, VIII*, 455, Sartre's emphases.)

> you read one of Murakami's books, what changes? Nothing. In fact, he affirms that lack of change. He comforts those who, while they have a certain amount of self-respect, lack the courage to make breakthroughs in their own lives, saying "Hey, it's okay for you to be bitter and lonely." Most people don't have the guts to get their hands dirty, which is why Murakami is so popular.[39]

The author may have been thinking about a very few special works of "literature", or she may have been thinking about anything by Murakami besides *Underground.* In any event, there is little doubt that researching and *writing* this curious, unclassifiable work, so far from "affirming lack of change" for Murakami, affirmed a very significant change for him.

Whether it will also have had that effect on his readers—especially in Japan—only they could say. For my part, I found it a difficult book to read on many levels, *except* in those places—his prefaces and postfaces—where the author analysed his own motivations and reactions. For once, he stopped playing those (apparently pointless) cat-and-mouse games that characterise much of his prose fiction, and broke cover to reveal an authentic intellectual in seemingly full flow of reflection upon his real prejudices and values. I suggest that, in *Underground*, Murakami aspired towards a committed intellectual usefulness which Sartre would have both recognised and admired.[40]

---

[39] Naomi Watanabe [*sic*], literary critic, in the July issue of *Cyzo* magazine, quoted in *Metropolis*, Tokyo, no. 797, 3 July 2009. The reference (no doubt unwitting) to Sartre's second best-known play, *Les Mains sales* (*Dirty Hands*), is a happy coincidence.

[40] At the time of editing (March 2011) the news is dominated by political earthquakes in North Africa and geological earthquakes in New Zealand and Japan, the latter followed by a devastating tsunami and potential nuclear disaster. As survivors flee from Sendai to Tokyo, or from Tokyo to Osaka—and the 1995 earthquake in Kobé is repeatedly evoked—one wonders whether, when and how Murakami might address this latest catastrophe to strike his homeland.

Works Cited

Asabuki, Tomiko. *Vingt-huit Jours au Japon avec Jean-Paul Sartre et Simone de Beauvoir (18 septembre–16 octobre 1966)* (traduit du japonais par Claude Peronny et Tanaka Chiharu). Paris: Langues et Mondes / L'Asiathèque, 1996.

L'Express (International), no. 3024, 18–24 June 2009.

Murakami, Haruki. *Underground: The Tokyo Gas Attack and the Japanese Psyche* (trans. Alfred Birnbaum and Philip Gabriel). London: Vintage, 2003.

Obama, Barack. *Dreams from My Father: A Story of Race and Inheritance*. New York: Crown Publishers (1995), 2004.

O'Donohoe, Benedict. "Contemporary Perspectives: Sartre, Clooney, McCarthy, Murakami", in Benedict O'Donohoe and Roy Elveton (eds.), *Sartre's Second Century*. Newcastle upon Tyne: Cambridge Scholars Publishing, 2009 (173–90).

—. "Sartre en Grande Bretagne" (translated into Japanese, abstract in French, 9–10), in Ishizaki Harumi and Sawada Nao (eds.), *Sartre, penseur pour le XXIe siècle? Actes du colloque international*. Tokyo: Editions Shichosha, 2007.

Sartre, Jean-Paul. "Autoportrait à soixante-dix ans" [Self-Portrait at Seventy] (with Michel Contat), in *Situations, X*. Paris: Gallimard, 1976 (133-226).

—. "Plaidoyer pour les intellectuels", in *Situations, VIII*. Paris: Gallimard, 1972 (375-455).

—. *Les Mots*. Paris: Gallimard, 1964.

PART IV:

SARTRE IN JAPAN

CHAPTER ELEVEN

HOW TO WELCOME AN INTELLECTUAL SUPERSTAR: SARTRE AND THE JAPANESE PRESS IN 1966

SUZUKI MASAMICHI

It may sound odd that it was in 1966 that the Japanese press spoke most about Sartre. The reason for this is that Sartre and Beauvoir visited Japan that year for the first and last time. During their stay from 18 September to 16 October, Sartre gave three lectures, and they both participated in round-table discussions and gave interviews, as well as visiting several regions. The three lectures were afterwards reproduced in *Situations, VIII* as "Plaidoyer pour les intellectuels".[1] However, their talks given on other occasions, the reactions to those speeches and the background to their visit are not well known outside Japan.[2] In fact, this important event has some interesting elements which we can use as tools to consider the question of the "Sartre phenomenon", of intellectuals or of the mass media creating social phenomena. More than forty years after Sartre's and Beauvoir's visit, and thirty years since Sartre's death, I propose to throw some light on this event in order to offer an occasion for rethinking and resituating Sartre as an intellectual superstar.[3]

To begin with, I will look at Sartre's lectures and the reactions of his audience. Next, I will look at the role of the mass media that transmitted

---

[1] Sartre 1972, 375-455.

[2] Asabuki Tomiko recounts their visit to Japan, from the point of view of their friend and interpreter, in her book *Vingt-huit Jours au Japon avec Jean-Paul Sartre et Simone de Beauvoir*, 1996, the Japanese edition of which was published in 1995. [Note that the Japanese practice of placing the surname before the forename—for example, Asabuki Tomiko—has been respected (Eds.).]

[3] An earlier draft of this chapter was given as a paper at the conference of the AHRC-sponsored workshop hosted by the UK Sartre Society at the Institut Français, South Kensington, in September 2009. (Eds.)

these exchanges. Finally, I will propose a review of the question of the intellectual in our time from another perspective. What in fact happened? How was it reported? And what would happen now?

Action and reaction

The celebrated intellectual couple was invited by a publishing company Jimbun Shoin (literally, Humanities Publishing) and Keio University. The former had almost finished the publication of *Sartre's Complete Works*. A young Japanese sociologist, Ishii Motoko, supposes that the invitation was a kind of memorial event for the company to mark this achievement, and that the head of the company judged it appropriate to invite the author before his popularity declined.[4] Sato Saku, a specialist in French literature, who was also an advisor to the head of the company, had asked Sartre to come to Japan the previous year. By contrast, at the French Embassy, there was a round-table discussion between Japanese specialists of French literature and the French staff, who branded Sartre as "out-of-date". One of the participants—Suzuki Michihiko—later revealed that, once he was informed of this, Sartre decided to accept the invitation.[5] The official invitation was sent in January 1966.[6]

It is quite natural that different people should have different expectations of such a big event. For some Japanese, Sartre was first of all a philosopher of existentialism, for others he was a committed writer, whilst other people felt embarrassed by what they saw as the incongruence of these two "Sartres". Indeed, there was an incident which might have caused some confusion: Sartre had announced that the subjects of the three lectures would be: "Literature and Language", "Commitment of a Writer", and "On Theatre". And it was only two weeks before his arrival with Simone de Beauvoir that he revealed a change of plan: he would focus instead on the question of the intellectual.[7] It seems that he found it important to address this question after reading about fifty books on

[4] Ishii Motoko, "A Study on the Introduction of J.-P. Sartre to Japan: From the Perspective of the History of Publishing", *Bulletin of Kyoto University Graduate School of Education*, no. 52, 2006, 93-107 (text in Japanese with a summary in English; see page 103).

[5] This fact was disclosed in discussion at the annual conference of the Japanese Sartre Society, held at Rikkyô University, Tokyo, in July 2009.

[6] "Round-Table Discussion: Sartre, His Personality and Literature", *Mita Bungaku* (that is, *Mita Literature*), December 1966, 78-101. The participants were Asari Keita, Sato Saku, Haniya Yutaka, Hirai Keishi, Hotta Yoshie, Yasuoka Shotaro.

[7] Ibid.

Japan[8], where the intellectuals had been severely criticized after their defeat over the revision of the Japan–US Security Treaty.[9] The Vietnam War—against which a protest movement, "Peace for Vietnam, Civil Federation", was organised—revealed all the more the seriousness of the situation. It was quite natural that many people should be eager to know what Sartre thought about these issues.

What the Japanese heard or read was, in a sense, a typical Sartre discourse. The first lecture, given on 20 September, was "Qu'est-ce qu'un intellectuel?" ("What is an intellectual?").[10] In this paper Sartre attempted to situate intellectuals in history, linking their origin to the birth of the bourgeoisie and explaining how the philosophers of the eighteenth century, *qua* "technicians of knowledge", became "intellectuals" who contradicted the dominant bourgeois ideology by their free spirit. This argumentation is in fact quite familiar to readers of *Qu'est-ce que la littérature?* (*What is Literature?*) or *Critique de la raison dialectique* (*Critique of Dialectical Reason*). The second lecture (22 September) treated the "Fonction de l'intellectuel" ("The role of the intellectual"): here, Sartre argued that the intellectual lives a fundamentally contradictory existence as a bourgeois fighting on behalf of the working classes. Such a "monster" reminds us of (Sartre's) Jean Genet or Goetz von Berlichingen. The third lecture (28 September) asks: "L'écrivain, est-il un intellectuel?" ("Is the writer an intellectual?"). In this one, Sartre classifies language into common language and technical language. A writer, he asserts, uses the first category, which can communicate several meanings at the same time thanks to the materiality of the words. Here we see again the dichotomy between two kinds of language that he introduced into *What is Literature?*, although the terms of the dichotomy were somewhat changed in the lecture. In *What is Literature?*, Sartre had insisted that only prose should commit itself, while poetry—which has recourse to the materiality and the polysemy of words—could not commit itself. Now, however, Sartre argued that the common language, with its material and equivocal words,

---

[8] Ibid., 78-79.

[9] In 1959 the revision of the Japan–US Security Treaty was at issue. The left wing was afraid that the new treaty, which obliged both countries to defend themselves collectively, might involve Japan in a war, and organised violent demonstrations, in which a large number of people took part. Once the new treaty was concluded, there remained a bitter feeling of defeat among the leftists.

[10] For consistency's sake, and to avoid confusion, we have used the titles of these three lectures as they are published in *Situations, VIII*, although their actual titles at the time may have been—or have been reported or remembered as being—subtly different. (Eds.)

was used by the committed intellectual whether as a writer of prose or poetry, the technical language being reserved for the specialist. With its rather abstract dialectic argumentation, clear-cut structure and dextrous rhetoric, Sartre's discourse constituted a kind of "dissertation", in the French sense of the word.

However familiar this procedure might be to Sartre's more or less passionate readers, there was something embarrassing for the public, even for his faithful readers. Sartre argued as if the difference between the bourgeoisie and the working classes were simple and clear-cut. But in Japan, at least, this was not necessarily the case. The sociologist Shimizu Ikutaro, professor at Gakushuin University, insisted that there was a high level of mobility between classes, that upward social mobility was normal, and that there were many intellectuals who came from the working classes.[11] Another critic, Muramatsu Takeshi, accused Sartre of sticking to the classical Marxist schema which presented the bourgeoisie as exploiting the working classes.[12]

Those who supported Sartre were well aware of this point. In a round-table discussion with him and Simone de Beauvoir, held on 12 October, Sakamoto Yoshikazu, Tsurumi Shunsuke, Hidaka Rokuro and Kato Shuichi (chairperson) pointed out that the dividing line between the bourgeoisie and the working classes had been becoming less clear, at least and particularly, in Japan. Admitting this, Sartre stressed the contradiction of the intellectual who shared the same interests as the working classes but who was forced to work for the dominant class.[13] And in the press conference held just before his departure, Sartre argued that in spite of the improvement of living standards, the salary of a Japanese person was still smaller than that of a European. He emphasised the importance of the role of the intellectual in a world where poverty was still prevalent.[14]

In a discussion organised by the editorial department of the *Asahi Journal*, without the presence of either Sartre or Beauvoir, Oe Kenzaburo pointed out that Sartre's discourse looked simple and schematic when it was summarised, and that this had provoked the criticism of it. But the

---

[11] Shimizu Ikutaro, "'The Function of the Intellectual' [literal translation of the title of Sartre's second paper]: Comments on Mr Sartre's Lecture", *Asahi Shimbun*, 12, 13 October 1966, evening editions.

[12] Muramatsu Takeshi, "An Objection to Sartre: His Unattractive Schematized Theory", *Yomiuri Shimbun*, 3 October 1966, evening edition.

[13] "A Talk with Sartre: About the Intellectual and the Nuclear Problem", *Sekai*, December 1966, 48-69.

[14] Reporter Nemoto [forename unknown], "What Sartre has left us", *Asahi Shimbun*, 21 October 1966, evening edition.

attractiveness of Sartre's argumentation consisted in its peculiar literary images.[15] After the departure of Sartre and Beauvoir, the philosopher Ichii Saburo, professor at Seikei University, proposed a counter-argument to Shimizu's claim. He contended that Sartre's theory held good, regardless of the mobility between the classes, because Sartre was simply revealing the self-deception of the intellectual who actually belonged to the bourgeoisie and was trying to work on behalf of the lower classes.[16]

Sartre also took part in a number of round-table discussions on a variety of topics: on 12 October, one about intellectuals and nuclear weapons; two days later, one on literature and thought, and another triangular discussion on Japan. On 15 October he attended a meeting of "Peace for Vietnam, Civil Federation". The subjects which Sartre did not address during his lectures were the focus of discussion in these forums. During the round-table discussion held on 14 October, Suzuki Michihiko insisted that all of Sartre's activities, whether literary or political, constituted a whole œuvre whose constituent parts could not be separated from each other, although he admitted that numerous Japanese readers did not approve of his political commitment.[17] It is relevant to point out that Shirai Koji, who was the chairperson of this discussion, had been deploring this change in Sartre, from "author of *Nausea*" to "committed writer".[18] However, in this discussion, Shirai Koji said only that there were some small differences between the opinions of the participants. They, all specialists on Sartre, put questions on almost every subject—from how he was influenced by Proust and the Surrealists, to how his belief in the power of language had changed—and Sartre duly replied. He also talked

[15] "A Round-Table Discussion: Sartre's Theory of the Intellectual—how should we judge it?", *Asahi Journal*, 16 October 1966, 90-99.

[16] Ichii Saburo, "A Reversed Theory on the Intellectual: Comments on Mr Shimizu's Speech", *Asahi Shimbun*, 31 October 1966, evening edition.

[17] "My Literature and Thought", *Bungei* (*Literary Arts*), December 1966, 220-46. The participants were Sartre and Beauvoir, Hirai Keishi, Suzuki Michihiko, Ebisaka Takeshi and Shirai Koji (chairperson). During another conversation, without the presence of Sartre and Beauvoir, Oe Kenzaburo supported Suzuki's opinion, expressed also by Kato Shuichi: see "A Round-Table Discussion: Sartre's Theory of the Intellectual—how should we judge it?", 98.

[18] Although a Professor at Keio University, one of the institutions hosting Sartre and Beauvoir, Shirai Koji missed no opportunity to voice this criticism: see, for example, "Welcoming Sartre", *Asahi Shimbun*, 5 September 1966, evening edition, or again "A Round-Table Discussion", etc., 94-95. Ten years after Sartre's death, he published an attack on Sartre entitled "Jean-Paul Sartre's 'Crime'", in *Shokun!* (literally *Ladies and Gentlemen*), May 1990, 224-33.

about the "commitment" of Mallarmé and Genet[19], about why he had abandoned *The Roads to Freedom*[20], and why he had never joined the Communist Party. Each of these questions had already been addressed on previous occasions, or would be clarified on later occasions.

In the round-table discussion of 12 October, Oe Kenzaburo insisted that it was imperative to oppose the nuclear armaments of all countries, whether the USA or China. Sartre accepted this position, adding however that it was necessary to emphasise the accusation against the US, which would not be easily persuaded.[21] At the meeting of the "Peace for Vietnam, Civil Federation", held on 15 October and attended by Sartre and Beauvoir, Hidaka Rokuro agreed with Sartre on this point.[22] At the same meeting, the novelist Kaiko Takeshi pointed out the responsibility of France for the Vietnam War and the apparent indifference of the French people to this problem. Beauvoir replied that *Les Temps modernes* had discussed it in several issues, adding that it was moreover one of the items at the top of the agenda for the French Left. On the other hand Sartre, while admitting France's responsibility, stressed that it was the USA which was actually waging the war.[23]

Media

It goes without saying that the number of people who actually heard Sartre speak was rather limited. As is often the case with a superstar, not all of those who wanted to see and hear him were admitted into the conference halls. The role of mass media was important, therefore, not only in providing information for those who were excluded from the halls, but also in attracting the interest of those who might otherwise be rather indifferent. And because the most famous intellectual couple was coming, it was the "press", in rather a strict sense, which led the way. At this time,

---

[19] Cf. interview conducted in 1960 by Madeleine Chapsal, in Michel Contat and Michel Rybalka (eds.), *Les Écrits de Sartre*, 1970, 262.
[20] Cf. Simone de Beauvoir, *La Force des choses*, 1963, 214.
[21] *Sekai*, December 1966, 59-64.
[22] "The Vietnam War and Anti-War Principles", *Sekai*, December 1966, 81-121. Other participants were Iida Momo, Kurihara Yukio, Tsurumi Shunsuke, Umihara Shun, Komatsu Sakyo, Tsurumi Yoshiyuki, Oda Makoto, Shibata Michiko, Hariu Ichiro, Kaiko Takeshi, Shinmura Takeshi, Kasahara Yoshimitsu, Suzuki Michihiko, Hirai Keishi, Kuno Osamu, Takeuchi Yoshimi, Fukasaku Mitsusada, Kubota Hanya, Tanigawa Gan, Muto Ichiyo.
[23] Ibid., 87-94.

Japanese TV was considered to be turning the whole nation into idiots.[24] On the other hand, it has long since been normal in Japan that a family subscribes to one daily newspaper, and so the national daily papers have enjoyed a high level of sales. The national newspaper companies also publish weekly magazines or books and, moreover, they more or less fund the TV networks, so that a national paper is considered to be linked to a TV station on an ideological or political level. Furthermore, it is through advertisements in newspapers (or displayed in railway carriages) that people know about other printed media, such as magazines or books. Thus the influence of the national daily newspapers seems to have been particularly strong in Japan. I shall limit my examination to two national dailies, which contrast with each other in their ideological tendencies but have the biggest circulations, and therefore provide data on similar bases.[25]

It is possible to classify articles in Japanese newspapers roughly into three categories: those which claim to report "facts" and which are written by a journalist who is part of the newspaper company; those which express the opinion of the author who is part of the company; those which express the opinion of the author who is not part of the company. Although the tendency has been changing in recent years, articles of the first category are often anonymous, and this was almost always so in the 1960s. The narrative of a text which claims to present "facts" is written in the third person taking an omniscient point of view, which does not however exclude emotional expressions. It goes without saying that, in articles of all three categories, the values held by the editors of each company are more or less, and differently, reflected.

The *Asahi Shimbun* (literally *The Rising Sun Newspaper*) sponsored Sartre's and Beauvoir's second and third lectures, although its publishing company was not reported as being one of the sponsors of their visit. However, its liberal and/or leftist position, with a touch of elitism too, fitted well with its support for the subversive intellectual couple. Around the time of their visit to Japan, in particular, the number of articles

[24] It is not possible to get precise information about the TV or radio news programmes reporting Sartre's and Beauvoir's visit. According to the *Mainichi Shimbun* (25 September 1966), on 25 September, 2 October, 7 October and 14 October, their first, second and third lectures, and the triangular discussion of 14 October, respectively, were all broadcast on NHK radio and TV.

[25] In 1966, the *Asahi Shimbun* had a circulation of about 5 million, while the *Yomiuri Shimbun* had about 4 million: see Kusayanagi Taizo, "On a Contemporary Kingdom, the *Asahi Shimbun*", *Bungei Shunju*, November 1966, 108-122 (117). Recently the two dailies have had a circulation of about 8 million and 10 million respectively, according to the Japan Audit Bureau of Circulation.

concerning Sartre and Beauvoir rose sharply. From their arrival on 18 September until their departure on 16 October, *Asahi Shimbun*'s readers were informed not only about their lectures, round-table discussions and interviews, but also about their sightseeing and other travels, by lengthy articles accompanied with many photographs. Especially for the three lectures, there were feature articles which occupied almost a whole page, consisting of a presentation and summary of the lecture, by an anonymous journalist, and a commentary by a specialist.

The narrative of the anonymous journalists insisted passionately on Sartre's popularity. As early as April 1966 (the official invitation had been sent in January), the visit of Jean-Paul Sartre—"more highly regarded in Japan than in his own country"—was announced. On 1 September, it was reported that there was "already a rush of applications to attend [his] lectures". The morning edition of 21 September reported that the first lecture of "Monsieur Sartre, who [was] extremely popular among the Japanese students", had been a great success, describing how only 500 students—selected at random from those who had applied to hear him speak—were admitted into the lecture hall, and how other students had had to watch the event on television in seven other rooms. As for the second lecture on 22 September, sponsored by the *Asahi Shimbun*, it was reported in the evening edition of the day that 2,000 "passionate Sartre fans", chosen at random from 30,000 applicants, "had listened attentively to the simultaneous translation without making any noise except for their passionate applause at the moment of Sartre's and Beauvoir's appearance in the hall".

The title and subtitles of an article are often designed by an editor, although the expressions may be borrowed from the text. In any case, their function of attracting the readers is most important, and at the same time they represent the values held by the author and/or the editor. In the morning edition of 21 September, readers saw the headline in bold characters: "Deep Impression on the Audience". As a subtitle they read: "The Hall of Keio University Was Completely Full". The title and the subtitle of the article reporting the second lecture in the evening edition of 22 September were verging on the sensational: "Arch-Enemy: the 'False Intellectual'. Monsieur Sartre's Severe Tone. In Front of 2,000 People in Hibiya Public Hall".

Let us now look at the commentaries. On 5 September, Shirai Koji contributed an essay, entitled "We Welcome Sartre", and in the evening edition of 21 September, there was a commentary on the first lecture by Hirai Keishi (an assistant professor at Tokyo University). After the third lecture Kojima Terumasa, a professor at Kobé University, wrote a general commentary on the three lectures for the evening edition of 28 September. It is true that even Hirai or Kojima, who appreciated Sartre's lectures in general, seemed a little embarrassed by his schematic argumentation. And Shirai warned against an excessive idolisation of the visiting superstar. But the general tone of these comments was positive for the special guest's lectures, partly sponsored by the newspaper company.

On the other hand, an anonymous but apparently in-house journalist wrote a column entitled "Monsieur Sartre's Thrilling Talk", in which he mocked one of Sartre's television appearances.[26] This was the three-way discussion organised on 4 October and broadcast on 14 October by NHK (*Nippon Hōsō Kyōkai*: Japan Broadcasting Corporation), during which Sartre, Shirai and Kato discussed Japanese traditional theatre such as Noh and Kabuki, novelists including Tanizaki and Mishima, and architects such as Tange. The journalist in question found it extremely amusing that Sartre never talked within the framework prepared by the organisers, turning a question about traditional Japanese theatre, for example, into a problem of class conflict. However, reading the transcript of the discussion myself, I must say that Sartre's discourse does not seem to me half as subversive as the anonymous columnist claimed.[27]

It is not clear to me how Shimizu Ikutaro managed to get his rather categorical criticisms published in the evening editions of 12 and 13 October. According to him, Sartre did not understand the complexity of the situation in Japan after the struggle over the Japan–US Security Treaty, and he branded as "false intellectuals" scientists and engineers who were, in fact, working honestly and modestly. It should be noted that in the 1950s, Shimizu, a passionate reader of Sartre, was an active left-wing militant opposed to the revision of the Japan–US Security Treaty. He translated *Les Mots* (*Words*) with other translators just after its publication. But in the 1970s he began to support the revision of the Japanese Constitution and Japan's acquisition of nuclear arms. His "conversion" was probably not manifest at the time of Sartre's visit, and his reputation as a Sartre supporter recommended him to the newspaper. Even if the editor was shocked to read Shimizu's articles, he could no longer refuse them. But then Ichii Saburo counter-attacked, in the evening edition of 31 October. He found Shimizu's reaction "too emotional", alleging that—just

[26] He signed the column with the Japanese letter "ra", which was quite a normal custom in those days: it might be the initial of the author's surname, forename or nickname.

[27] See "The Occident and Japan" (translated into Japanese by Furuya Kenzo), in Hidaka Rokuro and Hirai Keishi (eds.), *Three Talks with Jean-Paul Sartre*, Jimbun Shoin, 1967, 131-57.

because Shimizu was disillusioned after his defeat in the battle against the Japan–US Treaty—he was disgusted with everything that reminded him of the past. I do not know whether the editor simply accepted Shimizu's articles and then Ichii's refutation, or whether he asked Shimizu to write the articles in order to have them refuted by another critic, and thus build a controversy around the superstar that was Sartre.

The *Yomiuri Shimbun* (literally *Reading to Sell*), a newspaper with a conservative reputation, provides a contrast to the *Asahi Shimbun*. Although this paper had carried more articles on Sartre than the *Asahi* before his visit, and the number rose higher in 1966, the increase during his visit was smaller. Moreover, the narrative of the articles was less passionate and more critical than in the *Asahi*. The announcement of the visit by Sartre and Beauvoir appeared as late as 14 July, Bastille Day. Besides coverage of their arrival in and their departure from Japan, the reader was provided with an essay before their arrival, but with summaries only of Sartre's three lectures, a critical commentary, a couple of column inches criticising Sartre, a report on his visit with Beauvoir to Kyoto, and some short articles reporting their other activities.

An anonymous journalist of the newspaper reported on their arrival in the lobby of the airport, where, according to the morning edition of 19 September,

> [...] several girl students looking like fans of Sartre were visible. Almost 100 journalists, not only from the newspaper or broadcasting media but also working on women's weekly magazines, rushed to the press conference which was held in the special waiting room of Japan Airlines.

Is it not possible to detect a kind of embarrassment and irony rather than excitement in the narrative? The article reporting the first lecture was apparently almost as passionate as that in the *Asahi*, but the narrative sometimes toned down the enthusiasm with some detachment: "Just after the War, existentialism was booming, while students these days are probably attracted by the sort of problems Mr Sartre poses, like 'the role of the intellectual' or 'political commitment'." While in the morning edition of 21 September and the evening edition of 22 September of the *Asahi*, the feature articles on the first and the second lectures were preceded by a kind of introductory article with sensational titles in large characters, the *Yomiuri* published only one article on each lecture, consisting of a presentation and a rather short summary.

The less enthusiastic posture of the *Yomiuri* is more evident in the commentaries. It is true that Hirai Keishi, who would later comment on Sartre's first lecture for the *Asahi*, contributed a long passionate essay before his arrival[28], and that Yanaihara Isaku, a professor at Doshisha University, wrote a fascinating report of Sartre's and Beauvoir's visit to Kyoto, but with a much greater range of criticism.[29]

The evening edition of 3 October featured an anti-Sartre page. A critic, Muramatsu Takeshi, wrote "An Objection to Sartre", with a subtitle in large characters: "His Unattractive Schematized Theory". He criticized Sartre as being someone who presented a stereotyped class division between the bourgeoisie and the working classes, and who condemned "humanism" as a notion invented by the former in order to exploit the latter. The author found in Sartre's lectures the discourse of a rabble-rouser and was surprised at the Japanese intellectuals who were charmed by such a schematic theory. On the same page, Hayashi Kentaro, a professor of history at Tokyo University, questioned the "divinization of Sartre" who stuck to Marxism as if it were holy writ. In the morning edition of 9 October, an anonymous author admitted, in his front-page column, that he felt so suffocated reading Sartre's novels or philosophical works that he had never read any of his books through to the end. And just before the departure of Sartre and Beauvoir, Aida Yuji, a professor at Kyoto University, referred ironically to a "Sartre boom", which he compared to the sensation caused by the Beatles' visit to Japan (30 June–2 July 1966). He deplored the Japanese intellectuals' enthusiasm, which was, according to him, "a phenomenon we [could] never be proud of" (see the *Yomiuri* morning edition of 16 October).

It is difficult to know whether the less enthusiastic, or rather critical, posture of the *Yomiuri Shimbun* towards the subversive intellectual star was due merely to its own conservative stance. This became more explicit from the end of the 1970s when the current head, Watanabe Tsuneo, took editorial command. However, it should not be forgotten that there had been articles in the paper attacking Sartre since 1947.[30]

---

[28] "What We Expect of Sartre", *Yomiuri Shimbun*, 9 September, evening edition. The author insisted that Sartre and the Japanese shared the same feeling about the experience of the war, but that they should understand Sartre's evolution. He expected that Sartre would complete the *Critique of Dialectical Reason*, thereby playing the role of Jean-Jacques Rousseau who had paved the way ideologically for the French Revolution.

[29] "A Holiday in Kyoto", *Yomiuri Shimbun*, 10 October, evening edition. The author, who was also a friend of Giacometti, showed Sartre and Beauvoir the sights. He reported that, whilst admiring gardens or architecture, Sartre also showed an interest in the lives of people.

[30] See, for example, Shirai Akira, "Sartre's Bubbles", *Yomiuri Shimbun*, 14 July 1947, morning edition; or Yama (probably the initial of the author's surname), "Sartre's Magic", *Yomiuri Shimbun*, 8 June 1962, evening edition.

On the other hand, weekly or monthly magazines took responsibility for publishing complete translations of Sartre's lectures and of the round-table discussions. The *Asahi Journal* (9 October 1966) offered the translation of Sartre's second lecture by Matsunami Shinzaburo (the Japanese translator of *Being and Nothingness* and a professor at Waseda University), and Hiraoka Tokuyoshi (assistant professor at Waseda). This weekly periodical was published by the *Asahi Shimbun*, and its political stance was more radical and left-wing than that of the daily newspaper.[31] *Chuokoron* (literally *The Central Public Opinion*) was in charge of the translation of the third lecture undertaken by Furuya Kenzo. The stance of this monthly was centre-left and/or progressive.[32] And it was *Sekai* (literally *The World*) that carried the transcriptions of the discussion of 12 October on the intellectuals, and that of 15 October on the Vietnam War. This monthly is published by Iwanami Shoten (The Rock and Wave Publisher), one of the biggest Japanese publishers, which produces rather "serious" and/or classical works and is reputed for its "progressive" position. And the publisher Jimbun Shoin which—with Keio University—had invited Sartre and Beauvoir in the first place, published in one volume the three discussions held on 4, 12 and 14 October, plus the speech Sartre made at the meeting of the 15th.[33] Thus the "progressive" and/or left media played an active role in propagating in written form Sartre's oral interventions. On the other hand, we cannot find articles on Sartre in the 1966 issues of "conservative" magazines such as the monthly *Bungei Shunju* (literally *Years of Literary Arts*), well-known as the awarder of a literary prize comparable to *Le Prix Goncourt*.[34]

Conclusion: And now?

We have seen how the Japanese intellectuals and public welcomed Sartre in 1966. But to what extent was the climax of the "Sartre

---

[31] Because of falling sales, its publication was "suspended" in 1992. In April 2009 it was "revived" for one issue only, featuring "The Japanese Social System on the Verge of Collapse".

[32] In 1999 the publishing company had financial difficulties and its publishing activities passed to the *Yomiuri Shimbun*, so that the political stance of *Chuokoron* is said to have become conservative.

[33] See Hidaka and Hirai (eds.).

[34] This monthly published essays by Ebisaka Takeshi and Asabuki Tomiko in 2000, respectively: "Jean-Paul Sartre: he gave away every book he had read because he denied property", January 2000, 336-38; and "Sartre: an unforgettable person", February 2000, 228-29.

phenomenon" in Japan shared by the whole nation? Was it only a big event staged by the liberal and/or left-wing media? Or did the conservative and/or right-wing media try to play down—even deliberately ignore—the highly subversive intellectual phenomenon that was Sartre? This is not an easy question to answer.

Nowadays, there are no charismatic figures comparable to Sartre: it is said that the age of the "great" public intellectual has gone. In spite of that, or because of it, the problematic of the intellectual has frequently been discussed.[35] In Japan, an international symposium about the intellectual was held in 2007, and a book of the proceedings published in 2009.[36] From among the questions discussed in this rich work, I propose to focus on a single problem in order to conclude this chapter, and at the same time to open up new areas of consideration.

Referring to "Plaidoyer pour les intellectuels", Tachibana Hidehiro says that, during the 1980s, people criticized those intellectuals who concerned themselves with what lay outside their field. But he insists that it is just these intellectuals who are capable of relativizing the problem, while specialists can treat it only from their specialized point of view. And he cites Noam Chomsky as a remarkable example of an intellectual who has always expressed his opinion on events in the contemporary world.[37]

I refrain from deciding whether or not intellectuals should concern themselves with what lies outside their field. As a matter of fact, a non-specialist intellectual can rarely intervene in a problem which needs specialized knowledge.[38] I would rather like to point out another question: it is now specialists who speak out to a wide public, mobilizing their

---

[35] See, for example, Christophe Charle, *Naissance des "Intellectuels":1880–1900*, Paris: Éditions de Minuit, 1990, and Michel Winock, *Le Siècle des intellectuels*, Paris: Seuil, 1997 and 1999.

[36] "The Intellectuals in the 21st Century. France, East Asia and Japan", held 21–23 March 2007 at the Japanese-French House in Tokyo; proceedings, edited by Ishizaki Harumi and Tachibana Hidehiro, published as *The Intellectuals in the 21st Century. France, East Asia and the World*, by Fujiwara Shoten, 2009.

[37] Tachibana Hidehiro, "The Problematic of the Intellectual", ibid., 300-318 (see 307-309).

[38] In 1966 a theatre critic, Yamazaki Masakazu, criticized Sartre's third lecture, in which Sartre argued that a writer used the common language, which communicated by its polysemy. According to Yamazaki, every field of study or activity was so specialized that a writer was no longer capable of understanding anything. He employed the common language just because it was the only language that he could use (see Yamazaki Masakazu, "I Ask Again: What is it to Narrate in Our Times? A Doubt about Sartre's Theory of Language", *Chuokoron*, December 1966, 244-51).

specialized knowledge. Very often what they argue goes beyond their field of study. Their books sell well. When some unusual incident happens, the media ask for their opinion. But it is difficult for non-specialist readers or viewers to judge their discourses, which present their moral or political values based on more or less simplified scientific theories. On the other hand, readers or viewers might "apply" vulgarized theories to a variety of problems, without having sufficient knowledge to examine their relevance.

As examples in Japan, I mention the names of two scientists. Kayama Rika, a professor at Rikkyô University, is a psychiatrist who is also known as a social commentator. Her political position is reputed to be left-wing and/or progressive. Criticizing, with a touch of mockery, the recent nationalistic tendency in Japan, she argues that "the incompletion of the Œdipus complex", helped by "splitting" and "dissociation", produces young people who articulate naively their love of Japan or their father.[39] Yoro Takeshi, emeritus professor at Tokyo University, is an anatomist. He argues that human actions and thinking are dominated by physiological operations of the body, especially those of the brain. Having been a victim of the students' violence in 1968, he is sceptical of the liberalist education supported by progressives. He finds it absurd to encourage young people to develop their "individuality" because individuality is innate in our particular heredities, whereas what is important for the maintenance of community is to share our common sense(s).[40]

Each of them has written more than fifty books and gives lectures or interviews on a variety of occasions. One could say that their influence is not slight, although there are plenty of counterarguments to their opinions. However, they are far from being charismatic figures comparable to Sartre or Simone de Beauvoir, or other "great" intellectuals. The question is whether these specialists should be regarded as a new type of intellectual. In any case, it is undeniable that those specialists who justify their moral judgments by mobilizing their specialized knowledge have increasing influence in our time—a time when nobody has a general view of the world, but everybody is anxiously seeking something sure and solid.

---

[39] Kayama Rika, *Petit* [sic] *Nationalism Syndrome.*
[40] Yoro Takeshi, *The Wall of a Fool.*

Works Cited

Asabuki Tomiko. *Vingt-huit jours au Japon avec Jean-Paul Sartre et Simone de Beauvoir* (trans. Claude Peronny and Chiharu Tanaka). Paris: Langues et Mondes / L'Asiathèque, 1996. (The Japanese edition was published by Dohosha Shuppan in 1995.)

Beauvoir, Simone de. *La Force des choses*. Paris: Gallimard, 1963.

Contat, Michel and Michel Rybalka (eds.). *Les Écrits de Sartre*. Paris: Gallimard, 1970.

Hidaka Rokuro and Hirai Keishi (eds.). *Three Talks with Jean-Paul Sartre*. Jimbun Shoin, 1967 (all of the original texts in French are translated into Japanese).

Ishii Motoko. "A Study on the Introduction of J.-P. Sartre to Japan: From the Perspective of the History of Publishing", *Bulletin of Kyoto University Graduate School of Education*, no. 52, 2006, 93-107 (text in Japanese with a summary in English).

Ishizaki Harumi and Tachibana Hidehiro (eds.). *The Intellectuals in the 21st Century. France, East Asia and the World*. Fujiwara Shoten, 2009 (texts in Japanese).

Kayama Rika. *Petit* [sic] *Nationalism Syndrome*. Chuokoron Shinsha, 2002 (text in Japanese).

Sartre, Jean-Paul. *Critique de la raison dialectique, I*. Paris: Gallimard, 1960.

—. *Situations, II*. Paris: Gallimard, 1948.

—. *Situations, VIII*. Paris: Gallimard, 1972.

Yoro Takeshi. *The Wall of a Fool*. Shincho Sha, 2003 (text in Japanese).

CHAPTER TWELVE

AN INTELLECTUAL STAR REMEMBERED: SARTRE'S 1966 VISIT TO JAPAN

SUZUKI MICHIHIKO WITH SAWADA NAO[1]

Sawada:—Professor Suzuki, I want to ask you about the circumstances of Sartre's visit to Japan in September–October 1966. On the one hand, because I think that the situation as it was then is difficult to convey today, and on the other, because I think that you possess a lot of "inside knowledge". First: how did you, as a researcher on Proust, come to take an interest in Sartre?

Suzuki:—In 1954 I went to France to do research on Proust, and in 1958 I returned to Japan. There, the impact of Sartre's work before 1954 was entirely different from what it became after 1958. It was only then that I began to read Sartre seriously. This was also to do with the 1960s, but before I elaborate further, let me tell you about the difference between 1954 and 1958. Right after the war, Sartre was perceived as an "erotic writer", as represented by *Intimité* [*Intimacy*].[2] In 1947, the translation of *La Nausée* [*Nausea*; *Ôto* in Japanese] was published by Seijisha. Then *Les Chemins de la liberté* [*The Roads to Freedom*; *Jiyû e no michi*, 1950], and *Qu'est-ce que la littérature?* [*What is Literature?*; *Bungaku to wa nani*

---

[1] This interview was recorded shortly after the conference of the *Association japonaise d'études sartriennes* held at Rikkyô University, Tokyo, in July 2009. The transcript was kindly translated from the Japanese by Dr Simone Müller of the Department of Japanology in the University of Zürich, and the English text redrafted by the editors and Professor Sawada. Note that the Japanese convention of surname / forename (e.g., Sawada Nao) has been respected. (Eds.)

[2] *Mizu irazu* in Japanese, "Intimité" is in fact one of the collection of short stories first published in Paris in 1939 as *Le Mur* (*The Wall*), which helped to make Sartre's reputation before the war. It is interesting to note that the first English translation of this title also preferred the more enticing *Intimacy* to the more faithful *Wall*. (Eds.)

ka?, 1952] were also translated. As a student, I had read these books superficially. I had also read *La Nausée* in the translation by Shirai Kôji, published by Seijisha, but I didn't understand it very well. My interests focused mainly on Proust at that time, and it was my daily duty to read him in the original. Of course, I read the debate between Sartre and Camus which was a topic of discussion at that time, but I didn't have a clear preference for either position. So, that was roughly the state of my knowledge of Sartre when I went to France. There, I realised that Sartre's position in France was completely different from what it was in Japan.

Sawada:—What prompted that realisation?

Suzuki:—One event was the Algerian War, and another the Hungarian Uprising. When the Algerian War broke out, the overwhelming majority of the French thought that "Algeria belongs to France". This was a common assumption. Mitterrand too, in his position as Minister of the Interior, immediately came out in favour of this point of view. Only a few journals, such as Sartre's *Les Temps modernes* [*Modern Times*], and newspapers—*France Observateur*, *L'Express*—took different positions. This surprised me very much at first. I was especially impressed by Sartre's article "Le colonialisme est un système" ["Colonialism is a system", published in *Les Temps modernes* in April 1956] and by his foreword to Memmi's *Portrait du colonisé, précédé du Portrait du colonisateur* [*A Portrait of the Colonised, preceded by a Portrait of the Coloniser*, published in 1957].

Apropos of the Hungarian Uprising: one morning, a French friend ran into my cheap hotel and woke me abruptly by shouting: "This is by Sartre!" It was the article in *L'Express*, "Après Budapest". This indicates the degree to which Sartre's position aroused attention. I mentioned this in an article that I sent from France to the newspaper *Nihon Dokusho Shinbun*. They let exchange students write, so I wrote about the Hungarian Uprising. This must have been in early 1957, as it was around the time that I read "Le Fantôme de Staline" ["Stalin's Ghost"; "Sutârin no bôrei"] in *Les Temps modernes*.

So, I reconsidered my opinion of Sartre, and when I returned to Japan in 1958, his image there was completely different from the one I had left in 1954. The translations of *L'Être et le néant* [*Being and Nothingness*; *Sonzai to mu*, 1956–1960] and of *Saint Genet, comédien et martyr* [*Saint Genet, Actor and Martyr*; *Junkyô to hankô*, 1958] were being published. Plus, Sartre's *Collection of Philosophical Articles* had just come out [*Tetsugaku ronbun shû*, 1957]. This *Collection* included, as you know, *L'Imagination*, *La Transcendance de l'ego* and *Esquisse d'une théorie des émotions.*[3] Above all, Takeuchi Yoshirô's *Sarutoru tetsugaku nyûmon* [*Introduction to the Philosophy of Sartre*, 1956] had been published.[4] This played a major role. I was still writing various articles on Proust, such as "Le 'je' proustien" ["The Proustian 'I'"], and other French studies at that time. When I finished that work, I felt like doing some research on Sartre and I read *La Nausée* for the first time in the original. It turned out that the original, when properly read, was actually quite intelligible [*laughter*]! *La Nausée* is a well crafted novel which truly creates a vivid picture. At the same time, I read *La Transcendance de l'ego*, but the edition later published by Vrin (Paris) had not yet appeared, so we photocopied the article from *Recherches philosophiques*. I think the journal in question belonged to Mori Arimasa.[5] So that's how I finally started my essential research on Sartre.

Sawada:—In the 1960s, you started publishing books on Sartre?

Suzuki:—No doubt I was different from other Sartreans, in that I had read a lot of Proust and paid attention to the Algerian War, but in 1962 I started to write literary essays on Sartre. My first essay was: "*Ôto* to sono shûhen" ["On *La Nausée* and its surroundings"], published April 1962 in the review of Hitotsubashi University. Next came "Sarutoru no seiji to bungaku" ["Sartre's literature and politics"] in March 1963. I think that one was written for Iwanami Shoten's journal, *Bungaku*. Based on those articles, I then published the book *Sarutoru no bungaku* [*Sartre's Literature*] through Kinokunia Shinsho in February 1963. The Japanese translation of Francis Jeanson's *Sartre* was already available [1957], but otherwise there was almost no comprehensive study of Sartre's literature or theatre, and this might be the reason why, from then on, people began to ask me to write on him. Then came 1964, and *Les Mots* [*Words*] was published in France. At the same time, Sartre's assertion: "En face d'un enfant qui meurt, *La Nausée* ne fait pas le poids"[6], became a focus of discussion in Japan as well. Ôe Kenzaburô[7], for instance, wrote a long article on the subject of "literary debates on Sartre" in the magazine *Asahi Jânaru*. It became quite a journalistic topic.

---

[3] *The Imagination, The Transcendence of the Ego, Sketch for a Theory of the Emotions.*

[4] Takeuchi Yoshirô (b. 1924) is a philosopher and a specialist on Sartre's thought.

[5] Mori Arimasa (1911–1976) was a philosopher and an expert scholar of Romance languages.

[6] "Compared with a dying child, *Nausea* is not worth a penny." (Sartre, Interview with Jacqueline Piatier in *Le Monde*, 18 April 1964; see Contat and Rybalka 1970, 398-99.)

[7] Ôe Kenzaburô (b. 1935) won the Nobel Prize for literature in 1994.

Sawada:—In 1964 there was also the refusal of the Nobel Prize.

Suzuki:—At the time, I wrote several articles on that subject too. It became a journalistic topic as well. Moreover, there was the Vietnam War. In August 1964, the feigned Gulf of Tonkin Incident took place, which provided the pretext for the bombardments of North Vietnam from 1965 onwards. So the anti-Vietnam War movement naturally gained greater prominence. At that time, Sartre became popular among pacifist students.

Sawada:—You also wrote about that in Ikyô no kisetsu *[*Alien Season, *1968]: the way you experienced the Algerian War played an important role in drawing your attention to Sartre's statements.*

Suzuki:—A very big role, yes. I wrote about that in the foreword to *Sarutoru no bungaku* as well. Personally, Sartre got my attention when I learned of his political position in France. Of course, I had also read his works before 1954 but I couldn't claim that I understood him. As I didn't understand him, I put him aside. Then, by 1958, thirteen years after the end of the Second World War, the understanding of Sartre in Japan had developed. The mindset of France always becomes fashionable in Japan after a delay of ten or fifteen years. The same was true in the case of Structuralism. It takes that long to publish translations and interpretations and to develop a sense of understanding. In this respect, the period around the end of the 1950s and the beginning of the 1960s was an ideal time for doing research on Sartre in Japan. I think the time was ripe by then.

Sawada:—Sartre's visit to Japan was in 1966, but a French–Japanese round-table discussion on Sartre had been held in the course of 1965.

Suzuki:—Yes, that colloquium was organized by Abe Yoshio.[8] The French representatives were Maurice Pinguet and three cultural attachés of the Embassy. The Japanese representatives were Katô Shûichi[9], Hirai Hiroyuki[10], Takeuchi Yoshirô and myself. Abe Yoshio was the chairman. A questionnaire was distributed beforehand, asking basically: "Why is Sartre *en vogue* in Japan?" Supposedly the French found this curious. In France *Les Mots* became a topic of literary discussion because it happens to be *bien écrit*, yet—in theory, at least—Sartre himself already belonged to the past: "So, why do the Japanese like Sartre?" I was extremely annoyed. I told Abe that, as it was some time since I had come back from France, I would find it difficult to debate in French and I didn't want to participate. He replied: "But Katô Shûichi is coming as well!" When Katô

[8] Abe Yoshio (1932–2007) was a specialist in Romance languages.

[9] Katô Shûichi (1919–2008)—critic, physician, Professor at Sophia University, Tokyo—was a translator of Sartre's works.

[10] Hirai Hiroyuki (1921–1992) was a specialist in Romance languages, and a translator of Sartre's works.

and I met in France, he used to say: "It seems that languages mean nothing to me. You are young and you have studied languages, but for me communication is such a struggle." He had quite a complex about expressing himself in conversation. So I thought that, if Katô was coming, I might participate as well. However, as it turned out on the day, Katô held forth quite eloquently [*laughter*]. On the Japanese side, Hirai Hiroyuki's French was not brilliant either, and Takeuchi Yoshirô didn't speak it at all. So it was Katô and I who conducted the conversation, and I translated Takeuchi's remarks. Quite a crazy symposium, wouldn't you agree [*laughter*]?

Sawada:—Was it already decided at the time that Sartre would visit Japan?

Suzuki:—No, it wasn't. One of the French participants said something like: "De Gaulle would be pleased if Sartre joined the Cabinet, like André Malraux!" [*laughter*]. It was that kind of mood.

Anyway, this round table was a peculiar thing. All the French claimed that Sartre was useless. The Japanese, however, pointed out that his writings and actions, *Les Mots* included, were all connected, that Sartre was appreciated all over the world, that he was of significance everywhere: why, then, was it only the French who were too foolish to understand the fact? That was the gist of the argument. Then, after the symposium, we were told that the discussion would be printed in French, even though it really wasn't worth printing. Moreover, it seems that the Embassy sent the printed booklet to Sartre! So, Sartre and Beauvoir read it and were greatly amused. It could be that Beauvoir was trying to flatter me, but our round table might be one of the reasons why they came to Japan. When I first met her and greeted her with: "I am Suzuki", she said: "Ah, *that* Suzuki!" And when I asked: "How do you know me?", she replied that she had read the printed copy of the 1965 symposium.

But during Sartre's eventual visit to Japan, I felt quite uneasy. It was extremely hard to meet Sartre. Those of us doing research on Sartre had rather thought that we would be free to meet him whenever we wanted, but it turned out to be quite difficult to get in touch with him. When was the first time I met Sartre? It was on a very rainy day at an event in Nakano, which I had been told I could attend.

During their visit, as you know, Sartre and Beauvoir each gave three lectures. Satô Saku[11] had asked me to interpret simultaneously but I

[11] Satô Saku (1905–1996) was a specialist in Romance languages. He was a professor at Keio University which, along with the publisher Jimbunshoin, had invited Sartre and Beauvoir, and he was therefore responsible for their stay in Japan.

refused, insisting I was absolutely not up to the job. As it turned out, there were proper manuscripts of the lectures, as is customary with the French.

Sawada:—These lectures were later included in Situations, VIII[12], *but is there a big difference between the actual lectures and the publication?*

Suzuki:—He changed some details but the outline is roughly the same. Sartre's lectures were: "Qu'est-ce qu'un intellectuel?" ["What is an intellectual?"], "Fonction de l'intellectuel" ["The role of the intellectual"], and "L'écrivain, est-il un intellectuel?" ["Is the writer an intellectual?"].[13] They were intensively discussed in Japan. The magazine *Asahi Jânaru* had a column entitled "Chishikijin" ["Intellectuals"] at that time, and in one issue it published a round-table discussion between Abe Kôbô[14], Shirai Kôji[15] and Ôe Kenzaburô, called "Sarutoru no chishikijin ron" ["Sartre's theory of the intellectual"].

Sawada:—I understand that a huge mass of people attended the lectures?

Suzuki:—In 1966, the Beatles came too. Sartre's visit did not have quite as much impact as the Beatles' but, nevertheless, people poured in to catch a glimpse of Sartre and Beauvoir. The first lecture was at Keiô University, the second at Hibiya Hall, and the third one in Kyôto. Sartre's lectures revealed that there was no such term as "intellectual" [*chishikijin*] in Japanese at that time. There was, of course, the term "intelligentsia" [*interigencha*]. But the "intellectual" that Sartre meant was called rather "shinpôteki bunkajin", meaning a progressive and cultured person. In other words, "intellectuals" and "cultured men" were regarded as the same thing. In his first lecture, "Qu'est-ce qu'un intellectuel?", Sartre started with the Middle Ages, when only clerics could read books, then touched upon the *philosophes*, the philosophers and thinkers who composed the *Encyclopédie* in the eighteenth century, calling them "organic intellectuals" who were a product of the bourgeoisie. But then, at the time of the Dreyfus affair in the late nineteenth century, he claimed, the dilemma of the intellectual began—that was how he defined "the intellectual". This concept

---

12 *Shichuashion 8* in Japanese. Sartre's three lectures were published under the collective title "Plaidoyer pour les intellectuels" ("Apologia for the intellectual") on pages 375-455 of *Situations, VIII* (1972), but have also been published under separate cover as *Plaidoyer pour les intellectuels*. (Eds.)

13 Respectively, in Japanese: "Chishikijin to wa nani ka?", "Chishikijin no kinô", "Sakka wa chishikijin ka?"

14 Abe Kôbô (1924–1993) was an author whose work displays some influence of existentialism and of Franz Kafka.

15 Shirai Kôji (1917–2004) was a specialist in Romance languages and a translator of Sartre's works.

was new in Japan. I remember Takeuchi Yoshirô saying after the lecture: "Sartre's 'intellectual' is different from the 'intellectual' in Japan, isn't he?"

Sawada:—The content of these papers ranges from the historical situation of the intellectual to his social role. They seem to me like university lectures, but I was told that the reactions that followed were mostly hostile. Did the reception as a whole amount to this: "I didn't really understand"?

Suzuki:—Starting with Shimizu Ikutarô[16], there was a lot of criticism from people on the political right. Needless to say, there was nobody who had listened to the lectures and understood them immediately. Sartre's language is easy enough to understand when read, but initially I did not follow the lectures in the lecture hall either. Afterwards, I read a copy of the raw drafts and understood them. There were, for instance, people—even among so-called Sartreans—who perceived the intellectual as "someone who becomes famous thanks to his intellectual achievements, then uses his fame to meddle in things outside his field of expertise". (I criticised this point of view later, and was not afraid to name names.) In that case, he becomes a "false intellectual", one who merely criticises the authentic intellectuals. Of course, intellectuals are criticised for meddling in things which are not their business, but Sartre's main point was precisely that they do so because they relate conceptually to the problems they address. This was barely understood. Therefore, some people criticised Sartre's argument by claiming that "this is the official thinking of old Marxists". By contrast, Katô Shûichi said: "Good, isn't it? This is great!"

Sawada:—Afterwards, the lectures were comprehensively published in Situations. *Did Sartre redraft them for publication because he had been looking for an opportunity to focus more fully on his theme? He gave lectures everywhere, but very few of them were subsequently published in books.*

Suzuki:—Shortly before 1966, the phrase "*universel singulier*" ["singular universal"; "*dokujiteki fuhen*" in Japanese] had become a key term for Sartre. In his lectures, he used this term in approximately the same sense as "*être-dans-le-monde*" ["being-in-the-world"]. The focal point of the third lecture was that the "engagement of the author is the

[16] Shimizu Ikutarô (1907–1988)—sociologist, critic, and Professor at Gakushûin University, Tokyo—played an important role in the post-war pacifist (that is, anti-American) movement, but retreated from political activities after the disturbances surrounding the prolongation of the Japan–US Security Treaty in 1960.

activation and transmission of the lived being-in-the-world by the non-informative parts included in the common language".[17]

Sawada:—You refer to the concept of the "singular universal". This became an extraordinarily big problem area of Sartre's thought in his later years, didn't it?

Suzuki:—If we trace the term back, we end up at *Questions de méthode* [*Questions of Method*; *Hôhô no mondai*].[18] Sartre says the following: "Valéry is a *petit-bourgeois* intellectual, no doubt about it. But not every *petit-bourgeois* intellectual is Valéry." In other words, the *petit-bourgeois* intellectual is an objective, universal definition, but Valéry is singular. These are striking words. A similar sentence is: "The irreducible particularity of the individual is one means to experience universality." Moreover, the notions of the "internalisation of the outer world" and the "exteriorisation of the inner world" constitute a mindset that he maintained for a long time afterwards. There are also his claims that "*praxis* is a passage from objective to objective via internalisation", and that "the project is a mediation between two moments of objectivity". In other words, there were "problems of method" from the outset!

Next came the *Critique de la raison dialectique* [*Benshôhôteki risei hihan*]. At the end of the book—hidden by other tracts and thus easily overlooked—the subject of the intellectual comes up. Here Sartre says: "Among the bourgeois class only the intellectual, in other words only the product of bourgeois universalism, is able to notice the diverse conflicts of humanism, that is, its fundamentally infinite reach (towards all beings) and its limits." Here, the basis of his Japanese lectures was already formed, six years before he came to Japan. Moreover, *L'Idiot de la famille* [*The Family Idiot*; *Uchi no baka musuko*], published in 1971 and 1972, represents a sort of extension line. At the beginning, Sartre writes: "The fact is a person is never an individual. It would be better to call him a *singular universal*: totalised and thereby universalised by his time, he retotalises it by reproducing himself in it as a singularity."[19] In this manner, everything is connected, isn't it?

---

[17] Here and in subsequent exchanges where Professor Suzuki is clearly paraphrasing from memory, we have not attempted to locate the precise quotations he might have had in mind. (Eds.)

[18] First published in *Les Temps modernes* in September and October 1957, *Questions de méthode* was republished, in an enlarged text, as a prelude to *Critique de la raison dialectique, I* (*Critique of Dialectical Reason, I*) in 1960. (Eds.)

[19] "C'est qu'un homme n'est jamais un individu; il vaudrait mieux l'appeler un *universel singulier*: totalisé et, par là même, universalisé par son époque, il la retotalise en se reproduisant en elle comme singularité." (Sartre 1971, *Idiot, I*, 7.)

Sawada:—Did this get some attention during his lectures in Japan?

Suzuki:—Without necessarily looking for it, some people must have noticed the connection, but I'm not sure that anyone wrote about it.

A few days after the lectures, on the occasion of a literary round table with Sartre, I had three questions I wanted to ask him. The first one was this: at his third lecture he had merely talked about prose writers, he had deliberately excluded poets, limiting himself to "prose writers". Yet he mentioned a "common language", isn't that right? The "common language" differs from scientific language and mathematical formalism by including non-informative parts, parts that do not convey information. He says that these parts are similar to "things". This corresponds to the "poetic language" he described in *Qu'est-ce que la littérature?*, wouldn't you agree? I found this very strange. If you are limited to prose writers, you can't talk about Mallarmé's commitment, can you? So I said to Sartre: "I didn't really understand this point." However, when the discussion was subsequently published, it read: "I fully understood this point" [*laughter*]! Sartre's reply was vague at the time. At the end of the first chapter of *Qu'est-ce que la littérature?* there are some annotations that were added later, I think. He said the same thing that he wrote there, namely that in poetry there is also prose writing, and in prose writing there is also poetry. But, if so, is it really necessary to limit oneself deliberately to prose writers?

When he published *Situations, VIII*—could it be that he was concerned about this point?—he had changed this reference to "poets who call themselves prose writers", but I didn't really understand what that meant. What's more, phrasing it in this way simply gives rise to contradictions in other parts of the lecture.

My second question about the lectures was this: all writers can be positioned in a form of "universalisation", but at the same time all writers become a "singularity". So, if all writers are a "singular universal", and if all writers' works possess this quality, how can you then judge one work to be "good" and another to be "bad"? This is what I wanted to ask Sartre. In other words: "What are the criteria of literary critique?" Shortly before, there had been a debate between Honda Shûgo and Yoshimoto Takaaki[20], which had stimulated my interest in this question. Yoshimoto explained that it was not as simple as the proverb: "In the right hand the Koran, in the left hand the sword", but that one ought to imagine literature as being, in the right hand, the criterion of literary value since the beginning of

[20] Honda Shûgo (1908–2001) was a literary critic. Yoshimoto Takaaki (b. 1924)—thinker, poet, literary critic—was a leader of public opinion in Japan for many years.

mankind and, in the left hand, the totality of time in which the writer lives, and then see value arising from their point of intersection. Also inspired by that debate, I asked Sartre about that point, and he said: "It's a matter of tension". He meant that the tension between universality and singularity brings forth the value of literature. If this is true, then my third question arises: if there is tension between universality and singularity, then surely one must persistently expand and deepen "universal" things? In other words, I thought that, by expanding *savoir*, knowledge, this tension would only grow. To this Sartre replied: "I absolutely agree with you." So, I was a bit disappointed [*laughter*].

*Sawada:—Sartre often used to answer: "It's as you say", didn't he [*laughter*]?*

Suzuki:—I think Sartre may have had his autobiography, *Les Mots*, in mind, because there he said that, since he had been born a *petit bourgeois*, he had good reason to become neurotic. Of course, he had the capacity to see himself universally and objectively and, since he wrote from that perspective, he consistently deepened his own knowledge, and when he tried to express himself in a singular, individualistic way, he naturally experienced tension. But this was a difficult concept to grasp just by hearing his lectures. So, in summary, my three questions for Sartre were about the distinction between "poetry and prose", the validation of "critical criteria", and the issue of "knowledge". Also—and this has nothing to do with the lectures—I wanted to tell him: "It's great that you have made your way to Japan, but I wish you had come in a freer way!" [*laughter*]. I think it would have been good if he had met people like Yoshimoto Takaaki or Tanigawa Gan.[21] But Oda Makoto, with his "Let's see everything" attitude, simply went barging into Sartre's hotel uninvited![22] Maybe we should have done so too, but I guess we didn't want to be thought a nuisance.

Sawada:—Sartre himself was not the kind of person who rejected people who came to see him, but you are saying this was not the Japanese approach?

Suzuki:—Exactly. It was an invitation from Keiô University and Jinbun Shoin, but somehow everything felt arranged. However, since Oda Makoto was being very pro-active, Sartre and Beauvoir agreed to take part at a meeting of Beheiren. There, something funny happened. Someone had

[21] Tanigawa Gan (1923–1995) was a poet and critic.

[22] Oda Makoto (1932–2007) was a writer and a leading figure in the Japanese peace movement, the founder of the anti-Vietnam War activist group, *Beheiren*. *Let's See Everything* is the title of one of his works (*Nandemo mite yarô*, Kawade shobô, 1961).

volunteered to act as interpreter, and there were many speakers on the stage besides Sartre and Beauvoir. I was on the edge of the stage along with Umihara Shun.[23] I was having a whispered conversation with him when Simone de Beauvoir started to talk. Her French was easy to understand, but when the interpreter was supposed to translate, he said: "Sorry, too fast, I didn't get that!" So, Sartre and Beauvoir quickly called me over, but of course I didn't know what they had been talking about [*laughter*]! Finally Asabuki Tomiko[24] got up from the audience, came over and interpreted. So, from then on, I had to stand behind Sartre and Beauvoir, explaining the proceedings and interpreting.

After that, I attended a round table with Nakano Shigeharu[25], Iida Momo[26], Maruyama Masao[27] and Hidaka Rokurô[28], and I interpreted for Sartre with Katô Haruhisa.[29]

So, one way and another, Sartre came to Japan in 1966 and got a lot of public attention. That's when I met him for the first time, but afterwards, whenever I went to France and contacted him and Simone de Beauvoir, they always welcomed me willingly. Sartre wasn't around during my visit in 1967, but Beauvoir invited me to her apartment, and that year I also met Francis Jeanson at his place.

The following year, 1968, I went to France again and immediately got in touch with Sartre and Beauvoir. I think Asabuki Tomiko was there at the time, as well. The anti-Vietnam War movement was emerging and small revolutionary cells were being formed. Sartre told me: "I'm keen to introduce you to one of these cells" [*laughter*]. He said: "You'll be contacted by my secretary." So, I waited until I got a phone call, in which I was told: "Call this number." But when I did that, I was told: "You have the wrong number, try this one instead." I was redirected several times like this, until finally I was told to go to a certain place on a certain day. I felt sure it was a Maoist cell, or something like that. When I got there, they

---

[23] Umihara Shun (b. 1931) is a critic and a specialist in modern European history.

[24] Asabuki Tomiko (1917–2005) was a writer, a scholar of Romance languages, and a translator of Beauvoir's works. She accompanied Sartre and Beauvoir as their interpreter during their tour of Japan.

[25] Nakano Shigeharu (1902–1979) was a Marxist author, politician, critic and poet.

[26] Iida Momo (b. 1926) is an author and a critic.

[27] Maruyama Masao (1914–1996) was an influential political scientist and thinker. His philosophy later came to be called Maruyamaism (*Maruyama seijigaku*).

[28] Hidaka Rokurô (b. 1917) is a sociologist and one of the leading Japanese post-war "progressive intellectuals".

[29] Katô Haruhisa (b. 1935) is a specialist in Romance languages and a translator of French literature.

asked me: "Why have you actually come to our place?" When I replied that Sartre had said I should meet them, they all burst out laughing: "Sartre? Ha-ha-ha!" It was obvious they were sneering at him.

Sawada:—There was already that kind of atmosphere in France at that time, wasn't there?

Suzuki:—Yes, and I was bewildered by it. Shortly afterwards, *les événements de mai 68* [the Events of May 1968] broke out, and I took part in some demonstrations, too. Mutô Ichiyô[30] came over from Japan and we decided to join a *Comité d'action* [Action Committee]. At that time there were lots of Action Committees, and it felt like: "If three people gather together, an Action Committee is formed."[31] I joined the Writers' and Students' Action Committee. Maurice Blanchot, Marguerite Duras, and the surrealists J. Schuster and J. Mascolo, were also members. Soon, there were no students left, only journalists, and very few of us continued to meet. At first we used a classroom in the occupied Sorbonne, but after we were banished from there we used a large room in the Rue Pascal. We just met and talked. Only once did we organise a demonstration against "State oppression", but the information must have leaked, because we had barely gone ten metres before we were dispersed. Since we had nothing to do, I was asked to talk about Japan at the meetings [*laughter*]. In that situation, Sartre was not a suitable topic! It was only when we planned to distribute protest posters that we thought of contacting him, in order to borrow his name.

When they asked me to talk about Japan, I gave an account of the Kim Hiro incident, because I was a member of the Support Committee of Kim.[32] Schuster in particular listened with great interest, and as the Action Committee wanted to publish something, I was asked to contribute to its pamphlet. By then I had already been contacted by André Gorz and had decided to write an article for *Les Temps modernes*.[33] When I mentioned this, Blanchot said something like: "At the time of the *Manifeste des 121*

---

[30] Mutô Ichiyô (b. 1931) is a political critic and specialist in international politics.

[31] An allusion to a Japanese proverb: "If three women gather together, it becomes noisy" ("Onna sannin yoreba, yakamashii").

[32] In 1968, Kim Hiro, a Zainichi Korean—that is, a descendant of colonized Korea living in Japan—killed a number of Japanese *Yakuzas* (gangsters) and held a dozen hostages for more than three days, accusing Japanese society of ethnic discrimination against Koreans. As his standoff with police attracted an intense media spotlight, the issue of Zainichi Koreans gained a wide audience. Kim's "crime as performance" questioned the image of post-war Japan as a homogeneous nation in peaceful transition towards a democratic, capitalist, welfare society.

[33] See no. 268, October 1968.

[Manifesto of the 121], I suggested it was time to close *Les Temps modernes*, yet it's still published!" So, there were clear disagreements and differences between Sartre and the spirit of May 68.[34]

Before that, Sartre had given a speech at the Sorbonne when it was occupied by students. A big audience had assembled because Sartre was used as a crowd-puller, although he didn't know that yet. I felt a certain uneasiness when I met Sartre after May 68. Somehow, we didn't really agree about it, and I was shocked that he—who until then had always understood my rather poor French—didn't seem to understand me anymore. That was when I first thought he had grown old.

But Sartre gradually came to realise this. In 1969 or 1970, he was invited to address a student meeting, at which he was handed a note saying: "Sartre, sois bref!" ["Sartre, keep it short!"]. That startled him. Afterwards, he was chosen as a figurehead by the Maoist factions, especially within the group *La Cause du peuple* [the People's Cause], whose newspaper he willingly (and illegally) distributed. My uneasiness about Sartre increased from then on because the Sartre who took part in these activities was in fact doing so as a "celebrity". And that is somehow different from doing things on your own account. But I think it was also because Sartre had become old. Until *On a raison de se révolter* [*We Are Right to Rebel*; *Hangyaku wa tadashii*, 1975], I continued to write about him, but after that, when reading his interviews and other things, I felt distanced from him. So the Sartre of the 1970s doesn't feel familiar to me. Because of the strong impact he had made on me in the 1960s, I felt I had to refrain from writing introductory texts about his work and political actions in the 1970s.

Sawada:—You mentioned the question of Sartre acting as a celebrity. In Plaidoyer pour les intellectuels, *the nature of the intellectual is defined precisely by* not *behaving like that. You valued that highly, so this behaviour must have come as a big shock to you?*

Suzuki:—Yes. Plus, it was a shock that he was involved in the maelstrom of May 1968 but didn't really grasp the spirit of it. I don't think he felt it in his guts.

Sawada:—Is there a generational reason for that?

Suzuki:—It played a role, yes, and whatever you say, Sartre was just too famous, so he thought that people would approach him in any case. It came as a shock when he said, in "Autoportrait à 70 ans"[35] ["Self-Portrait

[34] The "manifesto" in question, signed by 121 French intellectuals, including Sartre and Simone de Beauvoir, asserted the right of serving French soldiers in Algeria to disobey orders on moral grounds—see Contat and Rybalka 1970, 359. (Eds.)

[35] Autobiographical interviews with Michel Contat, first published in *Le Nouvel*

at Seventy"], that he would be happy if his work were published in the *Bibliothèque de la Pléiade*.[36]

Sawada:—In Japan, too, the 1970s marked a frontier, and Sartre has not been paid much attention since then. How do you view that?

Suzuki:—I think one reason is that his method became more concise in the 1970s, but his writing skills declined. One gets the impression that he no longer had the vitality to move upwards whilst also going around, as he did in *Saint Genet*—which, of all his works, is the one I like best—but that he simply kept rotating around the same point. Also, because Japan takes an interest in contemporary French thought only after a delay of a few years, the media turned its back on Sartre, saying that his popularity in France had faded. I think the Japanese media are prone to that kind of flippancy.

Sawada:—I think that some of Sartre's works have considerable merit, independent of the "Sartre boom".

Suzuki:—I agree, and in the next few years of my life I want to focus on rehabilitating his reputation in Japan. To begin with, I shall publish a new translation of *La Nausée* this year. In roughly three years time, I intend to publish the fourth volume of *L'Idiot de la famille*, in collaboration with you, and a few years later, the fifth volume. I have read *La Nausée* already dozens of times, and I think it is a very modern novel. Roquentin comes across as a feckless scholar living on a bursary, like a wealthy idler with no aim in life. In this sense, he has something in common with the so-called "moratorium" people in contemporary Japan.[37] What's more, people who do not see the contingency of existence, and who refuse to look ahead, are called *salauds*, "bastards". Even though it is a novel written more than seventy years ago, it is not outmoded at all, and among Sartre's numerous unfinished works, it is a novel with a high degree of perfection. I think that's why he considered *La Nausée* one of his most successful works at the end of his life.

Sawada:—He must have rewritten it many times.

Suzuki:—According to Beauvoir's autobiographies, it was meant to become a philosophical essay at first. When she suggested that he adapt it more towards a novel, he amended it accordingly, including Husserl's

---

Observateur, 23 and 30 June and 7 July 1973, then reprinted in *Situations, X*, 1976 (133-226). (Eds.)

[36] "The Library of the Pleiades": luxurious, leather-bound, scholarly editions of the collected or complete works of great writers, published by Gallimard, Paris. (Eds.)

[37] A term coined by the writer Okonogi Keigo in the late 1970s with the title of his book *The Era of the Moratorium People*, describing an affluent but disoriented young generation of individualists. (Eds.)

phenomenological ideas, so that it became at once dense yet entertaining to read.

*Sawada:—*Les Chemins de la liberté *were written as a kind of sequel to* La Nausée, *but when that didn't work out, they took on quite a different character with the second volume,* Le Sursis, *wouldn't you agree?*

Suzuki:—Yes; judging by his letters, Sartre wrote extremely fast. He went on writing *Les Chemins de la liberté* at quite a speed, even after his conscription, but maybe his books couldn't "keep up with him", so to speak, and it was inevitable there would be a crash somewhere.

Sawada:—Up to the second volume of Les Chemins *it is still carefully crafted, and there is also a particular structure to it. It would seem he still found time to write at that point?*

Suzuki:—I haven't re-read *Les Chemins* lately, but my original impression was that the first volume is a sequel to *La Nausée*, but the third volume is completely different: that was the post-war Sartre. In the second volume he used various writing techniques, it is quite complex, and since he devoted a lot of attention to the novel's form, I found it rather difficult to read the first time.

Sawada:—Let's return to Sartre's attitude towards the Events of 1968. Were there any signs that something was going to happen before May?

Suzuki:—There was the anti-Vietnam War movement—in Japan, the New Left movement, *Zenkyôtô*[38]—and there was the issue of American deserters. Also, the Kim Hiro incident had happened in February. So, before I left Japan, I was dashing to two or three different places every day, just to contact people. I didn't think it would be like that in France and I had stupidly changed all my Japanese Yen into Francs, but then the Franc was suddenly devalued because of the "Events" and I made a huge loss [*laughter*]! Careless of me! As for "signs", well, in Japan the university entrance exams were cancelled and we knew that we had entered a turbulent era, but still I didn't anticipate May 68. There was the SDS [*Sozialistischer Deutscher Studentenbund*, German Socialist Student League] in Germany, of course, and the anti-Vietnam War movement in France, and it was a time when people started to form small political cells, so I suppose that *something* should have been anticipated in France. Certainly, *after* May 68 got started, it was instantly clear that we should have seen the "signs". For instance, reading *Les Maîtresses de Lénine* [*Lenin's Mistresses*], in which Genet defended Daniel Cohn-Bendit, one

[38] *Zenkyôtô* (abbreviation of *Zengaku kyôtô kaigi*) was the "All-Campus Joint Struggle Council". Student organisations sprang up at universities all over Japan in 1968, as the riots took hold.

can see that, in the throes of May 68, he had naturally sensed the *Zeitgeist* and internalised it.

I have a lot of material on May 68 at home. The students at Nanterre, for example, where Cohn-Bendit studied, published some kind of booklet similar to the Japanese journal *Harahara tokei*.[39] Whilst Nanterre was on strike, their slogans included things like: "Learn from the Japanese *Zengakuren*!" [*laughter*].[40]

Sawada:—Was the Sartre of that time the same as the Sartre who had visited Japan?

Suzuki:—Well, he always had an open-minded, easy-going attitude, and one could talk to him about anything. I was mostly invited to some restaurant in Montparnasse to meet him, places like La Palette or La Coupole. I remember mentioning Kim Hiro and the American deserters, but Sartre and Beauvoir both showed much more interest in the former. When they asked me to write something about it I was introduced to André Gorz, who was also very interested, and that's how my article got published. When it appeared, there was an editorial disclaimer reading: "This is not necessarily the opinion of the Editorial Committee, nor of the Japanese Left." I said to Gorz: "Isn't it a bit odd to write something like that?" He replied: "I guess J.-B. Pontalis must have written it." When I got back to Japan, I received a letter from Simone de Beauvoir, asking me whether I had written a follow-up to it.

Sawada—Blanchot, who was in the Writers' and Students' Action Committee, became a big author from then on, didn't he?

Suzuki:—Oh, yes, legendary! Blanchot, Schuster and Mascolo had often taken common action since the "Manifesto of the 121" in 1960. Because Sartre had been in Brazil at the time, Claude Lanzmann handled things in his place and I think that, having contacted Sartre by phone, Lanzmann wrote the testimony for the court. At meetings of the Action Committee, famous writers like Blanchot and Duras sat down around a big table with me, an unknown foreigner, all talking and using the familiar form of address, "tu". The person who handled the practical matters was a young writer called Bellefroid, who was still unknown at the time. It was

---

[39] Started in 1974, this magazine gave instructions on manufacturing bombs and developing guerrilla tactics.

[40] *Zengakuren* (abbreviation of *Zen Nihon gakusei jichhikai sô rengô*) was the "All-Japan Federation of Self-Governing Student Associations", a Communist league of students in Japan, created in 1948, noted for organising marches and protests. They were involved in the anti-"red purge" and the peace-treaty movements, in opposition to the Korean War and the renewal of the Japan–US Security Treaty in 1960, and in the student movements of the 1960s.

Philippe Gavi [whose real name was Jean Contenay], the co-author of *On a raison de se révolter*, who took me there. A year earlier, he had been doing research on the problem of the American deserters in Japan and had asked me for an interview, and during 1968 I met him regularly in France.

If one looks at the time before May 68—the speeches of Sartre on the Algerian war and the group discussions of *Critique de la raison dialectique*—it is as if they were written *in anticipation of* May 68, as if May 68 retrospectively affirmed them.

But to return to our theme: I think it is very significant that Sartre formulated a theory of the intellectual in his 1966 lectures in Japan. In other words, Sartre—in his theoretical speculations—had the knack of anticipating what people would think, even if he did not always translate those theories into practice by his own actions.

Sawada:—Indeed, yes, Sartre has that attribute: he is excellent at grasping things he has not personally experienced, and putting them into words.

Suzuki:—A theory of the intellectual, such as Sartre formulated it in Japan, has not been published in such a highly conceptualised form anywhere else. At a stretch, I suppose one could say Gramsci has written a comparable theory of the intellectual.

Sawada:—That is because there is no perfect model. Sartre adeptly arranged things, so far as the "intellectual" is concerned, from the time of the Dreyfus affair, critiquing Benda's La Trahison des clercs *[*The Treason of the Clerks*], and then tracing a contemporary sketch.*

Suzuki:—Between 1994 and 1998, many books about intellectuals were published in France, because it was the centenary of the Dreyfus affair. It was Sartre who paved the way for Winock's book, *Le Siècle des intellectuels* [*The Century of the Intellectual*]. In this sense, he had always been at the leading edge. Nevertheless, towards the Sartre who came to Japan I felt a sort of familiarity: "Ah, this person is not a frightening old man, and it is even possible to talk to him informally." But, in France in 1968, I felt a sort of distance: "Ah, this man is, after all, a high-flying intellectual!" [*laughter*].

Anyway, when properly read, Sartre is definitely interesting, that's for sure, and I think we need not only a new translation of *La Nausée*, but of *Saint Genet* as well. *La Nausée* is an excellent book, but Sartre is more than *La Nausée*. It is extremely important that he evolved afterwards, although it is true that there would not really *be* any Sartre without *La Nausée*. It is often rightly pointed out that the work contains scenes in which the humanists are strongly criticised, isn't it? Yet Sartre doesn't really get to the bottom of things. Rather, Roquentin ridicules the alleged humanist who accepts the mundane conceptions of humanism or human rights. Sartre was "built", so to speak, after the war, as were his philosophical and political ideas that we might otherwise call "humanist", and I see no contradiction between the Sartre of *La Nausée* and the post-war Sartre.

Sawada:—Using that terminology, we can say that Sartre only criticises people who approach humanism through the "universal". His own humanism asks how the human person can be possible as a "singular universal", and within that project he remains consistent.

Suzuki:—Yes, that's right! The interesting thing about Sartre is that he definitely didn't limit himself to the "universal", for it necessarily included the "particular".

Sawada:—In the case of Japan, the figure of Sartre is strongly connected to post-war times, but when reading La Nausée *and* Les Chemins de la liberté, *I feel in retrospect that the time* between *the wars is extremely important. I mean,* La Nausée *is set in the 1930s, isn't it?*

Suzuki:—Exactly! Céline, Proust, Malraux, Joyce, surrealism—they are all included in *La Nausée*. They had all been part of Sartre's formation through the 1910s, '20s and '30s.

Sawada:—It's interesting that, in one sense, it became a work that anticipated the post-war era.

Suzuki:—It was the same with Camus and *L'Étranger*. They were both authors whose works were widely read in Japan as post-war literature. Sartre was almost unknown before *La Nausée*.

Sawada:—It must have been reviewed as early as 1938, but I think it was not really understood by an average audience. I think it's interesting that the contemporaneity of La Nausée *only became clear later on. I hope that, with a new translation, many more things will become clear. A new translation of* Les Chemins de la liberté, *in which I am also engaged, will shortly be published by Iwanami Bunko. In this context, I think it is really important that a new translation of* La Nausée *is being published as well. Meanwhile, thank you so much, Professor Suzuki, for sharing your reminiscences and reflections with me today.*

Suzuki:—You are very welcome, the pleasure has been mine!

Works Cited

Benda, Julien. *La Trahison des clercs* (1927). Paris: Grasset, 2003.

Camus, Albert. *L'Étranger*. Paris: Gallimard, 1942.

Contat, Michel, and Michel Rybalka. *Les Écrits de Sartre*. Paris: Gallimard, 1970.

Jeanson, Francis. *Sartre (par lui-même)*. Paris: Seuil, coll. Écrivains de toujours, 1955.

Sartre, Jean-Paul. *L'Age de raison (Les Chemins de la liberté, I)*. Paris: Gallimard, 1945.

—. "Après Budapest, Sartre parle", *L'Express*, no. 281 (supplement), 9 November 1956 (13-16).

—. *Les Chemins de la liberté*: see *L'Age de raison*, *La Mort dans l'âme*, *Le Sursis*.

—. *Critique de la raison dialectique, I, précédé de Questions de méthode*. Paris: Gallimard, 1960.

—. *Esquisse d'une théorie des émotions* (1939). Paris: Hermann, 1975.

—. *L'Être et le néant*. Paris: Gallimard, 1943.

—. "Le Fantôme de Staline", *Les Temps modernes*, nos. 129-130-131, November–December 1956–January 1957, and in *Situations, VII*. Paris : Gallimard, 1965.

—. *L'Idiot de la famille: Gustave Flaubert de 1821 à 1857, I, II, III*. Paris: Gallimard, 1971, 1972.

—. *L'Imagination* (1936). Paris: PUF, 1969.

—. *La Mort dans l'âme (Les Chemins de la liberté, III)*. Paris: Gallimard, 1949.

—. *Les Mots*. Paris: Gallimard, 1964.

—. *Le Mur*. Paris: Gallimard, 1939.

—. *La Nausée*. Paris: Gallimard, 1938.

—. (with Philippe Gavi and Pierre Victor). *On a raison de se révolter*. Paris: Gallimard, 1974.

—. "Préface", in Albert Memmi, *Portrait du colonisé, précédé du Portrait du colonisateur*. Paris: Gallimard, 1957.

—. *Qu'est-ce que la littérature?*, in *Situations, II*. Paris: Gallimard, 1948.

—. *Saint Genet, comédien et martyr*. Paris: Gallimard, 1952.

—. *Situations, VIII*. Paris: Gallimard, 1972.

—. *Situations, X*. Paris: Gallimard, 1976.

—. *Le Sursis (Les Chemins de la liberté, II)*. Paris: Gallimard, 1945.

—. *La Transcendance de l'ego* (1936). Paris: Librairie Philosophique J. Vrin, 1972.

Winock, Michel. *Le Siècle des intellectuels*. Paris: Seuil, 1997 and 1999.

CONTRIBUTORS

JEAN-PIERRE BOULÉ
Jean-Pierre Boulé is Professor of Contemporary French Studies at Nottingham Trent University and the author of a number of books, notably on Sartre, including *Sartre médiatique* (1992) and *Sartre, Self-Formation and Masculinities* (2005). He is the co-founder of the UK Sartre Society and Executive Editor of *Sartre Studies International.* His *Existentialism and Contemporary Cinema: A Sartrean Perspective,* co-edited with Enda McCaffrey, is also published in 2011, and he is preparing (with Ursula Tidd) a companion volume, *Existentialism and Contemporary Cinema: A Beauvoirian Perspective* (due 2013).

MICHEL CONTAT
Michel Contat is Director of Research Emeritus at the *Institut des Textes et Manuscrits Modernes* (ITEM / CNRS / ENS) in Paris. He is the author, with Michel Rybalka, of *Les Écrits de Sartre* (Gallimard 1970) and of numerous articles and books on Sartre, the latest being *Pour Sartre* (PUF 2005). He is also editor of Sartre's *Œuvres romanesques* (1982) and *Théâtre complet* (2005) in the Pléiade edition at Gallimard, and of Sartre's *Écrits de jeunesse* (Gallimard 1990). He has been Chair of the French *Groupe d'études sartriennes* since 2009.

GARY COX
Gary Cox is the author of *How to Be an Existentialist, or How to Get Real, Get a Grip and Stop Making Excuses* and *The Existentialist's Guide to Death, the Universe and Nothingness*, as well as of several books specifically on Sartre, including *The Sartre Dictionary*. He has a doctorate in Philosophy from the University of Birmingham, where he is an Honorary Research Fellow. For more information about Gary Cox, go to: www.garycoxphilosophy.com

JOHN IRELAND

John Ireland is Associate Professor of French and Francophone Studies at the University of Illinois at Chicago. He has written extensively on twentieth-century French literature and theatre, with a particular focus on Sartre. He is a member of the ITEM / CNRS *Équipe Sartre*, where he has collaborated on a number of projects and publications, including Sartre's *Théâtre complet* in the Pléiade collection in 2005. Other publications include: *Sartre: un art déloyal: Théâtralité et engagement* (Jean-Michel Place 1994).

DERMOT MORAN

Dermot Moran is Professor of Philosophy at University College Dublin and a Member of the Royal Irish Academy. He is the author of *Edmund Husserl: Founder of Phenomenology* (2005) and of *Introduction to Phenomenology* (2000), and editor of *The Routledge Companion to Twentieth Century Philosophy* (2008).

FRANÇOIS NOUDELMANN

François Noudelmann, Professor at the University of Paris VIII, has written several books on Sartre: *"Huis clos" et "Les Mouches"* (Gallimard 1993, 2006), *Sartre ou l'incarnation imaginaire* (L'Harmattan 1996), *Jean-Paul Sartre* (Adpf 2005), *Dictionnaire Sartre* (co-editor, Honoré Champion 2004). His most recent publication is *Le Toucher des philosophes: Sartre, Nietzsche et Barthes au piano* (Gallimard 2008). He frequently teaches as Visiting Professor at Johns Hopkins University and New York University.

BENEDICT O'DONOHOE

Benedict O'Donohoe read for a first degree in French and also took his doctorate at Magdalen College, Oxford. He is now Deputy Director of the Sussex Centre for Language Studies and Head of Modern Languages at the University of Sussex. He has spoken and published widely on Sartre in the UK, the US, Canada, Japan, Ireland, France and Switzerland. He is the author of *Sartre's Theatre: Acts for Life* (Peter Lang 2005), the editor of J.-P. Sartre, *Les Jeux sont faits* (Routledge 1990), and co-editor of *Sartre's Second Century* (CSP 2009). He is a former Secretary and President of the UK Sartre Society and UK Reviews Editor of *Sartre Studies International.*

MICHAEL GILLAN PECKITT

Dr Michael Gillan Peckitt received his doctorate from the University of Hull, UK. His research interests are in phenomenology, German idealism and Japanese philosophy, particularly the Kyoto School. His most recent publication was a chapter entitled "Resisting Sartrean Pain" in Katherine J. Morris (ed.), *Sartre and the Body* (Palgrave Macmillan 2010). He has also co-edited an issue of the journal *SWIF Philosophy of Mind Review* with Dr Luca Malatesti. Michael is currently working as an independent scholar on a comparative study of continental and Japanese philosophy, funded by the British Academy.

NAO SAWADA

Nao Sawada is Professor of French Literature at Rikkyô University in Tokyo. He is the author of a number of books, notably on Sartre: *Yobikake no keiken, Sarutoru no moraruron* (*The Call to Adventure: An Ethical Reading of Sartre,* 2002). He edited the book, *L'Héritage de Jean-Paul Sartre* (Actes du Colloque international: "Que faire de Jean-Paul Sartre? Perspectives littéraires, philosophiques et politiques", 2001). He is the co-founder and former Secretary of the Japanese Society for Sartre Studies. He has translated into Japanese many of Sartre's books, including *Les Mots* (*Words*) and *Les Chemins de la liberté* (*The Roads to Freedom*). He has also translated a number of novels of French contemporary authors such as Philippe Forest and Tahar Ben Jelloun.

NAOMI SEGAL

Professor Naomi Segal is Director of the Institute of Germanic and Romance Studies and Professorial Fellow at Birkbeck, University of London. She has chaired or served on numerous national and international committees including (currently) the Standing Committee for the Humanities of the ESF, HERA, the British Academy Panel for Europe, the *Institut Universitaire de France* and (previously) the AHRC (1999–2006) and the AUPHF (1996–2004). She is the author of seventy-three articles and eleven books, most recently: *Consensuality: Didier Anzieu, Gender and the Sense of Touch* (2009), *Indeterminate Bodies* (2003), *Le Désir à l'œuvre* (2000), *André Gide: Pederasty and Pedagogy* (1998), and *Coming Out of Feminism?* (1997). She is currently co-editing four other collections and researching for two further monographs: *Six Strays: Fictional Dogs from 1845 to 1992*, and *Eurydice's Revenge, or: The Haunting of the Replacement Child.*

MASAMICHI SUZUKI
Masamichi Suzuki, Professor of Intercultural Studies at Hosei University in Japan, received his doctorate from the University of Paris X with a study on *La Violence dans les œuvres romanesques de J.-P. Sartre: Théories et fantasmes* (1996). He has translated into Japanese several articles on Sartre. His recent research interests have been in discourse analysis of mass media texts as well as literary works.

MICHIHIKO SUZUKI
Michihiko Suzuki is Professor Emeritus at Dokkyo University in the greater Tokyo area. He is the author of a number of books, notably on Sartre, including *Sarutoru no bungaku* (*Sartre's Literature*, 1963) and *Sarutoru to sono jidai* (*Sartre and his Time*, 1971). He is co-founder and President of the Japanese Society for Sartre Studies. He has translated into Japanese many of Sartre's books, notably *La Nausée*. He has also translated Proust's *A la recherche du temps perdu*. In addition to his academic work, he has long campaigned for Korean residents in Japan.